D1242941

Cowboy Dances

CHEYENNE MOUNTAIN SCHOOL DANCERS AT CENTRAL CITY, COLORADO, DURING DRAMA FESTIVAL.

Cowboy Dances A Collection of Western Square Dances

by

Lloyd Shaw

With a Foreword by
Sherwood Anderson

Appendix Cowboy Dance Tunes
arranged by
Frederick Knorr

The CAXTON PRINTERS, Ltd.
Caldwell, Idaho
1948

First printing July, 1939
Second printing April, 1940
Third printing December, 1940
Fourth printing April, 1941
Fifth printing December, 1941
Sixth printing October, 1943
Seventh printing August, 1945
Eighth printing October, 1946
Ninth printing January, 1948
Tenth printing October, 1948

Manufactured in the United States of America
by Ganis and Harris, New York, N. Y.

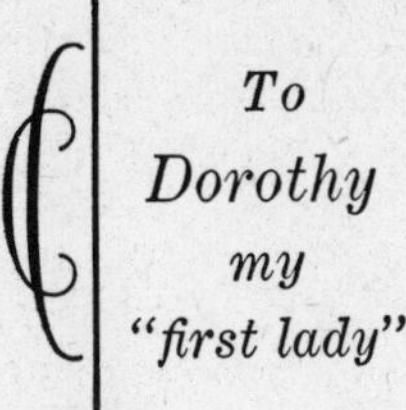

To
Dorothy
my
"first lady"

Foreword

Dear Lloyd Shaw

I AM a little afraid that anything I could write for the book would have to be, perhaps too much, the result of a very passing impression. I came up there out of low country. It was a day of sharp and rather glorified impressions, the great hills, some snow clad, deep gulches, great sense of space. I was rather breathless with wonder.

I came to see your dancers, and they seemed to me very real and very much a part of America. There was a kind of rough grace, sincerity, feeling of fun, joy in living. We have had so much, in our romantic literature, of the cowboy, shooting up towns, saving fair virgins, being always so faultlessly noble under a rough exterior that I was very thankful to see something of a more authentic old western life brought back in these dances.

I think there was something the feeling of an early America and its joy in a huge new land, something really virginal, joyous, good. I felt real play spirit. I wanted to stay, take it in, soak it in, see more and more of it.

I think indeed that you have done something very real. The feeling of fun, some joy in living, is too much gone out of most of us. You seem to be keeping it alive in these dances, and if this passing impression of mine is of any value to you, you have certainly my permission to use it.

Very sincerely,

Sherwood Anderson

Marion, Virginia

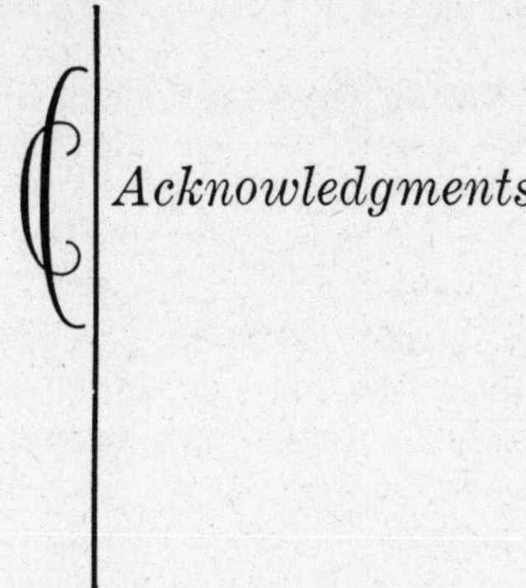

Acknowledgments

IN A COMPILATION such as this, where so many have helped, even when they did not know that they were helping, it is almost impossible to render the thanks that are due. There are the fine groups of old-timers who have taken me in and let me dance with them and have answered all the "greenhorn" questions I could ask. There are the different dancers and callers whom I have met only casually, but many of whom have dropped a phrase or an idea that I have laid hold upon. To all of them my heartiest thanks!

Many of the calls are such common property that it would be impossible to assign them to any given caller; but of the many callers I have known I want to give special thanks to Guy Parker, Emerson Howard, W. S. Uhls, A. E. Christensen, Theiron Gilbert, and Clarence McComb. None of them, however, can be held responsible for any errors that may have crept into the book. Just a few days ago one of them said to me, "Well, professor, you don't call 'em the way I do. But that's all right with me, if you're satisfied." Alas, I am not. I owe much to the fiddlers, also, "E. G.," Nick, Fred, Smokey, and Dad; and to Harriett Johnson—my accompanist—who has so often and so patiently helped me "work out a new find."

One of the most difficult parts of preparing the book has been to secure photographs of the actual dances that would adequately show the action of each figure. Loyde E. Knutson has taken well over five hundred pictures from which I might choose my illustrations. For these fine pictures and for his splendid co-operation I acknowledge a special debt of gratitude.

In the specific preparation of the book I wish to express appreciation to Henry Ford for permission to adapt the

Singing Quadrille from one of his publications and to John A. Lomax to use James Barton Adams' delightful poem, "At a Cowboy Dance," from *Songs of the Cattle Trail and Cow Camps*. Also I wish to give my special thanks to Jack Allison for the pictures taken at Central City. And thanks to Lefty Hays and to Doli Shaw, my daughter, for the diagrams, and to Marshall Morin for lettering them, and to Dub Smith, my "strummer," for the little music scores. Lastly, to my wife and daughter more than thanks for so carefully going over and over the manuscript for me, and for having so patiently listened while I talked and talked and talked.

L. S.

Preface

FOR MANY YEARS a group of young people at the Cheyenne Mountain High School has been working in the field of the European folk dance under my direction. They have been called upon to give exhibitions of those delightful peasant dances before all sorts of audiences and in widely separated places.

As we went ahead, demonstrating these folk dances of Europe, we became more acutely aware of the fact that there was, all about us, an old American folk tradition of purely Western dancing that we should explore. Already we were using the New England Quadrilles, New England Circle Dances, such as Soldiers Joy or the Cicillian Circle, many of the line dances or contra dances, such as Money Musk, Pop Goes the Weazel, Speed the Plough, and others. But we could not seem to get hold of the purely Western square dances that our cowboys had enjoyed on the ranches and in the cow towns of the West.

We could find no printed instructions or calls in spite of diligent searching; and our experiences with old-time callers were most discouraging. There was nothing we could get our hands on. At last a rancher down below Cheyenne Mountain, who had been a cowboy in his early days and had since called many an old-time dance, came to me and asked if I could furnish one set (four couples) of my dancers to join with a set of his young people in a square-dance contest that he was entering. It was just the start we needed.

Guy Parker was not only a "caller," but also something of an artist and poet in his own right. He understood my young folks, and it was no time at all until we were in the full swing of his dances. We refused our share of the prize money that we had helped him win in the contest, so in order to pay us back he insisted on coming to the school and teaching us all the old dances he could remember.

Once started, it was easy. To our surprise we found there were little groups of old-timers who got together regularly for the old-fashioned dances, out on the plains, up in the mountains, even in the city itself. They most generously welcomed us to their dances. By writing down calls on old envelopes or scraps of paper, I soon found quite a collection accumulating. One thing leading to another soon brought me into contact with many fine old callers. I could swap some of my variations for some of theirs. And they generously gave me of their store.

I soon found myself on the trail of the old square dance, wherever I went in the West. It was a mild sort of research in Western Americana and proved most delightful.

Now, instead of merely demonstrating these fine old dances, we found ourselves being asked to teach groups how to dance: high school, college, adult groups, all finding it a most contagious sort of fun.

Gradually we perfected a technique by which we could soon get any group quickly through that trying period of "initial diffuse movements," and before the evening was half over they would all be dancing with a reckless abandon, and near enough correctly to make the evening a hilarious success.

But, of course, they could not carry on by themselves. Closely directed, they could dance. But without help it all slipped out of mind and was lost. I tried to have some of the old-time callers help them, but it would not work. In the first place, they were not teachers and did not quite know what to do with a bunch of "plumb greenhorns." In the second place, so many of the old-fashioned callers use a sort of running doggerel, mostly rhythm, that is often hardly recognizable as words. Only to the experienced do their inflections mean anything, and to them it is the inflection rather than the unrecognizable word that directs them through the figures. With beginners, most of these callers proved more of a confusion than a help.

After much inquiry and patient searching I was able to find only one little pamphlet of directions and calls, and it was difficult to get hold of. Dozens and dozens of leads were given me, but whenever I ran them down they were "call books" of New England Quadrilles and not the cowboy dances that I was seeking.

It seemed to me that if the groups we had started were to carry on, they would have to have a manual, not only of directions and calls, but a book that could lead any group of beginners through the first confusing stages of the dance.

In the summer of 1936 I was invited to bring a set of my dancers to the famous play festival at Central City as an experiment in early-day fun. The dances caught like fire. In the old dining room of the famous Teller House we held forth and we found young society folk, actors from the current play, visiting artists, celebrities, everyone dancing with us. For the next two summers we took over the old William's Livery Stable at Central City and danced every day for the two or three weeks of the festival. With these shifting crowds we had to refine our technique so that they could catch on quickly. This experience convinced me that any group could start out alone if simple progressive directions and a manual of the simpler calls were available. This little book is the outgrowth of that conviction.

I hope that later I may be able to assemble a more complete book of calls, with all the variations and all the more intricate changes added. I have nearly a hundred dances now in my own notebook and I am convinced there are more than twice that many extant. I would very much appreciate it if anyone having other calls or variations of calls would be good enough to write them down and send them to me. Perhaps then we could get them all collected in one volume. And credit, of course, will be given in the proposed book to each contributor who sends in a new call.

Such a book would of course be a reference book of calls, with definitions of terms used, and instructions properly and logically and somewhat coldly arranged.

But this present volume is no such thing. It proposes to be a very personal, chatty sort of manual. I wish to write it as if I were standing at your elbow and helping you with your first dance. It is not primarily intended for those groups that are already successfully organized with a caller and plenty of calls of their own, and already dancing well. Of course, if they should chance upon the book and find anything of value in it for themselves, I should be very glad. But this book is intended for beginners, who are beginning at the very beginning. And it hopes to give them enough help to carry them into a new realm of most delightful fun.

In many different places I have seen groups of beginners trying to do these old dances. Without an experienced caller, without authentic calls, without much of an idea of the form of the old dances, they try to make up for their lack with a boundless enthusiasm. They need help. The time seems ripe for a revival. Seeing these old dances take hold so contagiously makes me hope that they may spread to hundreds of groups all over the country who are eager for good, wholesome, social fun.

But besides the dancers and the young of heart who wish to "shake a wicked hoof" around a square, I have found an increasing number of people who are interested in the old dances for their historic and literary significance. They are a living bit of the colorful days of the Old West. Beaten out by hand in the crude forge room of necessity, they are an authentic witness of the life of our fathers. Perforce the work of amateurs, of pioneer spirits, they were fashioned from old fragments of dances that had been carried by ox team from many lands. Each phrase of their apparently meaningless chatter appears to have a significance and a history that makes it fascinating to the student of words or of peoples.

I have had letters from many writers and students about the dances, and a book might be written for them alone. But it would lose its flavor. The dances would be like dead ants preserved in the amber of the past. We want them stingingly alive and danceable. We want them as real as the varmints the cowboys sang about—

"The sand burrs prevail
And so do the ants
And those who sit down
Need half-soles on their pants."

Unless you are half-souled, don't sit down with them in your study chair. Get a group of friends together and dance them. Then their literary significance and their full flavor will be yours.

Coombe-Corrie
January, 1939

Table
of
Contents

PART II—THE CALLS

THE DANCES

APPENDIX—COWBOY DANCE TUNES

List of Illustrations

Part I

The Dances

At a Cowboy Dance

Git yo' little sagehens ready;
Trot 'em out upon the floor—
Line up there, you critters! Steady!
Lively, now! One couple more.
Shorty, shed that ol' sombrero;
Broncho, douse that cigaret;
Stop yer cussin', Casimero,
'Fore the ladies. Now, all set:

S'lute yer ladies, all together;
Ladies opposite the same;
Hit the lumber with yer leather;
Balance all an' swing yer dame;
Bunch the heifers in the middle;
Circle stags an' do-ce-do;
Keep a-steppin' to the fiddle;
Swing 'em round an' off you go.

First four forward. Back to places.
Second foller. Shuffle back—
Now you've got it down to cases—
Swing 'em till their trotters crack.
Gents all right a-heel an' toein';
Swing 'em—kiss 'em if yo' kin—
On to next an' keep a-goin'
Till yo' hit yer pards agin.

Gents to center. Ladies 'round 'em;
Form a basket; balance all;
Swing yer sweets to where yo' found 'em;
All p'mnade around the hall.

Balance to yer pards an' trot 'em
'Round the circle double quick;
Grab an' squeeze 'em while you've got 'em—
Hold 'em to it if they kick.

Ladies, left hand to yer sonnies;
Alaman; grand right an' left;
Balance all an' swing yer honies—
Pick 'em up an' feel their heft.
All p'mnade like skeery cattle;
Balance all an' swing yer sweets;
Shake yer spurs an' make 'em rattle—
Keno! Promenade to seats.

JAMES BARTON ADAMS

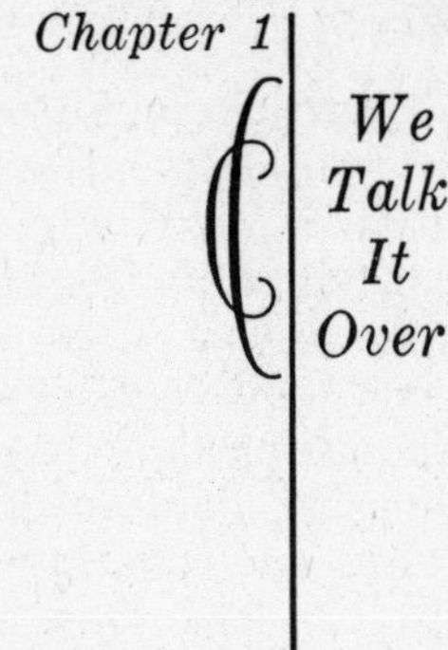

Chapter 1 We Talk It Over

VERY OFTEN at some dinner table or in some informal group, the discussion has turned to my strange enthusiasm for the old dances of the past, and I have found enough interest and curiosity developed to lead directly to the formation of a little group of friends who decided to join with me and to try a bit of the dancing for themselves.

It is the natural way to start—talk it over and then try a dance or two. One has to know what it is all about first. One naturally wonders where the dances came from, what their relationship may be to other forms of dancing. Are they still being done today? Just what do we mean by a square dance? Where is the sport?

So let's talk it over informally. Much that we say will have to be speculative. But guessing is good fun, and it often arouses more interest than a cold array of scientific and carefully classified facts.

When it comes to finding the origins of the Western square dance, for instance, one simply has to speculate. The dances and the calls, except in rare cases, were never written down, but were transmitted from caller to caller by the oral route. And all the footnotes and references and authorities are lost in the process.

One old caller said to me in answer to my question about a certain call, "Well, I reckon I don't know! My daddy always called it this away. But he said his daddy had a plumb different way, and I never felt sure about it. There's something the matter with that call, and I don't like it. I never use it unless I got to." A year later, in another place, I found what I suspect of being a variation of the old granddaddy's call. At least it was more complete and gave sense to the bobtailed lines he had used.

But where did the granddaddy get the original call? We can only guess. Back in the mist of the past, moving down from father to son, from community to community, the old calls spread without chronicler and without record. Usually something was lost at each step from the original call, until some semicreative natural genius, who liked to keep a continuous patter of words going all the time, filled in the omission with new words of his own, and a new variant was born.

But someone always protests that he has seen many an old call book—his aunt or his cousin still has a copy in the family trunk. I have patiently run down dozens of these old books, and so far they have always been call books of New England quadrilles. And that is a different fish. New England turned naturally to books. But these old Western square dances grew up without benefit of letters.

Had these Western dances been the dances of scholars, every variant would have been recorded and fully annotated. Chronologies and pedigrees and records would have been kept. But these were the dances of country folk, who kept all their essential knowledge written only on the uncertain pages of memory! They were the dances of laconic folk who didn't tell all they knew even under questioning! They were often the dances of secretive folk who were somewhat jealous of their special talent and special knowledge.

So all we have to go by in our speculations is the internal evidence presented by the dances themselves. Fascinated with bits of this evidence, I have pieced out the following theory as my own explanation of the possible origin of the Western dances.

I believe the two main sources to have been the New England Quadrille and the Kentucky Running Set. In addition, perhaps the Mexicans contributed something in the way of steps, but their dances are usually not "called." And lastly, I feel sure that some of the figures of the Western dance were borrowed directly from old European folk dances.

It will pay us to have a look at the two main probable sources of our Western dance.

The New England Quadrille

The New England or early American Quadrille was, of course, an adaptation of a European dance. Usually France is given credit for the origin of this form, although dances executed by four couples arranged in a square figure with a couple on each side of the square are found in the peasant dances of nearly all the European countries. Undoubtedly many of these contributed to the formal Quadrille which was finally perfected in France and in England.

The Quadrille at the height of its favor was usually danced in five parts, with a pause in the music between each part and usually a complete change of the music for each part. This tradition of five parts still persists in our American Quadrille even when two parts are combined. It is amusing to read in the introductions of some of our old call books, that a Quadrille is always danced in five parts, and then to search in vain through the book for a single dance that has all five parts still separate and distinct. Most of them are numbered, "one-three-five," or "one-two-four," still preserving the tradition while saving only three parts of the dance. This probably developed through having only three parts to the music with two pauses. Even then the American forms of the dance retained all five parts, but with two pairs coalesced.

Unlike a Western dance, in the Quadrille the head couple was numbered "one," the opposite couple "two," the side couple to the right "three," and the side couple to the left, "four." In the first figure, after a general introduction, the opposite couples maneuvered with each other in a variety of patterns across the set. In the other figures all four couples maneuvered together around the square which became a circle of dancing action. Only occasionally did the first couple execute a maneuver with the right-hand couple, then on to the opposite couple and finally to the couple on the left, thus working as it were around the square. In the more formal quadrilles, this movement was always in the fourth part and was named "The Visit." But this pattern of working around the set is the standard form of the Western Square Dance, as we shall later see.

The music for the Quadrille was precise, measured, and accurately correlated with the figures and with the calls. For proper execution the dancers should have been trained by a dancing master. These conditions were, of course, quite impossible on the ranches of the West.

Do you recall that fine description of a dance in Owen Wister's *The Virginian,* where the cowboys swapped the swaddling clothes of the sleeping infants? Imagine what that bunch would have done with a French dancing master counting "one-two-three." Distances were great in the West. Dances could not be the affair of one small community. From a hundred or more miles in every direction the dancers would come. Some had just moved into the country from Iowa. Some had drifted up from Texas. Some had followed the herds down from summer grass in Montana. They could not possibly do a precise and measured Quadrille. They needed something simple in pattern that a man could learn quickly, if he knew something like it back on his own ranch, and with a good running call that would tell him what to do even if he didn't. Thus developed a true Western dance built on the New England square framework.

There are many call books available for the New England Quadrilles; but I believe the best book for anyone who is interested in these fine old dances is *Good Morning,* by Mr. and Mrs. Henry Ford. Mr. Ford has done a splendid thing in preserving the very best of these fine dances. He has brought together the most skillful of the old fiddlers, the finest of the old callers, and with his staff of expert assistants has made a complete study of the Quadrille. In his book are full and excellent directions for dancing not only the old Quadrilles but also most of the lovely "round dances" which were the favorites of an earlier generation.

Any group wanting to have joyous fun, the exhilaration of "real dancing," and the fascination of working out the lovely patterns of these classic Quadrilles can do no better than to turn to *Good Morning* and dance it through from cover to cover, though they will have to see many a "good morning" dawn before the job is done.

These New England Quadrilles are so well known that it is only natural that they should popularly be thought the chief source of the Western dance. And they surely contributed much, especially through such forms as the Singing Quadrille and similar dances in which the call is sung, with words and music fixed.

But probably the Quadrille is only a tributary. The main stream, I believe, heads in the Kentucky Mountains.

The Kentucky Running Set

In the mountains of Kentucky, and throughout the Southern Appalachians, an old form of dance called the Running Set has survived. Cecil Sharp, the great authority on Country Dances of England, discovered the dance on his visit to this country in 1917, and proclaimed it as one of the purest and oldest dance forms of England. When first told of the dance, he avoided it because he believed it to be "a rough, uncouth dance, remarkable only as an exhibition of agility and physical endurance." When he finally chanced to see it danced, he was fascinated by its beauty or aesthetic quality and by its historic significance. He made a careful study of it and wrote a booklet on his findings which he published as Part V of his authoritative study of English dancing, *The Country Dance Book*.

In this little volume one immediately recognizes the source of much that we find in the Western Square Dance. The call and the spirit of the running set are much closer to the Western form than is the New England Quadrille.

In the Running Set as many dancers as wish to may join the figure, standing in couples in a huge circle. The dance can follow many patterns, but here is a typical form. After an introductory *circle left* similar to the introduction of the Western dance, the first couple moves to the second and executes a special figure, then on to the next couple and repeats this figure. As they go on to the fourth couple, the second couple *follows up* and executes the same figure with the third couple, and then follows behind the first couple and repeats the figure with each couple in the ring. As soon as possible, the third couple *follows up* and dances with the fourth, and then follows around the ring. This goes on until every couple has followed in a sort of looping or crocheting chain stitch of continuous and furious dancing.

The figures that they execute between couple and couple not only bear a resemblance to the Western figures but in some cases are identical. And the do-si-do, with which each couple ties off when they finish the circle, survives in an altered form in the Western dance.

Miss Ida Levin has published more recently a little volume called *Kentucky Square Dances*. In this, the same Running Set is danced as a square, and the similarity to the Western dance is even more evident. While saying that any number of couples may participate in the Running Set, Mr. Sharp, it should be pointed out, also says that it is usually danced as a square with four couples.

He concluded, after a careful study from internal evidence of the Running Set, that it is the earliest known form of English Country Dance, earlier than any dance described in Playford's famous *English Dancing Master* (1650), the earliest known book on English dancing. The complete absence of courtesy movements is one bit of evidence for this conclusion. There is no French bowing or saluting before the dance begins. In Playford's dances the court influence is already felt and the courtesy movements have been introduced.

Mr. Sharp was, of course, delighted with his discovery of this earliest form of English dance. And not only does he feel its connection with the May-day Round, which was the source of all English country dances, and which was a "pagan quasi-religious ceremonial," but he definitely traces three of the figures which he found in the Kentucky Mountains back to their ancient pagan ceremonials; one he connects with well worship, one with druidic tree worship, and one is in the serpentine form of the Hey with its established religious or magical significance.

It is not surprising that this missing link of the English Country Dances should be found in our Appalachians. Etymologists have pointed out for some time that the phrases and words and pronunciations of these hill people are almost pure Elizabethan English. Isolated and changeless in their mountains, they have preserved the pure English of Shakespeare, which we in our modern development or degeneration laugh at as the talk of hillbillies. In the same way they have jealously preserved the ancient dance forms. Their ancestors in northern England and in the lowlands of Scotland as stubbornly preserved the true dances of their people and would have nothing to do with the innovations which Playford describes as the dances of London. When these people moved to this country, they still held their ancient forms unchanged and crystallized, fossils, if you will, for all time.

And these Kentucky Dances are surely the chief forbears of the Western dance. The names of some of the dances are identical: *Lady Round the Lady, Birdie in a Cage, Ladies in the Center, Figure Eight.* Unlike the Quadrille, whose couples are numbered in opposite pairs, the couples here are numbered "one-two-three" around the circle to the right as in our Western dance. With a little preliminary explanation any group of Western dancers could instantly pick up and execute the Kentucky dances in no time at all. Through the Ozark Mountains of Missouri, where they are still danced in an intermediate form, these dances probably moved on to the West and developed a distinct form of their own to suit the needs of our early pioneers.

To be sure, our Western dance has the courtesy movements, such as *Honors right and honors left,* and much bowing and saluting of the ladies. And this, of course, is derived from the New England Quadrille, along with such figures as *Right and left through, Two ladies change,* etc. But primarily, and at its very heart, I believe the Western dance stems back to the pagan ceremonials of our English ancestors by way of the Kentucky Running Set.

The Tide Comes Back

A book has just come to my desk which interests me very much. Written most delightfully by two simon-pure New Englanders, Tolman and Page, it gives a picture of the present-day New England dance as done in New Hampshire. They call it *The Country Dance Book,* probably quite unaware that Cecil Sharp had used that title before them. And as they say, "like a frog hollerin' for his own puddle," they describe their village dance quite unconcerned and entirely unaware of the square dance as danced in other parts of the country.

The fascinating thing to me is the internal evidence in the dances they describe of the impact of the Western dance on their present-day New England forms. The waves that rolled out from Kentucky and New England have washed together and broken against the cliffs of the Rocky Mountains and have now surged back with a new impulse that is apparently felt all over New England. The tide comes back.

The modern dances they describe are freer, a little more irregular, a little more hilarious. I am sure they would distress a dancing master of half a century ago. And the "prompter" of that elder day with his clipped, terse directions, is being replaced by a "caller" who fills in with a constant line of patter which never ceases, and which has a suspiciously Western tang.

And why not? There has been a constant interplay between the East and the West in every other field of interest. And our pioneer cities in the West also had their formal dances given by the "best people" fifty years ago, and the quadrilles and lancers were as exact and precise as any in New England. But gradually the sagebrush and the cow camp pushed in on them with an uncouth modification of the Kentucky dance, and the do-si-do put on a white collar, celluloid perhaps, and mingled with those "best people."

I treasure a little leather-bound manuscript book of dance calls written in letter-plate longhand by a doctor-druggist in one of our Colorado cities of half a century ago. He called their dances for them and he must have called them elegantly. Every dance is as formal and precise and measured as his beautiful chirography, and it is 100 per cent New England throughout the book.

Tolman and Page describe a couple of dances which they say originated in New York. (Is not New York almost the "West" to them?) In some parts of New England, they say, "These dances were regarded with contempt reserved for the foreigner. But the newer generation found them fun to do and so they became established." And there is the whole story in a nutshell. The modified Western dances were carried back to New England by returning sons, and the young people found them fun to do.

Where were they modified? I have a friend from Indiana who feels that they started there, but another friend from Illinois feels that his state deserves the credit. Iowa could make out one of the finest claims, if Missouri didn't have so much to say. And Kansas can do some "hollerin' " on her own account.

We of the Rocky Mountains must be careful not to consider all these states to the east of us as part of "the East," and our dances as "Western." Here in the high, dry country, alas, Texas and Oklahoma, Montana and Wyoming, Arizona and New Mexico, all feel they have a more important part in the picture than even my beloved Colorado. And from across the mountains come voices from Utah and Idaho and California calling, "If you want to see the real Western dance, come out here!" The waves chop back and forth against each other and confuse us as to the original impulses.

Perhaps one day they will all quiet down to one great American folk-dance form. Perhaps on the great natural proving ground of the cattle range, the last American frontier, where virile youth wanted an hilarious good time, the cowboy dance proved to be the survival of the fittest of the American folk dance forms, and may be this great American dance.

It would shock my New England friends to hear an old Colorado rancher ask me if I ever danced *Hell's Victory.* From his description I was sure of the dance and told him it was *Hull's Victory,* not "Hell's"——"*Hull's Victory* with his famous ship *The Constitution.*" "No, no!" he says, "it's *Hell's Victory!* Called it that ever since I was a boy!" The waves chop back and forth. And it won't be long until a Western docey-doe will feel quite at home in a New England parlor.

The Music

It is often asked if it is not almost impossible for a modern group to try these dances because it would be so difficult to find an old fiddler who could give the calls. And there is always surprise at the answer that very seldom does the fiddler do the calling. All you need is floor space, a piano, and anyone who knows the call—and the dance can start without any special music. The cowboy dance is not bound to the tradition of any unusual set of musical instruments. Every saloon and every dance hall had its honky-tonk piano. The piano is part of its authentic tradition.

For beginners any of the old standard, monotonous, rhythmic tunes, played on the piano in 2/4 or 6/8 time, such as "Turkey in the Straw," "Arkansas Traveler," or the famous old jigs and reels will do. To be any fun the dances have to be held up to a good tempo, and I prefer the 2/4 time. The 6/8 time is apt to be rather fatiguing to your musician, repeating itself indefinitely through the long figure of the dance. It is very apt to become slow with a little rocking-horse repetition. And yet I must admit some of the best old fiddlers seem to prefer this slower 6/8 rhythm.

I have asked some of my fiddler friends to list for me their favorite tunes for square dancing. They have each listed ten personal favorites which I have grouped as "a"; then the ten that they play frequently but not so often as "b"; and finally, the ten that they play only occasionally.

However, they say it depends on the time and the crowd as to which is their favorite and they never feel quite alike. Since the names as well as the tunes are traditional and oral, I have left them in their original spelling to illustrate this point.

Emerson G. Howard's favorites are:

a. Soldiers Joy, Wild Horse, Heel and Toe Polkie, Mississippi Sawyer, Flute Music, Girl I left Behind Me, Paddie won't you Drink Some, Don't You Want to go to Heaven Uncle Joe, Durang Horn Pipe, and Grey Eagle.

Selections For Waltzes—

b. Over the Waves, Peek a Boo, Doris Loan, My Little WEE Dog, Bohemian Waltz, Rock the Little Baby to Sleep, Dream Waltz, He's Sleeping In the Klondike Vail to Nite, Matcaisy, and Home Sweet Home.

c. Red Bird, Buffalo Girls are you coming out to-nite, Irish Wash Woman, Wagner, Louie Reak, Fisher Hornpipe, Golden Slippers, Turkey in the Straw, Give the Fiddler A Dram, and Casie Jones.

You will notice that "E. G." has put in ten favorite waltzes in place of group b of the square dance tunes. I am tempted to comment on many of the tunes in these lists, but a few comments will illustrate my point sufficiently well. Take the Dream Waltz in the above list as an example. "E. G." tells me that he had played all night for a dance down in Woodward County, Oklahoma. At dawn he lay down for a little nap before having to go to work. When he awoke a strange tune was singing itself in his head. He got out his old fiddle and played it till he had it set in his mind. It is his "Dream Waltz," and other fiddlers who learned it from him call it "Emerson's Dream." The tune "Wild Horse" he heard and liked at a show. He didn't know what it was but later another fiddlin' friend heard him playing it and told him it was called "Wild Horse." He has called it that ever since. There was an old fiddler by the name of Louie Reak who claimed that he himself had "made up" a tune that he played. You will find it under the name "Louie Reak." But I must drop the stories and get on with my lists.

Smokey Minson's favorites are:

a. Ragged Annie, Hoe Down, Soldier Joy, 8th Day of January, Arkansas Traveler, Turkey in the Straw, New Money, Texas Break Down, Lop-eared Mule, and Waggoner.

b. Love Nobody, The Girl I Left Behind Me, Haste to the Wedding, Buffalo Girls, Old Joe Clark, Do Rang Hornpipe, D and G Rag, Woe Mule, Irish Wash Woman, and Dill Pickle Rag.

Nick Nichol's favorites are:

a. Turkey in the Straw, Irish Washer Woman, Soap Suds Over the Fence, Sugar in the Gourd, Arkansaw Traveler, Soldier's Joy, Chicken Reel, The Girl I Left Behind Me, Buffalo Girls, and Devil's Dream.

b. Little Brown Jug, 8th of January, Ragged Annie, New Money, Texas Breakdown, Waggoner, Dill Pickle Rag, Haste to the Wedding, and D and G Rag.

c. Lop-eared Mule, Durang Horn Pipe, Leather Breeches, Sally Goodyn and Old Susanna.

Dad Ead's favorite tunes:

a. Flat Wood—Square Dance, Never Saw the Like Since Getting Upstairs, Long-eared Mule, Leather Britches, Durang Hornpipe—own arrangement, Tennessee Wagoner and Missouri Wagoner, Virginia Reel, Eads Two Step, Dick Reavis D Cord Reel, Arkansas Traveler.

b. Smokey Mountain Buffalo Gals, Sallie Goodin, Irish Washwoman, Eads Country Dance Reel, Old Dick Reavis G Cord, Brushy Branch, Texas Breakdown, Laplace March, March Italia, Life on Ocean Waves.

c. Fisher's Hornpipe, Sailor's Hornpipe, Devil's Dream, Just an Old Time Waltz With You, Over the Waves Waltz, Paddie Won't you Drink Some, Haste to the Wedding, Salt Lake City Two-Step, Missippi Sawyer, Husking Bee, Gullie Hoppers Dance.

For a small group of beginners who are just learning the idea of the dance, a piano is quite sufficient. But if the group begins to get good, they will want authentic music, which means that a good old-time fiddler must be found, and it is surprising how a little inquiry will usually discover one in any community. Most carefully schooled violinists simply cannot produce the authentic flavor. "Fiddlers" have mastered a proud craft all their own. They consider it a disgrace to be a "note-reader." They have learned to fiddle by ear from some other old-time fiddler. And they usually learned to fiddle when they were little boys.

What they lack in concert technique, they more than make up in dexterity and endurance and inviolable rhythm. They usually tuck their fiddle under their chins in the standard fashion, but they hold it at any bizarre angle that suits their individual fancy. One of the best fiddlers I know never tucks his instrument under his chin, but holds it in the crook of his elbow, lying out along his forearm, curling his long fingers up around the strings with amazing dexterity, and swinging his bow in long sweeps back and forth in front of his waist. Another fine fiddler I know, because of an accident, had to give up the standard position for awhile, and perfected a style in which he holds his fiddle propped up vertically on his knee, strings away from his body like a tiny cello, and ready for a nice long comfortable sweep of his bow arm. He found this position so good that he never changed back again.

When you have found your old fiddler, he will usually have to furnish his own pianist. For since he is not a "note reader," a regular pianist, with printed music before her, worries him till he cannot play. He usually knows a "woman" who can either play chords to his music or who can elaborate those chords into a full and figured melody. But they must be teamed and used to each other or the fiddler cannot play at all. With these two old-time musicians it is customary to have a "strummer" who beats out the rhythm with either a guitar or a banjo. Sometimes drums are added to these three. Or a big base fiddle, plucked, not bowed, gives worlds of good rhythm. In fact, one of these good big-toned "bull fiddles," and an accordion, to accompany your old-time fiddler, makes a combination that is hard to beat.

A modern jazz orchestra with its saxophones and clarinets, somehow cannot supply authentic flavor. If a real old-time orchestra cannot be found it is almost best to limit oneself to a good pianist, who is in sympathy with the old jigs and reels and willing to try for the real old-time flavor.

There are many old-time books of music. Perhaps as good as any for the pianist to begin with is the *Pioneer Collection of Old Time Dances,* published by the Paull-Pioneer Music Corporation. But she must remember that one simple old tune of eight or sixteen bars will have to be repeated through all the seven or eight minutes it takes to dance a square, with whatever variation that she can invent. Or if she must, she can modulate into another tune now and then in the middle of a dance.

But not so with the old-time musicians. When I call a dance, most of my fiddlers ask me to let them know each "call" just before I call it, because they want to be prepared to give that call the old tune which their experience has taught them is best for it. And they hold that tune through to the bitter end of the call. For the special old-time round dances, or couple dances, such as the varsouvianna, the schottische, and the polka, there is, of course, special music.

But we have gone a long way from our dinner party and their discussion of the origins of the Western square. By now they will be wanting to know just how a Western dance is done. If they get really interested, it may be necessary to place cubes of sugar on the table in a sample square and maneuver them around through some sweet little dance. But a real discussion of the figure and steps of the dance had better wait until the first real dance, when we can get a set of dancers out on the floor to demonstrate it all for them.

Chapter 2

The First Dance

WHEN a group of beginners are brought together for their first dance, doubts and embarrassments and reluctance are apt to be manifest. For this reason it is best to have no audience present to add to this embarrassment. There is always a group of the curious who like to sit on the side lines and watch others pioneer and who say that perhaps they will try it later. It is hard enough to go through what the psychologist calls the period of "initial diffuse movements" (and what the beginner calls "making a fool of himself") in learning a new set of reactions without having the curious smiles of the onlookers make the initial movements even more diffuse. So, for the best success, only those who are willing to try the dances themselves, should be invited to the party.

If one full set of experienced dancers can be present they will prove invaluable. They can first demonstrate the dance to be learned (and we learn most quickly by imitating what we have seen), and then the demonstrator set can split up and one of its experienced couples can take its place as the first or head couple of each set of beginners and lead them through the figure with a great economy of time.

The Caller

The success of the first dance will depend upon the effectiveness of the "caller." The hostess, or the chairman, may make all arrangements and get the dancers and accoutrements together, but it is the "caller" who will have to put the dance over. Once started, the dance is in his hands. A committee of explainers and directors only outbabbles the tower of Babel itself. The caller must give all the commands, all the explanations, all the directions. Of course, having explained a movement and asked the dancers to try it in a "time out" period, then and only then can the leading couples, and all the experienced dancers present, help and explain personally to all who do not know.

At first blush, it would seem that a professional caller would be necessary. But I have found that many experienced callers are at a loss in teaching beginners. They are expert at calling for experienced dancers. But they are not natural teachers and are at a complete loss to make things clear to beginners. Then, too, they have often developed a nasal twang, or a lightning patter; they are extremely picturesque and colorful and interesting and are perfectly intelligible to experienced dancers who are used to them, but completely unintelligible to a beginner. An experienced dancer, who not only knows the caller but also the call itself, can make a change on the slightest variation of intonation or inflection. But to a beginner it is only "gibberish"—it is "jaberwocky"; and he is completely confused—while the professional caller considers him unbelievably stupid. He thinks he told him what to do and that only a fool would fail to do it. But if the beginner cannot understand him he has told him nothing.

A good amateur caller then should first have the voice—loud, clear, and distinct. He should have done enough public speaking to enunciate distinctly and to be able to throw his voice so that it will cut through the stamping and laughing and chatter of the dance hall as sharply as a knife. For if he is not heard he might just as well be absent.

At times he may prefer to sing his call and this is very effective. But he must remember that singing is never as clear, as easily understood, as the spoken word, and his first duty is to be understood. Thus he usually compromises by using a sort of singing chant, speaking his words distinctly but pitching them on a musical tone and giving them a chanting or singing quality. This note or tone must be in key with his orchestra, that is it must be on one of the elements of the chord of the key in which the orchestra is playing. His voice then, like the "bull fiddle," is simply chording with the orchestra. The simplest chord, of course, is made up of three tones, the tonic, the dominant, and the third. He will find that he usually pitches his voice instinctively on the dominant, though he will often shift back and forth to the other two notes. He must not be self-conscious about the special note or its technical name, but he must make sure that the note he uses is in harmony with his orchestra at all times.

He, of course, must be thoroughly familiar with the calls before the dance begins. If it is all new to him it means not only preliminary study, but he will probably have to get a few friends together beforehand and move them around and work it all out until everything is perfectly clear to him and practiced enough to be running smoothly. Our caller must have an infallible sense of rhythm, not only of the fiddle, but instinctively timing his phrases with the four- or eight-bar units that the music itself is built on. This must be instinctive, for with different groups on the floor, some fast and some slow, he never calls his dance twice alike. If he ever fails in the rhythm of his phrasing, the dancers find the dance no fun at all, even though they may not be able to analyze the source of the trouble.

This means that the caller often has to start his call phrase on the weak part of a musical phrase. If both his call and the musical phrase are built to the count of eight, it would be theoretically best for them to start together on the count of "one." But if the dancers get behind, the "one" of the call may have to fall on the "five" of the music, starting this on the second half of the musical phrase. Take, for example, the call "Two gents swing with the elbow swing" on page 172 and count it out on the four fingers of your left hand. You will find you have counted through your four fingers exactly four times. But now put a set of dancers before you and try it, and you will find they simply can't keep up with that mechanical perfection of four sets of four counts. They have too far to go around each other, too much floor to cover. Now you will have to introduce waits (two counts each time, since one beat of wait would throw the next phrase out of step). Perhaps it would count something like this:

Two gents swing with the elbow swing
(Wait, wait)
Opposite partners elbows swing
Now two gents with the same old thing
(Wait, wait)
Now your partners elbows swing.

Our caller must also possess an unerring geometric

sense, that is a spatial sense of moving and interrelated pattern. We all recognize the presence or absence of a color sense or a sense of smell or a sense of taste. We would not expect a person without an "ear" or a sense of tone to participate in group singing, or a "color blind" person to execute a painting. And yet I am convinced that though psychologists have never recognized it, there are as many people who lack a "spatial," a "geometric" sense as there are those who lack a sense of color or of tone. And we find that they are never able to learn how to square dance. In spite of an otherwise high order of intelligence and in spite of endless instruction, the pattern means nothing to them and they are forever running off in the wrong direction. It goes without saying that an infallible spatial or geometric sense is essential to any good caller.

Then he should be a natural teacher, which so many of the old professional callers, alas, are not. By natural teacher, I mean, he must not only be able to make his ideas perfectly clear, but if the beginner does not understand one way he must be able to explain in another and another until it all comes clear. This means that he must not only be able to analyze every detail of the dance, but he must be able instantly to analyze the difficulty that stands in the way of the beginner.

Not only is this clear-headedness essential in teaching the dance, but it is very necessary in the midst of the calling. He will see the whole pattern weaving itself out before him on the floor. Here a set of more experienced dancers may be running ahead of his call. There an especially slow set is falling farther and farther behind. He must keep them together. He must put more command in his voice, and make the fast ones wait and the slow ones catch up. (In extreme cases he has to stop the dance and beg the fast ones to wait for the call, and the slow ones to follow the call even if they have to leave out a section in which they have bogged down. Everyone must follow the call on the instant or it will be bedlam.) Ten or twenty sets on a floor all moving exactly to the call is a sight to be remembered.

Always there will be distractions. Someone always wants to talk to the caller in the very middle of his call. And even though he does not listen he is severely distracted. Fast sets, slow sets, new arrivals, little accidents, all tend to distract him. But he must keep his eye on that unfolding pattern, and carry it on, and keep his place exactly timed in every call.

It is not an easy job. I have seen experts who regularly got their calls out of order, or left one couple completely out. And I have seen many experienced callers who could not keep two sets together in a dance. It is a special trick and not nearly as easy as it looks.

Yet there is always some simple-minded, rather loud-mouthed individual who keeps asking to be allowed to do the calling simply because he enjoys his own noise and loves to be at the center of things. Experienced dancers may carry on in spite of him. But beginners will fall in confusion before him, their enthusiasms all laid low.

The quick, intelligent, capable caller that I have described will find one more river yet to cross, and that is his own first embarrassment—and his finest qualities only make this river seem wider. He will feel everyone look at him most peculiarly on his least faltering or his tiniest mistake. But he must carry on clearly and smoothly and forcefully, in spite of the embarrassment. It comes mostly from the newness of his job. All good callers have had to swim this river. He may be tempted to carry cards in his hands to read from, but they are apt to make it worse. He had better put it all in his memory, and then plunge in. Soon he will find it going smoothly, and he will know the delight of controlling a great unfolding pattern of human beings through the contagious beauty of a dance.

But, it will be asked, does not the fiddler do the calling? No, not very often in a Western dance. I know many fiddlers who are also good callers, but they never do both jobs at once. "Calling is hard enough," they tell me, "without having to keep the fiddle going too." In the old New England Quadrilles, where the dances are more symmetrical, the calls very much shorter, and the changes always occurring on a change of the music, which is the particular music for that particular dance, the fiddler can and often does do the calling. But in the Western dance it is very rare indeed.

Circle Two-Step

If the party is large it often pays to start with an "ice-breaker," such as the Circle Two-Step. This gets them all used to laughing and trying together, mixes them up thoroughly and breaks down all barriers and stiffness, and gives them all a chance to become familiar with a few fundamental elements of the old dances.

Have all the dancers stand holding hands in a great circle around the hall and all facing the center of the room. Men and women must alternate. Two or three extra women or a few extra men together in the circle will spoil the dance. The caller must see to it that they are evenly and alternately distributed.

He must then explain that the woman on each man's right is his partner, that each will constantly get new partners in this dance, but always the woman to the right is the man's partner. It is well to explain further that in all old-time dancing not only is the woman on the right the man's partner, but he must get the habit of always putting his partner on his right when he takes a position in the circle or in a square or when he promenades the hall. As soon as each man learns always to put his partner on his right side much of the confusion of learning is eliminated.

Now the caller briefly explains the few directions or "calls" that he will use during the dance, and has the group walk through them slowly before the music begins.

Circle right—Still holding hands, each dancer turns to the right and walks with a light gliding step around the circle in that direction until the call is changed.

Circle left—Each dancer, turning to the left and still holding hands, walks with the circle in the opposite direction, or to the left. The caller must explain that he will never call these circles in the same order and that they must get used to listening for the "call" and following the "call" on the instant, whatever it is.

Forward and back—The whole circle, holding hands, walks forward, beginning with the right foot, four steps toward the center, closing in the circle, and then walks four steps back.

Grand right and left—Each man, turning to the right, faces his partner and takes her right hand (she having turned to her left and faced him). Partners walk past each other holding right hands for a moment and then releasing them so that the man can take the next lady in the circle by the left hand, while the lady takes the next man by the left, and in this fashion they keep marching, each taking each new person they meet alternately with the right and then with the left hands. The men find themselves marching around the circle to the right, or counterclockwise, in a sort of serpentine through the oncoming line of ladies, taking the first by the right hand, the next by the left, and so on alternately until the call is changed. The ladies, in the meantime, are marching to the left, or clockwise, around the circle, passing to the right and then to the left of the individuals in the oncoming column of men.

(Note: This, of course, is only half of the regular call. But I have found it simpler to start beginners this way, and not to mention the "allemande left" with which this figure always begins until they have become thoroughly familiar with the simple right and left.)

Dance that pretty gal around or simply *Everybody dance*—Each man chooses the nearest girl to him, the one whose hand he has just reached, and swings her into an old-fashioned two-step, anywhere around the floor. Quite often the two lines are moving unevenly, and there will be a concentration or surplus of girls in one place, while in another part of the circle there will be a surplus of men left without partners. It must be explained that each man must run across the circle as quickly as possible and choose the first unengaged girl he meets as his partner. It often helps for some man who is dancing by her to call out *Here's an empty* so as to make it easier for the lone men to find these stray women, and incidentally this always puts more laughter into the party.

Form a grand circle, put your lady down on your right—All the dancers fall back to the wall and take hands again in a great circle. (Only for the first few times will it be necessary to call *Put your lady down on your right.* As soon as it becomes instinctive to put the lady on the right, we call only *Form a grand circle.* But until that time it is well to add this phrase and avoid the confusion that otherwise entails.)

Having explained the calls it is well to try it just once with the music, using the calls in the order in which they are given above. If the dancers get in trouble, it is necessary to stop and explain their difficulties. But usually they catch right on and you can go ahead.

As soon as the dancers are going nicely the call should be varied in order to get them used to following the call. The *Circle right, Circle left,* and *Forward and back* should never be given twice in the same order. But, of course, once the *Grand right and left* has been called, it must be followed by *Dance that pretty gal around,* and after a period of general dancing must be followed by *Form your grand circle.*

After the dancers have gone through the whole dance several times it may be necessary to advise them about the shuffling gliding step that is used, and about the carriage of the upper body.

The Steps

The Circle Two-Step offers a good chance to practice the steps that are used in all square dancing. And though some of the variants are seldom used in this circle dance, it may be best to discuss them all at this time.

The step most frequently used is a light, gliding, shuffling walk with a promenade rhythm. The knees are loose, the step is light and somewhat shuffling and in complete swing with the music. The best dancers hold themselves quite erect or stiff from the waist up, shoulders back and elbows high, wide, and handsome, the dip and sway of the body being mostly produced from the loose-jointed hips and knees. There is a grace and beauty and swing to a good dancer that is very catching.

Some dancers take a little leap or jump on each step, springing up and down quite joyously. This is usually the mark of a beginner. The old-timers are always so smooth that if you saw them dancing beyond a low wall, you would think they were whirling and spinning and moving on casters or wheels, such is the action of the upper body. Watching their feet, however, one is fascinated with the flash and speed and loose-jointed abandon. Nearly all of them put in frequent "breaks" or "two-steps." (The same step that is used in marching to get in step with the platoon.) In step and out of step they continually interpolate this little "break." Now and then they "stamp" to accent the rhythm. And the best dancers throw in a little jig or "hoe-down" without ever missing their step, just a flashing little flourish to add fun and beauty to the figure.

Once in a while, though very rarely, and always for some special call, the whole set may do a "hippety-hop," or skipping step. But this is very exhausting and is seldom seen.

It is best to discourage it in the Circle Two-Step, though some beginners instinctively try to do it.

I once saw a very fine group of dancers in a state contest use a slow "cakewalk" step, with arms folded high on the chest, head well back, and knees lifted very high on each step. It was effective, but all the old-timers around me insisted that it was not the real thing, that nobody ever danced like that in the good old days. I suspect, though, that even in the good old days special groups did whatever they pleased if it added fun to the dance, even as they still do today.

The most effective, the most fun, and the most fascinating step to watch is the good old gliding, shuffling, rhythmical walk, perfected until it has an uncouth grace all of its own.

When they choose their partners in the *Grand Right and Left* and dance freely over the floor they should use the old-fashioned two-step. This will prove a difficulty to some of them. Of course, the easiest solution is to let them one-step. But it creates more fun and gives the satisfaction of starting with a good old-time dance step if the two-step is more or less mastered. They came for an old-fashioned dance, and they are usually laughingly jubilant over their jerky two-step, no matter how badly they do it.

The Two-Step

The two-step is essentially a step-together-step or step-close-step, starting alternately to one side and then the other. Or it is analyzed more completely as follows, in which the directions are given for the man, the woman of course, using the opposite foot and the opposite direction from the man.

On the first beat of the music let the man slide his left foot out to the left, and before the second beat let him close his right foot to his left. Then on the second beat let him step backward in a short step with his left foot. On the first beat of the second bar of the music let him slide his right foot to the right and quickly close his left foot to his right, and on the second beat take a short step forward with his right foot.

If he repeats this through several bars of music, for practice, he will find that he is remaining almost in one spot, doing a sort of flattened square. But this will give him his rhythm and his steps most quickly, and when it is mastered he can step forward or back as he wishes and progress in any direction he may choose. To go forward, for instance, he will slide with his left, close together with his right, and take a short step forward with his left—then on the next bar of music slide with his right, close together with his left and take a short step forward with his right. He will repeat this series as long as he wishes to continue forward.

Since on the first beat there is the "slide" and the "close" and on the second beat of the music only the "step," some beginners find it easier to count the music "one-and-two-and," "one-and-two-and," etc. In this case they "slide" on the "one," "close" on the "and," and "step" on the "two," holding through the final "and."

The real two-step should be smooth and beautiful to watch. But in a Western dance it is quite in kind to make it joyous and bouncy. In fact, the man will find that if he spins continuously to the right while he dances (that is, in the "right face" direction), it is good fun to lift the lady off the floor as he "slides" (or just before he "slides") with his right foot. As he leads with his left he does a regular two-step, but always as he leads with his right he lifts his partner as high as he dares without spoiling her rhythm or her step, for she must come down exactly on the beat. And the faster the spin, the greater the centrifugal force, and the easier the lift. The ladies, bless 'em, seem to like it.

In fact if a group does not care to master a smooth two-step, it is wise for the caller to ask for a *Hippety-hop* and they will all fall into something sufficiently like the two-step to serve the purpose. And they will think they are having a very good time.

Allemande Left

After the dancers have the simple version given above so smoothly that the *Grand right and left* (where the trouble usually occurs) is faultless every time, the men all immediately starting to the right, or counterclockwise, and the ladies all going to the left, or clockwise, it is necessary for the caller to explain to them that a *Grand right and left* is almost universally preceded by a little introductory turn called *Allemande left.*

1. *Allemande* (After a preliminary swing each couple breaks holds.)

2. *left* (Each gentleman advances to his corner lady)

ALLEMANDE LEFT

3. *with your* (takes her by the left hand)

4. *left hand* (and completely encircles her)

ALLEMANDE LEFT

If they are a group who are interested in terminology and origins, he may want to discuss this familiar old word of the Western dance caller. It has been suggested that it comes from the French phrase "a-la-main" or "on-the-hand" and that "allemande left" is simply a corruption of "on-the-left-hand." But though it sounds reasonable enough, I doubt if there is a drop of French blood in the word. Nor do I think it is a corrupted form of the Swiss "allewander," their term for a "right and left" derived from the root "to wind." The spelling clearly indicates German. And we find that there was a famous old dance called the "Allemande" or "German," which was full of turns, the gentleman forever taking the lady's hand and turning around her. And I believe that "allemande left" simply means do a left turn around your lady as they used to do in the old "allemande."

If your dancers are enjoying your explanatory talk while they catch their breath, it may interest some of them to know that the "right and left" which is part of this figure is a very ancient step indeed. Three or four hundred years ago it was known through Europe as the *chaîne anglaise,* or the English chain. And even earlier in England it was called the "Hey"—the "shepherds' hey" that the earliest poets wrote about. This same interweaving chain survives in the "Grand right and left" of a Western cow camp. Shepherds' hey!

The caller will explain that the complete call is usually given in some such form as:

Allemande left with your left hand,
Then right hand to partner and right and left grand,

but that until they get more used to the call and the idea he will use a simpler form which goes:

Swing your left hand lady with your left hand,
Then right hand to partner and right and left grand.

In this maneuver of the *allemande* each gentleman faces left, instead of turning right to face his partner, and each lady faces right, so that the gentlemen stand facing their left-hand ladies. They take left hands and walk once around each other and back to their own positions. This leaves them now facing their partners, whom they take with their right hands and march past them in the old familiar *Grand*

5. *Right hand to partner* (He now gives his partner)

6. *and right* (his right hand and passes on beyond her.)

GRAND RIGHT AND LEFT

7. *and left* (He gives the next oncoming lady his left hand, passes her)

8. *grand!* (Gives his right to the next lady, and passing each with a left or a right)

GRAND RIGHT AND LEFT

right and left in the same direction and same manner as they first learned it. It is nothing but the *right and left* preceded by a little left hook, or complete turn, around the left-hand lady, holding her left hand as you circle each other.

It is so simple that it may seem labored to teach it in two parts in this way. But I have found, especially with a large crowd, that it saves a lot of confusion and innumerable collisions. Starting with the simple *Grand right and left* gets their directions established and the men get in the habit of always going right and the ladies always going left with a serpentine, touching alternate hands. Once this is established it is easy to add the preliminary left hook of the *Allemande,* and the trick is done. But try to teach the two maneuvers at the same time to a large crowd and you will have them all running off wildly in all directions, and the stampede will be hard to check.

When you start dancing again, after the explanation, it will be well for the first three or four times through the dance always to use the simpler call *Swing the left hand lady with your left hand.* It helps them get started. Once they are used to the figure, start calling *Allemande left with your left hand,* and use this more standard form always thereafter.

The Circle Two-Step is simple to learn and fun to do, and when you finally stop them (by simply having the music stop in one of the periods of the two-step) they will probably shout and clap and call for more. To keep their interest up you can then give them some other simple and popular variations.

Variations

After the two-step, instead of calling *form a grand circle* you may call:

Form a double circle—
Ladies on the inside,
Gents on the out!
Ladies on the inside,
Pretty side out!

In this case there will be an outer circle of men only, holding each other by the hands and facing inward in the regular fashion. Inside them there will be an inner ring of only women, facing toward the men (pretty side out) and holding each other by the hands in a circle. When the two rings have formed, call:

Everybody circle right. Since the two rings are facing each other it makes each go opposite the other or past each other. When they have passed far enough to assure a new partner for everyone, call: *Everybody pick the prettiest gal and dance*—and they are off on the two-step again.

Since the two circles must always go in opposite directions a new caller often calls *Ladies go right and gents go left* hoping to make them do so. But since the two rings are facing each other this means that they will then both go in the same direction or in a sort of double column. So, in order to send them past each other, be simple and call either *Everybody circle right* or *Everybody circle left,* and that will send the two rings past each other.

Once they are familiar with this variation the caller can call either figure after the two-step and arrange all the parts in any way to suit his fancy.

Another pleasant variation after the two-step is to call *Promenade now two by two.* They should march side by side, lady on the right and holding both hands crossed over in front like a pair of skaters. And as soon as they are promenading smoothly (to the right, of course, or counterclockwise), you can call *Gents go forward and the ladies turn back* (or *The ladies go forward and the gents turn back,* as your fancy dictates, and never twice alike). When they are well mixed you again call *Everybody choose the prettiest gal and dance.*

This variation is very helpful when the crowd is large and the hall is small, for then the *Grand circle* can hardly fit around the room without loops and scallops in the circle, and the allemande is very difficult to do with such crowding. When they *Promenade two by two* it makes the circumference of the circle just half as large and simplifies everything, in addition to being good fun.

A third variation can be enjoyed by calling *Promenade four by four* when two couples march four abreast with arms hooked in elbows. This often causes a little confusion by some couple being left stranded without another couple to fill out their four. But if they look around the circle they can usually find another single couple who are also stranded, and they can run across the circle and join with them to complete their four. When they are well arranged and marching smoothly four by four, you can call *Keep your four columns moving while the gents go forward and the ladies turn back.* This gets them milling even more amusingly until you call *Pick the prettiest gal and dance.*

Summary

To start the dance the caller often needs only to have the orchestra start a two-step and when they are all out on the floor dancing he can call *Form a grand circle* and go on with the dance.

A typical form for the whole call might be something like this:

Circle Two-Step

Form your grand circle;
Circle left (or *Circle right)*
Forward and back.
Now allemande left as you come down,
Grand right and left and so on around,
Right foot up and left foot down,
Make that big foot jar the ground,
Now dance that pretty gal around.

¤ ¤ ¤

Form a grand circle—

And so on as long as desired, introducing whatever variation he wishes after the two-step period and stopping the dance by stopping the music during a two-step.

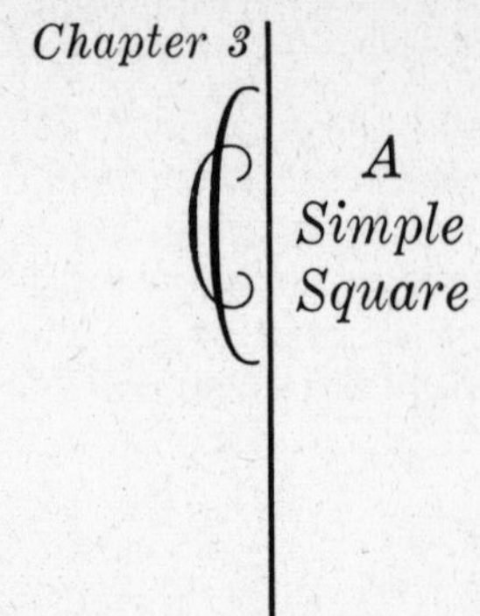

Chapter 3

A Simple Square

THE Circle Two-Step is so easy that your crowd will feel very confident and pleased with themselves as soon as they have done it a few times through. Now, laughing and friendly, with all their inhibitions stilled, they are ready for their first square dance.

While they are catching their breath from the Circle Two-Step is a good time to get them seated and give them a preliminary discussion on the theory of the square. It will help a good deal to put a set of dancers out on the floor in order to make your explanations clearer. If you have a demonstration set of experienced dancers it will make your

DIAGRAM OF A TYPICAL SQUARE DISTINGUISHING THE FOUR LADIES IN RELATION TO THE FIRST GENTLEMAN.

task even easier. But lacking them, you can put any four couples out on the floor and make things clear enough by moving them around.

The Positions

A set of dancers or a square is composed of four couples, each standing on one of the sides of an imaginary square, or towards one of the four walls of the room and each couple facing the center of the square (or the opposite couple). Where space is crowded this imaginary square need be only eight or ten feet across. But it is better, especially with beginners, to allow ten or twelve feet across for each square.

In each square and throughout the dance the lady's position is always to the right side of her partner. If this rule of always putting the lady on the right is carefully followed much confusion in learning can be avoided. In fact, the position of the lady gives her the name by which she is designated in the call. For each man the lady on his right is his "partner," the lady on his left is his "corner," the lady across from him is his "opposite," and the lady to the right beyond his partner is the "right hand lady," though she seldom figures in the calls. For each lady, likewise, the man on her left is her "partner," the man on her right is her "corner," the man across from her is her "opposite," and the man on the left next beyond her partner is the "left hand gent."

Each couple is numbered according to the side of the square on which they are standing, and they always return to this same or "home" position after each promenade or special maneuver. The couple standing nearest to and with their backs to the head of the hall is called "first couple." The couple to their right is called "second couple," the couple opposite them is "third couple," and the couple standing on their left is called the "fourth couple." The head of the hall is usually that end of the hall nearest the orchestra. If the orchestra is located in the middle of one of the sides, the caller should announce before the first dance begins which end of the hall is considered the "head." Since the "first couple" stands nearest the head of the hall they are sometimes called "head couple." And, of course, the "third couple" is called "foot couple." In this case the "second and fourth couples" are called "the sides," without differentiation between them.

Throughout any simple dance each couple is known as "first," "second," "third," etc., by the position they occupy at the beginning of the dance. And throughout this particular dance they always return to this same home position. For the second dance of the evening, however, they may each shift into a new *set* or *square* and take any position they happen to find open, keeping this position throughout any one dance. In a real old-fashioned square dance, where most of the evening is given to these old figures it is customary to call the sets out on the floor and to call two dances one after the other. These two separate dances are called the first and second "tip" of the set. And when the first dance is finished everyone remains standing in his position on the floor, laughing and visiting until the music starts again, and then the set dances the second "tip," retaining through it their same positions or numbers.

The Introduction

It must be explained that a square dance usually opens with one of several possible introductory figures. The following is perhaps the commonest form:

Honors right and honors left—Each man bows first to the lady on his right, that is, his partner, and then to the lady on his left. The ladies all return the bow, which is executed quite quickly.

All join hands and circle to the left—The whole square with joined hands moves in a large circle to the left, walking around in a clockwise direction. They usually get more than halfway around when the next call comes.

Break and swing and promenade back—At the word "break," hands are dropped all around, and each man takes his partner in a modified dance position, her right hand extended in his left, her left hand on his shoulder, and his right arm around her waist. Where this differs from the standard dance position is that instead of standing face to face, the couples often stand right hip touching right hip, the man's right arm having to pass across the front of his lady and his wrist around her waist. The lady, with her hip braced against her partner, throws her shoulders back away from him in order to take advantage of the centrifugal force of the swing. With short steps the couple swings completely around twice in a "right about face" or clockwise direction.

1. *Honors right!*

2. *Honors left!*

AN INTRODUCTION

3. *All join hands and circle to the left.*

4. *Break and swing!*
AN INTRODUCTION

5. *And promenade*

6. *Home.*
AN INTRODUCTION

Figure after figure in square dancing calls for this "swing" which is always done as above, and must be understood and mastered, if so easy a maneuver can be said to be "mastered," before one goes on with the dance. It is usually customary to make two complete revolutions when the "swing" is called for, but in some dizzy figures one revolution will be quite enough.

As soon as they have "swung," each couple promenades back "home," or back to the position they were originally standing in. They march two-by-two; that is, side by side, with the lady on the right side of the gentleman, and holding hands with the arms crossed in front of them as in the customary pair skating position; that is, the man holds the lady's left hand in his left hand and her right hand in his right with his right arm across above or in front of her left. (In skating it is usually crossed under the lady's the better to support her, but in dancing it is always crossed above.)

The promenade is always to the right, or counterclockwise. It occurs again and again throughout the figure of the dance, and the right-hand direction must become a habit.

Other introductory figures are used, but we can teach them with later dances. This *Honors right and honors left* is by far the commonest and is, therefore, the best to begin with.

After executing it the couples are back just where they started from, all facing the center as at the beginning, and ready for the dance proper to begin.

One of the easiest dances to start beginners with I have found to be:

Form a Star with the Right Hand Cross

This is in typical square formation with first couple visiting around to each of the others in turn, beginning with the second couple, going on to the third, and finishing with the fourth. Then the second couple visits around the square repeating the same figure in turn with each of the others, the third, the fourth, and lastly the first couple. Then the third and fourth couples each visit around the square in the same manner. While the first and second couples are doing the figure, the third and fourth couples merely stand and await their turn. In this type of square there are always two couples in action and two couples awaiting their turns. Of course, with experts the two odd couples may get in action too, just to make it more fun, but they have to scamper to be back in position in time to receive the visiting couple. And it is unwise for beginners to try this.

The simple figure used around the square in this dance is called:

First couple out to the couple on the right,
Form a star with the right hand cross.
Back with the left and don't get lost.
Swing your opposite with your right,
Now your partner with your left,
And on to the next.

The first couple simply walks over and faces the second couple. All four dancers grasp right hands at about the level of their heads, thus forming a star, and holding hands they march around to the left, or in a clockwise direction, until the next phrase of the call is given. They then let go their holds and each swings in toward the others (a right-face turn) and they grasp all four left hands at their head level and circle back to the right or in a counterclockwise direction.

On the last part of the call they let go each other's hands, and each man takes the opposite lady's right hand in his right and swings her completely around behind him. This brings them all into position so each man can then take his partner's left hand in his left and swing her around.

The second couple swings back into position and stands as they were at the beginning, while the first couple swings around and faces the third couple, with whom they repeat the whole figure, as the call is repeated for them.

The caller must be careful of his timing. It is best to allow just enough time in the *Right hand cross* for them all to take about four steps in this direction, then to reverse them with the *Left hand cross,* allowing time for only about four steps in this direction. Then let the opposites and the partners swing. In fact, it all times up with the music best if four or eight counts are allowed for each part of the figure.

As soon as the first couple reaches the third couple the caller must repeat the call again, and then again for the fourth couple. At the conclusion of this figure instead of calling *On to the next,* he usually says, *Balance home and everybody swing.*

At most dances and in most sets this *balance home* simply means *go home* or back to position. But with the more experienced dancers they not only *go home,* but separating from each other in a half curtsy they come together for the swing. At the same time the three other couples in the set *balance and swing,* that is, face each other and each takes four steps backward and then four steps forward to his partner and then they swing. It makes a graceful and finished maneuver in the set. For the *swing,* of course, all four couples take the modified dance position and swing around twice in place. He then calls:

Turn the left hand lady
With your left hand
Then right hand to partner
And right and left grand.

This is the same movement they learned in the Circle Two-Step. When they have all done the serpentine right and left and have again reached their partners he calls:

Take your partner
And promenade home.

Or, which means the same thing, he may call:

Promenade eight
When you come straight.

And each man taking the promenade position with his girl on his right walks counterclockwise around the square and back to his original place.

Before going on with the dance and sending the second couple around the square with the same figure, it is usually found necessary for the caller to straighten out some of the sets who have got badly mixed up. And it is best to take time out until the beginners get their difficulty cleared up.

In spite of the fact that they learned to do the *Allemande left* (or *Swing the left-hand lady with your left hand)* in the Circle Two-Step, they often have difficulty executing it in a square with only four couples. And I often find it helpful to walk them through this figure slowly without music until they get the idea fixed. Then too, some couples find it difficult to promenade back to their own positions, keeping their place in their square while they do so. Some couples, lacking a strong geometric sense, loiter or wander off into other squares or out around the hall or simply stand bewildered, while other couples "cut-the-pie" and get the square all mixed up. A few minutes taken to walk them slowly through the whole *Allemande* and *Right and left* to the *Promenade* is time well spent with beginners.

Another difficulty arises from the failure of the first gentleman to have his lady on his right when they present themselves to the third couple. If the lady is on the left side of him, it will put two ladies on one side of the *Right hand star* and two gentlemen on the other side. This will make the swinging of the opposites with the right hands very difficult and confused. The two ladies should be opposite each other and the two gentlemen opposite each other in the star. And this can be accomplished only if the lady is on her gentleman's right side as they approach the new couple.

As soon as all the difficulties are straightened out the music can begin again and the dance continue, going on where you left off and, of course, not repeating the introduction. The call continues:

Second couple out
To the couple on the right,
Form a star with the right hand cross, etc.

With an *on to the next* and *an on to the next* and then *a balance and everybody swing* the dance continues. Again they all do an *Allemande left* and a *Grand right and left* and a *Promenade to places.*

Then it is all repeated for the third couple around, and after another *Grand right and left* it is again repeated for the fourth couple all the way around. After the final promenade, the call is often given:

Promenade, you know where,
And I don't care.
Take your honey
To a nice soft chair.

And that set is over.

Since the call for the figure has to be repeated until it has been given twelve times, it is customary to alter it now and then for the sake of variety. Instead of *Form a star with the right hand cross* you may call:

Star by the right
And how do you do?
Back with the left
And how are you?

Or I have heard it called:

Right hands crossed
And how do you do?
Back with the left
And how are you?

All of which means exactly the same thing, and only adds variety to the calling. Another very easy square to execute with beginners is:

Forward Six and Fall Back Six

The same introduction can be used as in the previous dance, or you can call:

All jump up and never come down.
Swing your honey around and around
'Till the hollow of your foot
Makes a hole in the ground.
And promenade, boys, promenade!

Which means only that each couple shall jump up into the air and then swing each other around and around until the call is finished and they are told to promenade, when with the regular promenade position they walk once around the square to the right, or counterclockwise, until they come back to their regular position, where they stand until the caller puts them in action.

In the first part of the call proper it must be explained that as always in square dancing the instructions are for the men, the women having always to do the complementary or corresponding thing to the movement of the men.

The call starts with:

First couple out to the couple on the right (a)
And circle four;
Leave that girl, go on to the next (b)
And circle three;
Take that girl and go on to the next (c)
And circle four;
Leave that girl and go home alone. (d)

Though it sounds a little complicated, it is very simple to execute. (a) The first couple moves over to the right and faces the second couple. All four join hands and circle to the left, or clockwise. As they come around to the full circle (b) the first man lets go with both hands and moves on alone to the third couple. This leaves his lady standing with the second couple, still holding the second man's left hand with her right hand. The three stand in a straight row, with the second man in the middle between the two ladies.

The first man, having gone on to the third couple, joins hands with them, and the three circle once around to the left. (c) The first man and the third lady now break their hold with the third man and leave him standing alone, while they both go on to the fourth couple. As they advance to the fourth couple, and this is very important, the first man changes the lady from his left hand to his right hand, so she will be on his right side. (Remember that always when a couple approaches another, the ladies must stand on the right side of the men.) All four (the fourth couple, the third lady, and the first man) join hands and circle to the left once around. (d) Then the first man lets go his hold, and returns to his first position—*goes home alone.* This leaves the third lady standing to the left of the fourth couple, the three of them in a row.

This is simply a maneuver to move the first lady over to stand in a row of three, while the third lady stands with the fourth couple in a row of three directly opposite them. The first and third men stand opposite each other and alone.

The call continues:

Forward six and fall back six; (a)
Forward two and fall back two; (b)
Forward six and pass right through; (c)
Forward two and pass right through. (d)

On the call *Forward six,* or (a) each row of three on either side takes four steps forward toward the other, then four steps back, still facing each other, into place. As they are falling back the call should be so timed that (b) the two lone men start forward four steps. Then as they fall back to place with four more steps, (c) the six (the two side threes) should be moving forward and pass through each other's formation to the opposite side. (d) The two lone men then pass each other and also trade places.

In dancing, it is always customary to pass to the left as they do in English traffic, instead of to the right as they do in modern American traffic. To get a group of beginners in the habit of always passing to the left it is well to advise them to take right hands with the opposite person as they pass. This will assure them of passing correctly to the left. If some pass left while others pass right, the collision and confusion ruins the dance. So take time to teach them always to pass left by touching right hands while passing.

Our figure is now just as it was, except that everyone has traded places with his opposite and is left standing on the wrong side. The last call, therefore, has to be repeated to put them right.

Forward six and fall back six;
Forward two and fall back two;
Forward six and pass right through;
Forward two and pass right through.

Then continue with:

Swing on the corner (a)
Like swinging on the gate,
And now your own (b)
If you're not too late.
Now allemande left (c)
With your left hand
And right to your partner
And right and left grand.
And promenade eight
When you come straight.

Remember that each man's corner, or his corner lady, is the lady on his left. So to come out of his figure of symmetrical three's and one's, each man (a) swings the girl on his left. Then (b) he swings his own partner, or the girl on his right.

Then (c) they go directly from this swing into the *Allemande left and Grand right and left,* as in the previous dance. They then promenade back to their places.

The whole dance is repeated for the second couple, beginning the call with:

Second couple out
To the couple on the right
And circle four.

And after a promenade it is all repeated for the third couple, and finally for the fourth.

After the fourth, or final promenade, you can again call:

You know where
And I don't care.
Take your honey
To a nice soft chair.

With this the dance is over, and they are all pleased because the dance is so simple and symmetrical and such good fun. If the caller times it right it keeps them moving back and forth through each other with a fascinating sort of routine.

(Note: If any difficulty is encountered with the above explanations, it might be well to turn to pages 167 and 258 for the regular line by line explanations in the second part of the book.)

Chapter 4 — The Round Dances

IT WAS the custom at the old-time dances to form the sets for a square and while the sets were on the floor to dance through two complete dances or tips. Then a round dance would be played. And it in turn would be followed by the two tips of another square.

The round dances were couple dances, the couples free moving over the floor as in the modern ballroom dance. But our grandmothers' couple dances were always special dances such as the polka, the schottische, or the varsouvianna, or mazurka.

In the barn dances of today, or the so-called old-time dances of today, the same custom usually prevails of two squares and then a round dance repeating through the evening. But the round dance today is usually a one-step, or fox trot, or some modern dance. Only occasionally do they put in a real old-time round dance. The modern "old-time dance" which we see advertised is often a transition and shows signs of breaking down into a completely modern-time dance, with perhaps one or two squares dragged into the evening. When such a group as that to which this book is addressed sets out to play with the genuine old-time dance, nothing but the old-time round dances should appear on the program. The modern should be completely taboo. Alternate your evenings if you will, one being completely modern and one completely old-time. Do not alternate the two in the program of any one evening.

Even if you are teaching a group of beginners, the round dances must be introduced early in the evening, perhaps only one or two of them the first evening, repeating each later in the program to make sure it is well learned. But the variety introduced by the round dances is essential to a successful party. So it will be well before describing more squares to treat the commonest of the old-time round dances at this point, starting with the easiest. If the group gets so good that they later want a larger selection, you can turn to such a book as Henry Ford's *Good Morning* where these dances are completely described. But we shall limit ourselves now to those dances that are common in the West.

The Rye Waltz

This is the easiest of all of the round dances to teach and to execute. The couples take the regular dance position; that is, the man holding the lady's right hand in his extended left and his right arm around her waist while her left hand rests on his shoulder. The music is the old familiar Scotch tune "Comin' Thru The Rye." The first four bars are played rather fast in their regular 4/4 time. The last four bars are changed and slowed down so that each beat is modified to the 3/4 time of waltz rhythm, except the fourth or last bar which is left unchanged in its original 4/4 time; that is, the last four bars where the words begin "Ilka lassie has her laddie" become 12 bars of 3/4 time and one final and fast bar of 4/4 time. Then it is all repeated as many times as desired.

We shall describe the dance for the man, the woman, of course, using always the opposite foot in the opposite direction. Incidentally this Western arrangement is somewhat different from the Rye Waltz as danced in the East.

On the first bar of the music, the man keeping his weight on his right foot extends his left foot out to the side and lightly touches the floor with his left toe. On the second beat he closes his left foot back to his right. On the third beat he extends and points his left foot again to the side and on the fourth closes it again to his right. Then he sashays to the left for the four beats of the second bar. That is, he steps left and closes his right to his left, again he steps left and closes his right to his left, and then steps left and shifts his weight to the left, with a step-close-step-close-step rhythm. Then during the next two bars of the music, the whole thing is repeated to the right; that is, with his weight shifted on to his left foot he points right, closes his right to his left, points right again, closes again and then sashays to the right with a step-close-step-close-step.

Then the music changes to a slow 3/4 time, and the couple waltzes around the room for twelve bars of the music. For what would be the last four bars of the waltz section, however, the music changes back to the snappy 4/4 time of the original, and they hippety-hop again to the man's left with a step-close-step-close-step.

The whole routine is repeated as many times as desired, the music playing over and over and over again. (At some old-time dances you wonder if it will ever end.)

As one gets used to the step he will find himself dipping slightly in the first part with his right knee as he extends and closes his left foot away from and to his right. And he will find it natural to want to make the return a little longer swing and put his left foot behind or in front of his right instead of merely closing to the side of it. It is customary in this case to cross it first behind and the next time in front. So the left foot points to the side, then crosses behind the right, points to the side, and then crosses in front of the left—then the sashay. The lady, of course, does just the opposite, pointing right, crossing in front, pointing right, and then crossing behind.

A variation called the Scotch is sometimes introduced to add a bit of fun. The dance is just the same except that the dancers hop like a Scotch reel throughout the first part. That is, instead of standing on the right and pointing with the left foot, they hop on the right while they point with the left, and hop again on the right while they close with the left making the whole thing very bouncy and jolly.

We found another delightful variation current in the North Park of Colorado. Here instead of the point close, point close of the first four beats, they walk together to the left for three steps and close on the fourth; that is, still maintaining their regular dance position, they face slightly toward their extended hands (the man's left), and starting with the outside feet take three steps and close. The man walks left, right, left, and closes his right to his left, and the lady does just the opposite. Then they do the sashay, or slide close, to the right in the regular form. Now they walk three steps and close to the man's right and the lady's left. Then they slide-close back to the left in the regular form and follow it all with the customary waltz.

It is a pleasant and amusing variation and can be quite graceful, especially when they walk to the right, looking over their closed arms and moving with a long, gliding step, they can achieve quite a Spanish, tangolike grace.

The young dancers at our school have invented a wild variation all their own with which they amuse themselves mightily. They walk to the left three steps in the North Park way, but instead of closing their feet together on the fourth bar they pivot on their outside feet (the man's left, the lady's right), and do a complete revolution away from each other, coming together just in time for the sashay. They finish their walk in the other direction with another furious pivot preceding the sashay. And at the close of the waltz they do two complete revolutions away from each other in place of the slide-close sashay. They end with a deep bow if they get around in time. But this is just for fun and most decidedly is not an authentic variation of the Rye Waltz.

The Schottische

This is a delightful round dance, delightful both to do and to watch. The music can be found in the Pioneer Collection of Old-Time Dances referred to earlier. And Ford's arrangement is the form we like best, with three parts each with a full repeat.

In the usual form the dancers stand side by side, the man's right arm around the lady's waist, and the lady's left hand on the man's shoulder. Starting with the outside feet (the man's left and the lady's right), they take three light running steps and then hop as they swing their inside feet up and forward. Then starting with the inside feet (the man's right and the lady's left) they take three running steps and a hop while they swing their outside feet up and forward. Then, facing each other, the man takes the lady's right hand in his left, which puts them now in the regular dance position, and in this position they take four step-hops (beginning with the man's left and the lady's right foot) while they rotate once around to the man's right. The complete pivot leaves them facing forward again, and they let go hands and face forward, retaining only the waist-shoulder position, and repeat the whole thing.

To describe with more detail it may be best to note carefully the man's part, understanding that the woman uses always the opposite foot and the corresponding motion.

1. End of forward run swinging feet forward.

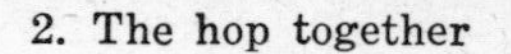

2. The hop together

THE SCHOTTISCHE

3. Hopping away from each other.

4. The rock.

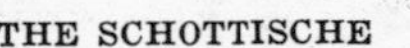

THE SCHOTTISCHE

The man standing with his partner on his right and holding her in a waist-shoulder position takes three light running steps forward, left, right, left, and then hops on his left foot while he swings his right foot up and forward. Then he runs again, right, left, right, and hops on his right while he swings his left foot forward. Now taking his partner's right hand in his left, he assumes the regular dance position and steps on his left and hops on his left, then steps right and hops with his right, and then repeats with a left and hop and a right and hop, all the time pivoting around in a right-face position. During the four hops he should have made a complete revolution and should be facing forward again. He lets go his partner's right hand, turns away from her so they are again side by side, and repeats the dance again as many times as desired. It often helps if the caller directs the men in their steps by calling left-right-left-swing; right-left-right-swing; left-hop; right-hop; left-hop; right-hop.

At most of the old-time dances I go to they do this over and over interminably at a rather slow tempo until I marvel at how they can keep it up. Occasionally some older couple will show some variation such as both stepping to the left with their left feet in the first part of the dance and hopping on their left feet while they swing their right feet up across and in front of their left. Then they step right and hop right while they swing their left feet across to the right. Repeating this again to each side, they are ready for the closed or dance position and do the step-hop while they rotate with the others. Or occasionally instead of the step-hop in the second part, they do a little modified, rather open two-step. The regular two-step, you will remember, is to step on the left on the first beat of the music and close the right to the left and quickly step again on the left to the second beat of the music, then do the same to the right, and so on. They do not quite close, however, in their modified two-step, but step left on the first beat and then step quickly and lightly on the right and immediately with the left again on the second beat. So, instead of a left-hop, right-hop, they do a left-right-left, right-left-right.

Even with these variations the dance is still apt to be a little monotonous, especially since either the two-step or the hop calls for a complete rotation always in the same direction with a consequent dizziness. And it is always quite slow. When I increase the tempo at the urgent request of my young people, the old-timers all cry out against it and say it is not the schottische until I sometimes wonder if it is not their age rather than their memory that keeps the tempo so slow, and if perhaps the young people even in the old times did not always prefer, and usually get, a little speed.

We were delighted when the daughter of one of the pioneer women showed us how her mother used to dance the schottische over on the western slope of the Colorado Rockies back in the eighties. And since her dance is in three parts with each part repeated just as the music is arranged, I believe it to be the true form, and we have adopted it as our standard form of the schottische. We have since had several old-timers confirm it as the original form. It offers enough variety to be great fun to do.

The first part is exactly as described above in our first description of the dance. It is repeated once as the music is repeated. Then the second part changes for the second part of the music as follows: Still holding the same waist-shoulder position, the dancers take the two sets of little running steps just as in the first part, left-right-left swing, right-left-right-swing, but instead of closing together in the familiar dance position and hopping together around to the right, they completely let go of each other, and turning away from each other, each hops independently, the man hopping on his left foot and turning in a left-face direction, and the woman hopping on her right foot in a right-face direction. On the first hop they turn away and are back to back, on the second hop (on the other foot, of course) they turn together and are face to face, on the third hop they turn back to back again, and on the fourth hop they finish face to face, and continue on until they are side by side in the waist-shoulder position and are running forward again on the repetition of this second part of the dance.

The third part of the dance starts with the run exactly as the other two parts, but instead of the second half of the run, the partners let go of each other, and while doing the second part of the run, they turn completely away from each other in one position, making a complete revolution. As they turn back together they resume the waist-shoulder position and instead of hopping they rock forward and back on alternate feet.

The whole step of this third part for the man (with the lady, as usual, doing the complementary or opposite step) is run left, right, left, and hop left as he swings his right foot forward, break hold with partner and with shorter steps in position walk right, left, right, hop while he turns left about face. Then side by side again and resuming the waist-shoulder position he rocks forward on his left foot and lifts his heel slightly instead of a hop, rocks backward on his right foot and again rises on his toe, rocks forward on his left and rises, rocks back on his right with a rise. He then repeats the third part.

As the music turns back to the first part, he starts at the beginning and repeats the whole dance as many times as desired.

The Varsouvianna

Perhaps the most graceful and most delightful of all the round dances is the Varsovienne. It originated in Warsaw, Poland, and from that city, with a few accidents of orthography, it took its name The dance spread all over Europe and took on different national characteristics. It moved on to our West, its name corrupted to Varsouvianna, and is a regular feature of our old-time dances. (So easy is oral corruption, I have even heard it unsmilingly called the "Varsity Anna.") It has its own special music, which can also be found in the Pioneer Collection of Old-Time Dances. Here it is called Ford's Varsovienne. For a real Western dance you should skip the first thirty-two bars of this music for it has been completely lost, and I have never heard it played in the West. Beginning with the thirty-third bar it is our authentic music. To be sure, since it is traditional with our fiddlers you can expect a little variation now and then from this printed score.

There are sixteen bars of this old standard Varsouvianna tune in the West. Our oldest pioneers tell me that these sixteen bars were always repeated once. Then there came sixteen bars of special waltz, which certainly improves the dance and keeps it from growing monotonous. And in the musical arrangement just mentioned (Pioneer Collection of Old-Time Dances) the following sixteen bars are the standard form used for this waltz. But when I tried to get one of my fiddler friends to play it so for me, with complete scorn for all "note-readers" he said he could not play that tune and broke into "Where, oh where is my little dog gone" in perfect waltz time, and it served just as well. He likes the waltz and now he always trots the little dog out and makes them waltz whenever he plays the Varsouvianna.

In the printed score the last variation following the waltz is perfectly authentic and is often heard in the West. It should be used for the second Varsouvianna step. But the first thirty-two measures of the printed score should best be omitted altogether.

This lovely dance is coming back in Western society. For several years they have been dancing it with a Spanish tempo in the ballroom of La Fonda, the leading hotel in Santa Fe. And in many of society's dances in Denver it is being introduced as a special number, though it is danced in its simplest form, over and over, and without the graceful relief of the waltz.

This simple standard form is danced as follows; the couple stands side by side, the man a little behind his lady. He holds her left hand in his left, shoulder high, and reaching across her right shoulder he holds her raised right hand lightly in his right. The two keep in step with each other, for the present. Later they will use opposite feet.

With their weight on their left feet they stand with their right toes pointed forward and touching the floor to the right. On the first note of the music (an introductory note, the third beat of the previous bar) they each sweep the right foot back over the left instep, dipping the left knee slightly as they do so. On the next count (the first beat of the new bar) they point the right foot out to the right front, again touching the floor with the toe, and on the next count step in behind the right with the left foot. Then they each repeat with the same feet (the right) to the same side, sweep, point, step. The third time they again sweep back with the right, point with the right, and step with the left. (But instead of stepping in close behind the right with the left they this time step to the left side with the left foot.) On the next count they close the right foot in behind the left, and on the next count point the left foot, the toe touching the floor, out to the front and to the left. That is, they both make a cross-over to the left. And as they do this left step-cross-point—the lady takes fairly long steps while the man takes very short steps and passes his partner over in front of him

VARSOUVIANNA (Standard Form)
1. *Sweep* (swing outside foot back over instep of other foot).

VARSOUVIANNA (Standard Form)
2. *Point* (out and forward with outside foot).

VARSOUVIANNA (Standard Form)
3. *Step* (close inside foot to outside foot).

VARSOUVIANNA (Standard Form)
4. *Point* (sweep and point as above).

VARSOUVIANNA (Standard Form)
5. *Step* (in behind partner).

VARSOUVIANNA (Standard Form)
6. *Cross* (pass to other side of partner).

VARSOUVIANNA (Standard Form)
7. *Point* (with partner on other side from start).

VARIATIONS OF VARSOUVIANNA
Closed position point.

VARIATIONS OF VARSOUVIANNA
Finishing with point.

VARIATIONS OF VARSOUVIANNA
Open position.

VARIATIONS OF VARSOUVIANNA
Open position.

VARIATIONS OF VARSOUVIANNA
Point.

from his right side to his left side so that when they point with the left foot she is standing on his left, his left hand over her left shoulder and holding her left, while his right hand holds her right hand out to the right of her right shoulder.

This may sound a trifle complicated, but is really very easy to do with the music, as the lovely old melody almost directs you to cross over and point to the left.

As the musical phrase repeats itself on a lower note, they repeat the whole thing beginning with the left and crossing to the right. That is, they sweep back with the left, point with the left and step with the right. Again to the left they sweep-point-step. Then again they sweep left, point left, and step out right with the right, cross with the left as the lady crosses over in front of the gentleman, and finish again pointing with the right.

Then the melody changes a little and directs them to cross back and forth twice, with the same cross-over step as the last half of the preceding; that is, they sweep back right, point right, step left, cross with the right, and point with the left; then (2) sweep left, point left, step right and cross left, and point right; then (3) sweep right, point right, step left, cross right, and point left; and (4) sweep left, point left, step right, cross left, and point right. The crossing foot always steps in behind the stationary foot.

Now this whole figure repeats itself as many times as desired. It is much pleasanter, however, to repeat it only once and then swing into sixteen measures of waltz before repeating it two more times, and so on.

I usually teach this step to a group by calling with the music:

Sweep, point, step,
Sweep, point, step,
Sweep, point, step, cross, point.
Sweep, point, step,
Sweep, point, step,
Sweep, point, step, cross, point;

Sweep, point, step, cross, point;
Sweep, point, step, cross, point;
Sweep, point, step, cross, point;
Sweep, point, step, cross, point.

Some teachers have them rise on the toe of the left foot as they sweep back with the right, then point with the right and close with the left. Although this is an accepted form, I think it a bit prettier to dip slightly with the left knee while sweeping the right foot back rather than to show much of a rise on the left toe. Or, if you want the movement very pronounced, you will direct them to use the old custom of hopping on the left while they sweep back with the right. And it is so instinctive for some people to put in this hop that they are apt to do it without your suggestion. But it is too jerky with a beginner, and I think it best to discourage the hop.

And that, over and over again, is all there is to the Varsouvianna as you find it at most of our dances. Once in a while you may see a couple do a turn back instead of a cross-over. That is, on the sweep-point-step-cross-point, instead of having the lady cross over in front of the man and get on his left side, she takes these short steps in position doing a rightabout-face as she does so, the man likewise doing a rightabout-face. This leaves them both facing directly backward and the lady now, of course, on the left of the man with his left arm over her shoulder. Then a left-about faces them forward and puts her on the right side, and so instead of crossing over she turns forward and back, and it proves a very graceful variation.

Using essentially the same steps, the different nations have developed a great variety of positions and styles. The Mexicans have the loveliest variations that I have seen. They carry through the step not only in the standard position, but in the regular dance position, in a back-to-back position, in a grand circle, and even in a grand right and left which is most delightful. And they do it all as a figure, with three couples working in and out from the points of a triangle.

Perhaps it was their influence, or a European influence, but in any case the oldest pioneers tell me that it used always to be danced here in the West in a variety of positions and each alternating with the waltz.

Miss Mary Kelleher, who gave me the three-part variation of the Schottische, has given me this arrangement, which in turn was brought by her mother from the western slope of Colorado where she danced it in the early days. It is the form we like best and that we always dance.

The first part is the same as the dance described above except that the partners use opposite feet, always pointing with the outside foot or the foot farthest from the partner. This makes it much more graceful and symmetrical, and is just as easy to execute as when the partners use the same foot and keep it, as it were, in step with each other.

To be more specific, the man sweeps back and points with his left foot while the lady sweeps back and points with her right. This lets them each point out and away from the other, making a most delightful position for the onlookers. On the cross-over she steps left and then points left while he steps right and points right, which makes the cross-over easier and much more natural. This greater ease makes me think that this is the original and correct position for the dance and that the other form is a corruption introduced because it was easier to teach beginners if you let them all keep in step with their teacher and with each other. In this older form it becomes natural for each "point" to be away from your partner, adding considerable grace to the dance. After repeating this first part once, all the couples go into sixteen measures of waltz.

In the second part the couples take the regular dance position; that is, with the lady's right hand resting in the gentleman's extended left hand and her left on his shoulder while his right encircles her waist. The first steps are the same as before, the gentleman sweeping back and pointing with his left foot, the lady with her right, and both looking and pointing in the direction of their extended arms. Since they are face to face, their two feet are almost together in the point, and their extended arms above the pointing feet. Instead of the cross-over they both walk with three short steps in the direction of their extended arms and then, turning together, point backward, the gentleman with his right and the lady with her left foot, and look back over their enclosing arms toward their pointing feet. Still looking backward, they repeat the movement, this time the gentleman sweeping and pointing with his right foot and the lady with her left, and then with three short walking steps in this backward direction they turn together and both point front again, or in the direction of their extended arms.

Now instead of the four cross-over steps back and forth, still in the dance position they take short steps in place, rotating half around to the right and pointing with the right. That is, each does a "right face" turn. Then they rotate back to the left and point again. Once more they rotate right and point, and then they return to the left and point, the lady always pointing with the opposite foot from the gentleman. This whole figure is repeated and again they waltz.

In the last figure they take an open position, side by side, the gentleman's right arm around the lady's waist and her left arm on his right shoulder, their outside arms hanging naturally at their sides. The first part of the step is the same except they move much more definitely forward and instead of the cross-over they turn together, letting go their waist and shoulder hold, and face each other and turn completely backward, taking a new hold this time with the gentleman's left arm around the lady's waist and her right hand on his shoulder, and they finish this measure pointing backward. The next measure in this reversed position, of course, carries them back where they started, and in place of the cross-over they turn together again, breaking holds, face forward taking their original hold and again finish by pointing forward.

They could, of course, repeat this turning back and front a couple of times in the last part, and they actually do. But instead of turning together to accomplish this, they turn away from each other, and, each pivoting around, they meet facing backward and both point. Then turning away from each other they turn until they face forward and point again; then away from each other and point backward, and away from each other and point forward again for the finish. They cannot hold on to each other at all in this last part, but the hands swing freely and usually come almost together over the pointing feet. The whole movement is flirtatious and graceful in the extreme. After repeating this whole last part they waltz again. And then the whole dance with all of its parts is repeated as many times as desired.

In teaching this last part it pays to use a "call" at first, as follows:

Sweep, point, step,
Sweep, point, step,
Turn together and point back,
Sweep, point, step,
Sweep, point, step,
Turn together and point front.
Turn back to back, point back,
Turn back to back, point front,
Turn back to back, point back,
Turn back to back, point front.

The rhythm of this call is a little tricky, but with practice it works, and without it beginners turn in wild confusion and get all mixed up.

The Polka

Another old-time round dance that is regularly used in the West is the polka—which is often called the "pokey" in cowboy parlance, perhaps from the square dance figure "Three by three in the pokey oh, three by three and on we go." If one traces back through the New England and European varieties of the polka he can get into deep water in a discussion of just what the polka is. But the Western dance by that name is extremely simple.

The couple stands side by side, either in the waist-shoulder position with the man's right arm around the lady's waist and her left hand on his shoulder, or in the cross-shoulder position, as in the Varsouvianna, where the man holds the lady's left hand in his left at the height of her shoulder and, crossing his right hand behind and over her right shoulder, holds her lifted right hand lightly in this position.

The music is Jenny Lind's Favorite Polka, which can be found in the Pioneer Collection of Old-Time Dances above referred to. In the West I have only heard the first sixteen measures, which are repeated over and over. The last twenty-four measures are never used.

The usual form of the dance is for each partner to stand with his weight on his left foot, and reaching forward with the right foot, to touch the right toe to the floor well in front of him, on the first count. Then bring the right foot back and touch the toe to the floor close beside the left foot on the second count. They then step forward on the right, close left to right, step right, and rise on the toe of the right foot for the next measure counting one-*and*-two-*and*. Then step forward on the left, close right, step left, and rise for the next measure; then step right, close left, step right and rise for the fourth measure. Then repeat the whole movement beginning with the left foot. That is, point forward with the left, count *one-and* and point back on the count *two-and*. Then left, right, left, rise; right, left, right, rise; left, right, left, rise. The whole thing can be repeated, first beginning right and then beginning left, over and over again, point front, point back and then advance straight forward with three sets of polka steps—then repeat. Most of the old-timers, in fact, do it interminably with no variation whatever.

In the regular polka step some of our dancers on the count *one-and, two-and,* simply take three steps and a rest on the second *and*, that is, left, right, left, rest, then right, left, right, rest, instead of left, right, left, rise. They rest the last half of the beat instead of rising. As a matter of fact this rise is not on a beat or even a half beat but is really slipped in as a grace note just before the step of the first beat of the next measure. Many people use a hop instead of a rise, and historically it is perhaps the more correct. But this hop also should be a grace note slipped in before the beat, rather than a hop on the beat itself. Now and then we find a dancer who has the subtle trick of it. But on a Western dance floor the great majority either hop, or rise, or rest, but always right square on the count. And, I imagine, it is more forthright and appropriate for a heavy cowboy boot. So take your choice.

Once in a while a couple will be seen doing the Heel and Toe Polka, although it is quite rare in the West. But it is seen often enough to merit a detailed description. In the Heel and Toe Polka the couples take the regular dance position, with the lady's extended right hand held in the man's left, and her left on his shoulder while his right

The cross-back under gentleman's arm.

The cross-over.

THE POLKA

encircles her waist. The man starts with his left foot, the lady with her right. The dance for the man is as follows (the lady, as usual, always using the opposite foot): With his weight on his right foot he touches his left heel to the floor (his toe pointed upward) on the counts *one-and,* then he touches his left toe to the floor close to his right foot on the count *two-and.* He then steps left on one, closes with his right on *and,* steps left again on *two,* and rests on *and.* Then looking backward over his right shoulder he repeats it all with his right foot—heel, toe, slide, close, slide. Now looking forward again to his left he repeats with the left—heel, toe, slide, close, slide. And, looking back, he does a final heel, toe, slide, close, slide to the right. For the next eight measures they do a regular polka, rotating slowly to the right. It is simply a step, close, step, hop, first leading with the left foot and then repeated with the right lead. The polka is often done with a bouncy little light step although it looks better to execute it smoothly, with the hop merely a rise on the toe or a lifting of the heel, or a complete rest can be used if the hop or rise are not enjoyed.

We were dancing once in Santa Fe, New Mexico, when a charming little lady who, they told me, had been reared on a cattle ranch near Las Vegas, protested that our Heel and Toe Polka was all wrong. "You should do it on a dollar," she cried. "We always boasted we could do it on a dollar!" So I asked her to dance with me, and found that what she wanted was the heel and toe as described in the last paragraph but instead of a slide-close-slide, she wanted a stamp-stamp-stamp done in position. Then to the other side heel-toe-stamp-stamp-stamp. All done without moving from one spot, and repeated again in position. Then we scampered all around the room in the eight bars of a regular polka. "There," she said, "that's the way the boys on our ranch always did it. That's the real polka."

The polka we like best is a sort of cross-over polka which we saw danced by a group from Walsenburg, Colorado. The first two parts were exactly like the regular polka, the partners side by side with the gentleman holding the lady's left hand in his left and reaching his right hand over her shoulder to hold her right hand shoulder high. They both touched their right toe forward and then back and then did three polka steps forward—right, left, right, hop; left, right, left, hop; right, left, right, hop. They then repeated all of this beginning with the left foot. On the next movement the man crossed the lady over and back twice as follows: First touching the right toe forward and then back, they followed by doing a cross-over step instead of a polka step. The gentleman let go the lady's right hand and still holding her by the left helped her turn in front of him with three steps, he in the meantime taking his steps in a stationary position. The lady was then on his left side, facing directly backward, their four shoulders in a straight line and facing in opposite directions. They now each touched their left toe forward and back, but since they faced in opposite directions this made a graceful position, with the left foot of each almost touching that of the other. Now instead of a polka step, the lady crossed back to place passing under the man's left arm, and doing a left-face turn as she passed under. She then stood again on his right side, and he reached over her right shoulder and again took her right hand. They touched right toes forward and back again and she again crossed over to his left side, facing backward. Then touching left toes forward and back, she crossed under his left arm and passed back into place on his right side. Now the whole dance was repeated as many times as desired.

The Waltz

The best of all round dances is the waltz. It is often danced as a single number, and in our Western dancing is even more often a part of one of the other round dances, and appears in many squares such as the Waltz Quadrille.

In the great majority of cases it is danced incorrectly. And the people who dance it incorrectly, alas, always insist that they are waltzing. They are really doing a smooth two-step to waltz time, a dance that is called the *redowa.* There was a time when it was listed on the old dance programs as such, but today its execution is hopelessly confused with the waltz and it has claimed the name of the waltz. A modern dance orchestra seldom plays a waltz. It is unpopular on a modern program. And I believe this is only because practically none of the moderns know how to waltz. In the days of Strauss it was the favorite dance and was done beautifully. It would still be a favorite, no other dance would compare with it, if it were only danced correctly.

In the three beats of waltz time the true waltz is danced step, step, close, while the redowa (or two-step in waltz time) is danced step, close, step. The first is graceful and beautiful while the other is a little jerky and unsatisfying. Yet notice that it is all a matter of timing. In a series of waltz steps, three bars for instance, it would be step, step, close; step, step, close; step, step, close. And the two-step or redowa would be the same thing on a different timing. It is step, close, step; step, close, step; step, close, step. In each case since there are two steps connected by a close; the beginner simply cannot see the difference between them. But in the waltz the first step is accented by holding it. It borrows nearly a quarter of a count from the next beat, and this gives the fascinating grace which made is so overwhelmingly popular in the days of Strauss. But the step, close, step somehow destroys this subtle rhythm and has relegated the so-called waltz to a place among the antiques.

I have never tried to teach a group of beginners but that one or two superior couples would dance away independently from the instruction, blithely and proudly doing the two-step or redowa. And when I called their attention to it they indignantly insisted that they were waltzing. Only a matter of timing made them wrong and yet this timing makes all the difference in the world.

And so if you would learn the delights of the true waltz you must take time and earnestly endeavor to overcome the instinctive and incorrect redowa. It will repay you abundantly in satisfaction.

Our grandfathers learned to waltz from a dancing master; and his commonest device in teaching them was "waltzing in a square." It will pay you to master it. Either chalk a square on the floor some twenty-two or twenty-four inches on each side, or imagine such a square. Stand with both feet together in the upper left-hand corner of the square. As you count one, step back with your left foot to the lower left-hand corner. As you count two, step back and diagonally with your right foot to the lower right-hand corner of the square. As you count three close your left

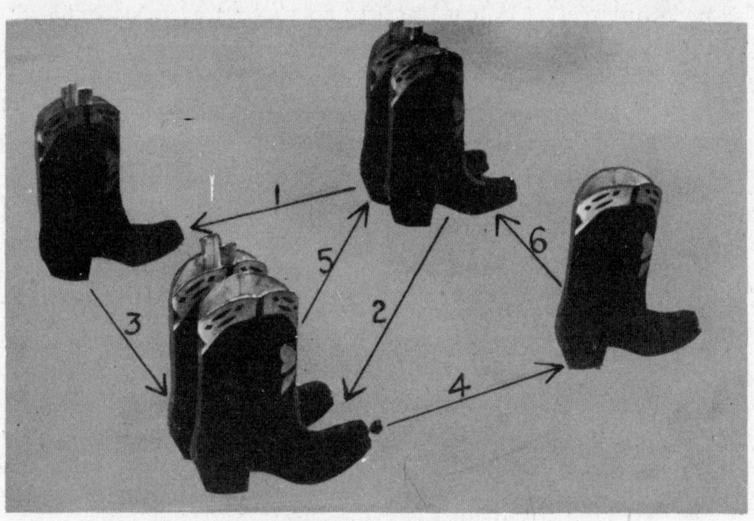

LEARNING TO WALTZ IN THE TRADITIONAL SQUARE
TWO MEASURES

First Bar of the Music

Count 1—Step straight back along the side of imaginary square with the left foot.
Count 2—Step diagonally to the other back corner of the square with the right foot.
Count 3—Close the left foot to the right foot.

Second Bar of the Music

Count 4—Step forward to the upper corner of the square with the right foot.
Count 5—Step diagonally to the corner of the square from which you started with the left foot.
Count 6—Close the right foot to the left foot.

Repeat this over and over until the waltz step becomes instinctive.

foot to your right so they are both together in the lower right corner. Now on the second measure count one again and step forward with your right foot to the upper right-hand corner of the square; count two and step diagonally forward with your left foot to the upper left, and as you count three close your right foot to your left, and you will again be standing with both feet together in the upper left-hand corner of the square. Now repeat this slowly with the count until your feet move instinctively. Then with the music repeat it again and again. It is simply an exaggerated waltz, first back on the left and then forward on the right, and thus around and around inside our practice square.

As soon as one becomes familiar with the step, he should accent the first step by holding it a little longer, even while dancing in his square, and thus establish the subtle rhythm of the waltz. He can take his partner in his arms in the regular dance position, and they can both dance in the prac-

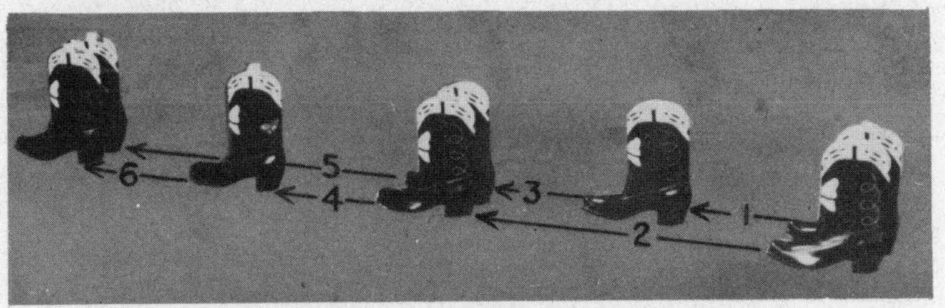

PURSUIT WALTZ OR WALTZING STRAIGHT AHEAD
TWO MEASURES

First Bar of Music

Count 1—Step forward on right foot.
Count 2—Take second step on beyond with left foot.
Count 3—Close right foot to side of left foot.

Second Bar of Music

Count 4—Step forward with left foot.
Count 5—Step on beyond with right foot.
Count 6—Close left foot to side of right foot.

Repeat over and over indefinitely.
To reverse take steps backward in reverse order.

tice square, she starting forward on her right as he goes back on his left, and she going back on her left as he steps forward on his right.

Once the waltz rhythm is established, most experienced dancers can carry on turning and pivoting naturally in a true waltz anywhere over the floor. But less experienced dancers will find it well to practice a forward step after they master the square. Moving in a straight line to music, they step forward on the right, then forward on the left, and then close the right to the left; then forward on the left, and forward on the right, and close the left to the right. Keep on moving forward with a left, right, close; right, left, close; etc., until the end of the hall is reached. Then for practice return by moving backward. Step back with the left, then back with the right, then close the left to the right. Continue backward with a right, left, close; left, right, close; etc., until back in position. Couples, of course, can practice this together in the regular dance position, the lady moving backward while the gentleman moves forward and returning vice-versa. In this pursuit or forward step it often helps to go around the square a couple of times and then start forward.

If this much is mastered the turn will probably come instinctively: but the old dancing masters had a device for teaching the turn that is quite enlightening and a surprising amount of fun to do. If you would like to try it, chalk a larger square on the floor, forty or more inches on each side, and with your chalk draw a diagonal in each corner chopping off about eight or nine inches of the corner. And when you are directed to step in a corner of the square you step along the side only as close as this diagonal, or truncation, will permit.

Begin this time by standing with both feet together in the upper left-hand corner and with both heels against the top line facing the center of the square. As you count one, step your right foot forward to the left side with the toe touching the left line immediately next to this upper left diagonal. On count two, step with your left foot so your left toe touches the left line immediately adjacent to the lower diagonal line (this, of course, leaves your back to the middle of the square), and on the third count, close your right foot to your left, leaving both feet together toeing the left side line next to the bottom diagonal. On the next count one, step with your left foot along the lower diagonal with the heel next to the near end of the bottom; on count two, step with your right foot so its heel touches the far end of the bottom line (you are now facing the center of the square); and on count three, close your left foot to your right, both heels against the bottom line. Continue for the next measure, on count one, with the right toe against the lower end of the right side; count two, the left toe touches the upper end of the right side (back now to the center); and count three, the right foot is closed to the left so both toes are against this side line. On the last measure, count one, the left heel is moved to touch the near end of the top line; count two, the right heel to the far side of the top (now facing

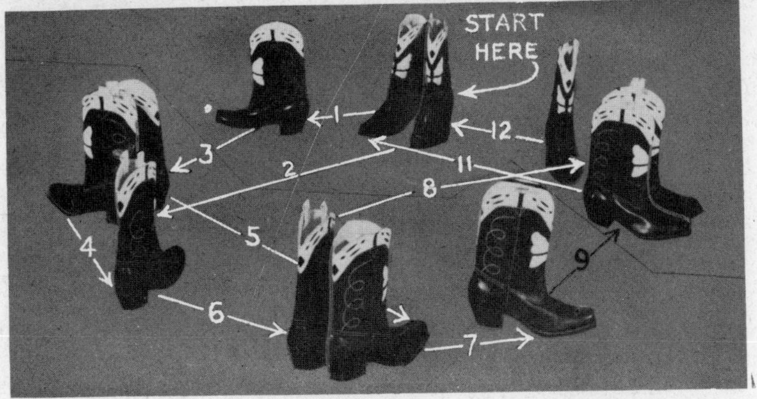

WALTZ TURN WITHIN A SQUARE

FOUR MEASURES

Stand near 12 at the right side of a square (whose sides are numbered 3—6—9 and 12) and which has its four corners clipped off (as 1—4—7 and 10).

First Measure

Count 1—Step with right foot and face out and to the right.
Count 2—Step with left foot to far end of that side.
Count 3—Close right foot to left foot.

Second Measure

Count 4—Step back with left foot to near end of next side of square facing in.
Count 5—Step to far end of same side with right foot.
Count 6—Close left foot to right foot.

Third Measure

Count 7—Step diagonally forward to near end of next side with right foot facing out.
Count 8—Step with left foot to far end of this same side.
Count 9—Close right foot to left foot.

Fourth Measure

Count 10—Step diagonally back with left foot to near end of the side from which you started.
Count 11—Step with right foot to far end of this side, putting foot down in original position.
Count 12—Close left foot to right foot and you are back where you started from.

Repeat over and over until order of steps and complete revolution become instinctive.

By starting at the other end of this side with the left foot the entire figure can be reversed.

center) ; and count three, the left foot is closed to the right and you are standing again at the upper left-hand corner as in the beginning, having made a complete revolution by facing out, in, out, and in again.

The little mechanical device of the square makes it rather delightful and surprising. Go around inside the square several times to music, and then reverse your turn by starting in the upper right-hand corner with both heels touching the top line. Then, of course, step forward with your left to the upper right side, then with your right to the lower right side and bring your left to your right in this lower corner. Then backward with your right to the nearest lower corner, and so on around the square revolving in an opposite direction from your first right lead.

Now you are ready for free waltzing anywhere on the floor. And if ever you get in trouble go back to the good old square again and master the difficulty. Constantly strive for the rhythm, for the first held beat, and for the subtle balance that makes the waltz a thing of joy.

You are apt to find rhythm your chief difficulty in getting started on the true waltz. Once started, the waltz takes care of itself. But it is important to start right. In an old dance book I once found the description of a waltz start that is so helpful and so graceful that most of our dancers always use it. And strangely enough it is very similar to the popular hesitation step of today, in spite of its age. On the first beat of the music the man steps back on his left foot so emphatically as to raise his right foot in the air in front of him. The lady steps forward on her right and lets her left rise parallel to his right. Balanced back in this position with their free feet raised from the floor and pointing from them they both rise on the toe of the foot on which they are standing on the second beat, and lower their supporting heels to the floor on the third. Their free feet still poised in the air, they are now ready to step out on them on the first beat of the second measure and to go into a regular waltz. That is, the man lowers his raised right foot and steps on this right on the first beat, then on his left, and closes his right to his left in a regular waltz. Meanwhile, the lady lowers and steps on her raised left foot and continues in the regular waltz.

It was an old rule that a waltz should always start with the man stepping back on his left foot and the lady forward on her right, but in this case the man balances on his left, the lady on her right, the gentleman counting the one-two-three of the waltz with a step, up, down on his left foot; the rhythm is established, and he is off to a perfect start.

On the Western dance floor some waltzers will be seen doing the Spanish waltz from our Southwest, pivoting and changing direction on each first step. That is, the man takes his first step directly to the side and as he puts his foot down he pivots on his toe so that he faces in the opposite

SPANISH WALTZ

TWO MEASURES

First Measure

Count 1—Stand facing north, step sidewards or west with the left foot.
Count 2—Pivot on the ball of the left foot and swing the right foot clear on beyond, and put it down at a distance. You are now facing south, feet separated.
Count 3—Close left foot to right foot.

Second Measure

Count 4—Step with right foot to the side—or to the west.
Count 5—Pivot on ball of right foot and swing left foot and place it on beyond. You are now facing north again.
Count 6—Close right foot to left foot.

Repeat indefinitely or reverse.

direction. At the same time he has swung his other foot on by and in the same direction as the first step and he then brings his feet together—then he repeats, leading with the other foot. This means that if he is facing south at starting he takes all steps sidewards and to the west and by pivoting alternately faces north, south, north, south, rotating continually as he advances with sideward steps always to the west. It is lovely to watch and fun to do.

Or on our Western dance floor we may see a modern

young couple who have just taken lessons in the modern waltz from a famous New York teacher. If we watch their footwork, they will probably advance in a series of lovely looping, elongated triangles. The first step forward, the second foot loops in toward it and then out to the side where the first foot joins it; that is, the second step swings close but stops out to the side even with the first step, while in the old waltz the second step swung clear on past as in natural walking. The diagram illustrates this.

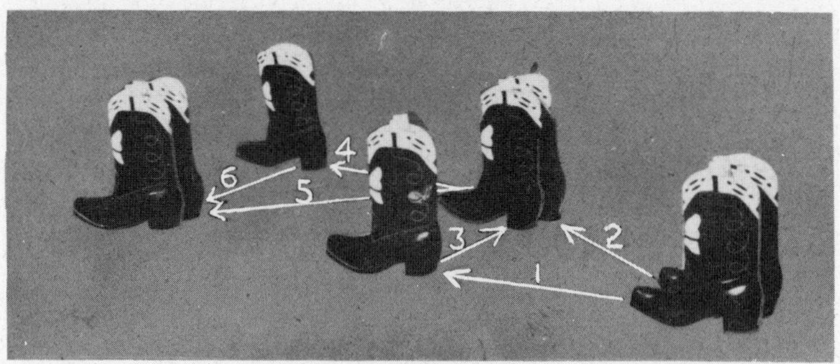

MORE MODERN PURSUIT WALTZ WITH SHORTER STEP

TWO MEASURES

First Measure

Count 1—Step forward with left foot.
Count 2—Step with right and place it out to right of the left foot.
Count 3—Close left foot to right foot.

Second Measure

Count 4—Step forward with right foot.
Count 5—Step with left and place it out to left side of right foot.
Count 6—Close right foot to left foot.

Repeat over and over, continuing forward, until steps become instinctive.

Ancient to modern, what is the waltz? Does it have a lovely little Viennese dip, or should it be so smooth and even you could carry a glass of water on your head without spilling a drop? Oh, here comes an old-timer, and from the look on his face the dear old man is going to tell me something is wrong. "Professor," he says in kindly reproach, "you are backing your lady. When I was a young feller we considered that such an insult that we'd fight the feller that backed a girl we liked." What spacious ballrooms or barn floors they must have had, when the man dared to back up so the lady could always go forward. Today a man must move forward, looking over his backing lady's shoulder in order to steer a course through the crowd that packs the floor. But I back up to please the old man, wondering if I can keep from knocking someone down while I do it. As I pass him again I smile proudly, but he beckons to me. "Did you tell our orchestra to play that fast?" "Yes," I confess, "I did." "Young man, a waltz is always slow and dreamy and you know that," and he winks at me with deep relish. As I back manfully away I recall that young Strauss was considered as dangerous and daring as a modern swing artist, and that he whirled his waltzers at a dizzy and exhilarating speed. Could it have been the sixties to the nineties that slowed the waltz down till it died? And will it someday come back again as a dance for the young, the loveliest and most joyous dance that ever graced a ballroom?

Chapter 5

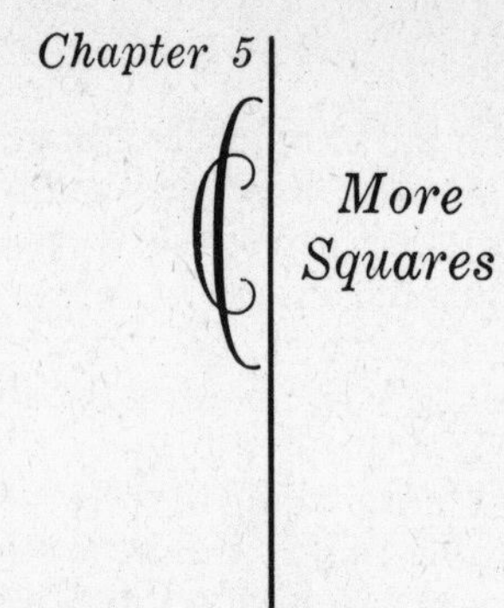

More Squares

The Docey-Doe

IT WAS the customary order at a Western dance to get the sets out on the floor and do two square dances, then do a round dance, then two more squares, and so on through the evening. But gradually the round dances became more and more the modern one-step, fox trot, etc., and the program, following the modern tendency, became mostly round dances with perhaps only two squares called during the whole evening. If you are reviving the old Western dance, keep your round dances in the background and build your programs two to one of squares.

If this is your first dance and you have just tried the Rye Waltz or some simple round dance, call your sets out on the floor for another dance. It is customary to call "*Form your sets for another square*" or "*Form your sets for a quadrille.*" And then the caller walks around the floor helping each set to form. If he finds a set lacking a couple he calls "one more 'two' here" until he fills out the set. And after all the sets are filled, one lone couple may come out on the floor looking for a set, and the caller will help them by calling out, "Three more 'twos' here, let's form another set. That's the stuff, thank you. Now two more 'twos!' Ah, here comes a couple. Now one more 'two,' please. Come, folks, come, let's get this dance started. One more couple, please." And he goes out and commandeers a couple from the side lines if he has to, and his floor is ready.

Ordinarily he would start the music and swing into a call without letting anyone but his fiddler know what was coming. But this is a first dance, and he will have to pause for a good deal of instruction. Perhaps right now he should teach the *docey-doe*.

This maneuver, usually spelled *do-si-do,* recurs over and over in most of the squares. Whenever a couple executes a figure with another couple they usually finish with a little subchorus *circle four and docey-doe.* Then, when they have gone around and done the same with all three couples and are back home, they usually all unite in a general chorus which is the *Allemande left and Grand right and left.* This subchorus, executed by fours, is so common that it must be mastered soon.

It is so important that it may be well to interpolate a discussion of it and its possible origin at this point. One of the common figures in the New England Quadrille, brought over from France, is the *Dos-a-dos* or *back to back.* This is executed by a lady and a gentleman advancing toward each other (as the opposite corners in the Virginia Reel), passing around each other back to back without touching in any way, and each walking backward to their original place. Of course, the French pronunciation was "dose-ah-doe"; and in London, or in Boston, where French was still current, it would be correctly pronounced. But in the Lowlands of Scotland or carried by those Lowlanders to the Appalachian Mountains of America there might be a corruption such as "do-si-do," and the figure could be and probably was developed into a more complicated and more joyous maneuver. The common Briton has a genius for mispronunciation. Note his "cross of the dear Queen," the "chère reine" corrupted into "Charing Cross," "Bethlehem" changed to "bedlam," the "contra dance" with its line against line called a "country dance." So *do-si-do* seems quite inevitable to me in an oral tradition. Years later when someone wished to write it down he mistakenly suspected it of a relationship with the old musical notation, the "so, la, si, do" of the upper scale, and called it *do-si-do.* As it moved west it sounded more and more like two words, "*docey-doe.*" When a literary friend who heard me call one night wrote me a note headed by a little drawing of a deer coming over a mountain and labeled "docey-doe" this impression of mine was confirmed; hence I deliberately depart from convention and spell the Western variant *docey-doe.*

Now in the Kentucky Running Set we find one of the first forms, a *circle four* with the four holding hands but with the men back to back or *dos-a-dos* while the women are face to face in the circling four. When they broke it was

1. Pass each other to the left, grazing right shoulders.

2. Step sidewards behind each other.

DOS-A-DOS

3. And still back to back, encircle each other on the opposite side.

4. Grazing left shoulders as you return to place.

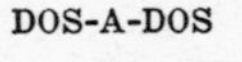

DOS-A-DOS

natural for each man to swing the opposite lady around behind him with his right hand and then *swing his partner with his left* and lead her on to the next couple. This simple form still survives, you will remember, in the *Form a Star with the right hand cross* which you danced earlier in the evening, except that the *circle four* was omitted, and the men were not back to back.

Later, it seems natural that the four would circle while all facing in, and a new movement would be required before they could conveniently swing their opposites with their *right,* and the more complicated it was the more fun it would be. So we find a form where each gentleman passes his lady beyond the other lady (that is, each lady passes between the opposite couple) from her partner's right hand to his left, then the two gentlemen swing in and pass each other back to back, *dos-a-dos,* still holding their partners by the left hand and continuing their pivots while keeping hold. They are now in a position and swinging in a direction which makes it inevitable to swing the opposite with the right and, of course, to finish by swinging partners with the left. This, to me at least, traces the evolution of the French *dos-a-dos* to the Western *docey-doe* with complete satisfaction.

Start very simply and very slowly, if you would save time. Let two couples stand holding hands in a circle of four, each gentleman's partner in his right hand, and the opposite lady in his left. Now let each gentleman break his hold with the opposite and pass his lady from right to left so that she passes between the opposite gentleman and his partner, of course, breaking holds with her partner to be able to do this, and then the gentleman takes her left hand in his left; that is, each gentleman passes his lady's left hand from his right hand to his left in such a way that at the moment of break between his two hands she passes beyond the opposite lady, and the opposite lady passes between him and his own lady. Now he continues the motion by passing her around behind him with his left hand, she, of course, doing a left turn. He must not turn with her, but must keep facing the opposite gentleman all the while. As she gets behind him he must, of course, let go her hand. Otherwise he would have to pivot around with her, and that would spoil everything. She continues encircling him, and as she comes around to his side she is in a position to be taken by her right hand by the opposite gentleman. So each gentleman passes his lady behind him with his left, releases her to let her go on around behind him, and reaches out with his right hand and takes the oncoming opposite lady. He passes her behind him with his right hand, releases her in the same manner so she can complete encircling him, and takes his oncoming partner with his left. As he turns her he puts his right hand behind her waist where her right hand palm upon her hip awaits it and walks with her to whatever position the continuing dance requires.

It all sounds very complicated in words, but is extremely easy on the floor once you get the idea. The gentleman beginners have three favorite ways of muddling up the *docey-doe.* The commonest error is in forgetting to face always the opposite gentleman, and in turning around or pivoting as they pass the ladies behind them. The second commonest mistake is trying to hold on to their partners while they pass them beyond the opposite ladies. This is, of course, physically impossible, as the resulting tangle will prove. And a few of the gentlemen forget to let go of the ladies as they pass them around behind them. But it would require an arm as long and supple as a boa constrictor to pass anyone completely around behind you without letting go hands.

The ladies, bless 'em, also have their favorite mistakes. Usually they try to turn to the right around the opposite gentleman instead of to the left around their partner as soon as they are released and are passing beyond the opposite lady at the beginning of the figure. But if they will concentrate on doing a "left turn" by giving their left hands to their own partners and circling behind them they will have no trouble. Then, often, when they circle their partners they seem to think the figure is over and refuse to encircle the opposite gentleman next. They must do a complete figure eight, encircling each man.

It often pays as a bit for preliminary practice for the two men to stand stationary, close, and face to face, and pass the ladies behind them in a series of figure eights. They will pass their partners behind them with the left hands and their opposites behind them with their right hands alternately over and over again until this essential part of the figure is established. And the ladies will probably never again encircle the opposite first after they have done a dozen or more figure eights around the stationary men.

1. *Four hands up*

2. *and here we go*

DOCEY-DOE

3. *Around and around*

4. *and a docey-doe!*
DOCEY-DOE

5. *A doe and a doe*

6. *And a little more doe.*
DOCEY-DOE

7. *Chicken in the bread tray*

8. *Pickin' up*

DOCEY-DOE

9. *the dough.*

10. *One more change*
DOCEY-DOE

11. *and home*

12. *we go!*
DOCEY-DOE

If the men will remember to face each other always and the ladies will remember to begin with a left turn—to do a figure eight beginning with the left turn—it will all go as smoothly as clockwork.

Now that the elements of this figure are mastered, let's slick it up a little. It is always preceded by a *circle four;* that is, the two couples, holding hands in a circle, circle around to the left until the call of *docey-doe.* It is often called *Four hands up and here we go, 'round and around and a docey-doe.* I expect it means four pairs of hands up and clasped, just as *Eight hands 'round* means eight pairs or eight dancers circling to the left. The dancers will find that it is just as easy to break into a *docey-doe* from the moving circle. But now it becomes instinctive and altogether correct for the men to move forward to seize the ladies' hands and to move backward as they swing them behind. They always more or less face each other, but weave back and forth with the ladies in a free-stepping and instinctive grace as they do so.

In fact, as the couples get expert, they will put in all sorts of flourishes. The commonest of these flourishes is for the men to swing past each other back to back as they swing their partners around with their left hands, and then, letting go, to continue a full pivot in order to take the opposite lady with the right hand. Then they pass the opposite gentleman again, back to back, as they swing the opposite lady with the right hand and do another full pivot in order to catch their partners with their left hands. This is the old form of the *docey-doe* described from the mountains of Kentucky.

I have seen some of our oldest Western pioneers precede the *docey-doe* with the call *ladies doe,* and the two ladies did a regular New England *dos-a-dos,* or *back to back.* They then called *and gents you know* and the two gentlemen did a *dos-a-dos* across their four. Then *circle four and docey-doe,* and they finished with the regular *docey-doe* described above. In fact, this *ladies doe and gents you know* has become just a bit of patter used by the caller while the four is executing the regular *docey-doe.* And beginners must never be worried by this patter, the caller is just amusing himself, sort of talking to himself in his sleep, and he has dozens of variants of this *docey-doe* call. Once you hear *docey-doe* swing into the figure and let the caller rave on as he pleases. One of the commonest bits of patter you will hear, if you can distinguish the words, will be something like this:

Four hands up and here we go
Around and around and a docey-doe.
A doe and a doe and a little more dough,
Chicken in a bread tray pickin' up the dough
And one more change and on we go.

And you will find it is timed so perfectly to the figure that as he says *on you go,* you have finished it all and are presenting yourself and your partner to the next couple for the next figure in the dance.

In some parts of the Western country I find what I consider to be a corruption or simplification of the *docey-doe.* It consists simply of the women doing a pair of figure eights around the men. It would follow the simple call:

Swing your opposite with your right,
Now your partner with your left,
Now your opposite with your right,
Now your partner with your left.

With no passing between and no turning left at the start it is easier for beginners to do. And I am convinced that that is how it happened—the original form was too difficult and was lost. And it is natural that these simpler variants should appear. The only difficulty is that each group thinks his variant is right. They will ask you quite innocently, "Do you do it the right way or the wrong way?" meaning "Do you do it my way or your way?" They seldom know anything of the history of the figure; they only feel that the way they first learned it, even if it were only last week, is the "old way" and any variation they learn this week, regardless of how ancient or authentic it may be is, of course, to them the "new way." It is truly inspiring to see the autonomous pride with which each group feels certain that it alone is authentic and the rest of the world is out of step.

The Lady Round the Lady and the Gent So Low

This is one of the simplest, the commonest, and the most popular of the dances that uses the *docey-doe.* And so, as soon as your sets have all mastered the *docey-doe,* it is a good call to begin with. Some fours may still be having trouble with their *docey-doe.* But if those who know how have demonstrated to the beginners, and helped them until they have learned it, and if each couple in the set has practiced it a few times with every other couple in the set, they should be ready for a dance and a chance to try it out.

You may use the first introduction that you learned in Chapter Three since it is the commonest and most usual form. Or if you want fun and action call:

All jump up and never come down
Swing your honey around and around
'Till the hollow of your foot
Makes a hole in the ground.
Promenade, boys, promenade!

All of which simply directs them to jump playfully up in the air (and how they love to jump high and silly!) and then take the swing hold (modified regular dance position, *see* Chapter Four) and swing around and around until the call comes to *promenade,* when they take crossed hands and march once around the square, to the right, and back to their own positions ready for the dance proper to begin.

Now call:

First couple out
To the couple on the right
With the lady 'round the lady
And the gent so low.

The first couple moves out to the second couple with the lady in the lead. The second couple separate from each other so the lady can pass between them and continue with a left turn by walking completely around the second lady. The first gentleman follows her around this lady. I am told that originally this was called *and the gent also,* but this was a little awkward and was sort of inverted to *the gent so low.* It is usually spelled "solo" when printed, perhaps because the man does a "solo" behind the lady. But since the accent is always on the second syllable as called, I have spelled it in the less frequent form.

The call continues:

And the lady 'round the gent
But the gent don't go.

The first lady now continues in a figure eight by circling with a right turn around the second gentleman. In the meantime, since "the gent don't go," the first gentleman, having circled the second lady, stops there standing beside her, and as his lady circles the second gentleman it brings her around between the two men ready for:

Four hands up and here we go
Around and around with a docey-doe.

Taking hands in a circle, the gentlemen opposite each other, and the ladies the same, each gentleman with his own lady in his right hand, they circle to the left and then execute the *docey-doe* described above. As they finish, the call goes on:

On to the next
With the lady 'round the lady
And the gent so low.
And the lady 'round the gent
But the gent don't go.
And four hands up, etc.

They do the whole thing through the *docey-doe* with the third couple. Then *on to the next* and they do it all with the fourth. Then:

Balance home and everybody swing.
Now allemande left with your left hand,
Right to your partner and right and left grand.
And promenade eight when you come straight.

They all do this general chorus figure of the *allemande and right and left* as described in Chapter Three.

Then the second couple is called out to the *couple on the right,* and the whole thing is repeated for them until they have danced the figure and the *docey-doe* with every other couple in turn, and finally *balance home* to join with all the others in another *allemande left and grand right and left.* It is then all repeated for the third couple, and for the fourth, and after this final *grand right and left,* the dance is ended with the call *promenade to your seats* or *promenade—you know where and I don't care.*

Or if you want to follow the regular Western fashion and dance two squares in succession, you will call *there you stand* or *that's it,* and they will finish their promenade and stand in their squares waiting for the *second tip,* or second call.

Now that the rudiments are learned you can turn to any of the calls in the second part of this book and try another dance. But some of them are quite complicated, and had better be left for a later day. Some of the easiest in the *docey-doe* pattern are *I'll Swing Your Girl You Swing Mine,* or *Two Gents Swing with the Elbow Swing.* In this latter the gentlemen can avoid mix-ups by remembering always to swing each other with the right elbows and to swing the ladies with left elbows. *Around that Couple and Swing at the Wall* is easy and popular, or *Dive for the Oyster.* This last looks very complicated, but is really very simple, and most groups like it best when they do it badly. As soon as they get it smooth, and there is no one to laugh at for his blunders half the fun goes out of it. So it is a great favorite with beginners, and even old-timers love it when they have beginners to astonish.

In the symmetrical selection of dances, *Ladies to the Center and Back to the Bar* is a favorite. Walk through it slowly first and stress the fact that the *star* must continue holding hands after they pick up the ladies on their arms. Once they get the idea of *allemande left just one and promenade the girl you swung,* and of always taking the new girl to the gentleman's home position, it will all go as smoothly as silk. And there are other dances in this section that beginners might want to try. *Swing the Ladies to the Center and Let them Stand* is very easy to do.

The *Down the Center and Split the Ring* type of dance is also easy. Perhaps the easiest to begin with is *Down the Center and Cut Away Six.* The *foot* sometimes forgets to swing but you can trust all the rest of the set to protest until they get to swinging. And some of the couples will have trouble in realizing that a *cut away four* is cutting around two on each side, and a *cut away two* means to go around one on each side. But beginners catch it quickly, and they always like it. By far the most popular, perhaps because it is the simplest of all of the dances in this section, is the *Waltz Quadrille.* After you have done it a few times the sixteen repetitions may grow unbearably monotonous. But in this case I always let each couple (really each gentleman) go down the center twice instead of four times, and it all comes out even in the end, and cuts the dance exactly in half.

There are many dances in the section where one lady or gentleman goes out that are very simple. For instance, *One Little Buffalo out around the Ring* is so easy as to be fool-proof, and it has a lot of laughs in it.

Once the group has done a dozen different dances they can try anything safely. Of course, such a dance as *Wave the Ocean* requires such a precision of timing that a general mixed group had better leave it alone or they will be mixed indeed. But any group that has worked together for any time at all can soon have it running smoothly, and their mastery of its timing will accentuate their pleasure in it.

Endings and Beginnings

There are only a few introductory figures current in the West, but it is well for the caller to have his group used to all of them, and to keep variety up by changing as often as possible. You will find them all in the second section of this manual. Any introduction will serve as well as another for any dance, with very few exceptions, and the caller must always strive for variety. To keep the interest up he must make them follow the call, and never let them know what is coming next. If some wise set runs ahead of the call with too much overconfidence, he had better change the call suddenly and leave them hanging out on a limb. It is good discipline and good dancing.

And so with the endings. In the second section you will find them all. Any ending can be used for any dance, and the caller should always use a different ending so the dancers will keep their ears pricked up for the call, and their interest on the alert. Only in the case of one or two dances is any particular ending more appropriate than any other. But in every other case scramble them joyously.

In the ending:

> *Swing your opposite across the hall;*
> *Now the lady on your right,* etc.

there is sometimes trouble on the first trial because the ladies, in their enthusiasm, cross over to meet the gentlemen, instead of standing still as they should, and waiting for the gentlemen to come to them. But the chief trouble comes from the gentlemen not being able to tell which direction to go for the *lady on the right.* This is because some of them may be facing the center of the square when the call comes, in which case they will really get the right lady; but those who have their backs to the center at the moment, of course, go in just the opposite direction and grab the wrong lady. It is easiest for the men to remember to move on in their regular promenade direction (which, of course, is a circle to the right), and take the next lady, in which case it makes no difference how they were facing when the call came.

There are two endings which have an identical execution, but the calls are worded differently.

Promenade in single file
And just let me remind you
To turn right back in the same old track
And swing that girl behind you.

This call usually comes after a swing, and all that must be remembered is to put the ladies down in front of the gentlemen before the single file promenade begins; then turning back (with a turn to the outside) the gentlemen swing each lady in turn and put each one down in front of them until after four promenades they get their own ladies again.

Promenade in single file
Lady in the lead in Indian style
Turn right back and swing 'em awhile.

From this call the dancers, of course, do exactly the same thing, repeating four times until they meet their own partners. But my dancers always take this call literally and on the words "in Indian style" they all crouch in war-dance tradition, and with their hands over their mouths, give a series of war whoops. It makes a pleasant variation, and the dancers seem to enjoy it. So I always alternate these two calls while doing the series of four repetitions, and it seems to work out better that way.

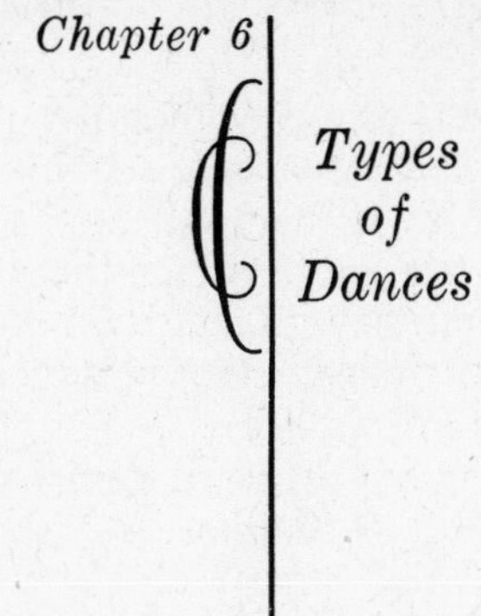

Chapter 6 Types of Dances

THERE were four distinct types of dances in the old American dance program. They were the square dances, such as the quadrille; the longways dances, such as the *Virginia Reel;* the round dance, such as the *Polka* and *Waltz;* and the circle dances, such as the *Cicillian Circle* or *Soldiers' Joy.* In our Western dances, only the modified square and a few of the round dances managed to survive. I hear references to the old circle dances done here forty years ago, but I have never seen one on a modern program in the West. Only the *Circle Two-Step* has carried on, and this is so simplified that it has little in common with the fine old-time circle forms.

Also, the splendid longways dances such as *Speed the Plough, Lady of the Lake, Hull's Victory, Pop Goes the Weasel, Money Musk,* etc., are only names in this part of the country, or revivals in some of the schools. At one old Western dance I attended the caller announced "Pop Goes the Weasel." I was delighted and got my young people out on the floor and all lined up for a good longways dance. But no one else lined up. They stood about the floor in couples, and as the fiddler started the familiar tune they all took a regular dance position and began to two-step.

Which of the old verses do you remember? Is it—

'Round and 'round the cobbler's bench
The monkey chased the weasel.
The monkey thought 'twas all in fun
When pop goes the weasel.

Whichever verse you do remember, you recall that the fourth line is always "Pop goes the weasel." And when the music reached that line, each gentleman turned his lady under his left arm (pushed her under, if you will, with the right hand that had been around her waist), and she flew away from him to her full arm's length. At the end of the rope, the extreme limit of their holds, he gave a mighty jerk so that she flew through the air and almost flattened herself against his chest. If she was still conscious, they started two-stepping again with a high hop and a joyous abandon until the music directed him to "pop" her again. It was funny and full of laughs. Any hilarious group will find it amusing for a few times. But it is a sad descent from the old dance of the same name.

But you will say that the *Virginia Reel* still survives. No, I have never seen it with the country folk. It has strangely survived in schools and in society groups as the only example they know of the longways dance. I say strangely because I do not consider it nearly as fine or as much fun as many of the others. And my young people almost refuse to dance it, they have become so tired of it since they have been called upon to demonstrate and to teach it so often. However, I am sure your group of beginners will want to dance it largely because they feel somewhat on familiar ground. And you should encourage them. My only suggestion is to break up the dance from the long double line it is usually danced in to the old traditional grouping of many shorter lines. It is best to have only six couples in a reel set, the gentlemen in one line and the ladies in the other, and as many of these short sets arranged crossways of the hall as the space will permit. Then it does not take so unbearably long to get through the dance once. In fact, with only six or eight couples in each set, we usually cut its time in half by having the first two couples form a bridge (after they have marched around and come together) and all the other couples passing under. This gives a complete new set of corners. Otherwise, the head couple becomes the foot couple on the second repetition, and they have a second turn on the corners with all the saluting and turning and *dos-a-dosing* to repeat. To be sure, in this shortened form only every other couple gets to reel down through the set. But they won't notice this if you don't tell them.

If you have many short sets for the *Virginia Reel* crossways of the hall, it is almost necessary to call the dance. It not only helps the beginners when they get on a corner and have to lead, but it keeps all the sets together and saves a lot of confusion on the floor. If a set gets through reeling before the others, it, of course, waits for the call before going on with the dance, and soon they will all be working together at the same tempo.

I have shortened the call and modified it to the present form as best suiting my purposes. I assume that everyone is sufficiently familiar with the dance so that detailed directions are unnecessary.

Head lady salute the foot gent.
Opposite corners salute.
Head lady turn the foot gent with the right hand 'round.
Opposite corners turn with the right.
Head lady turn with the left.
Opposite corners turn with the left.
Head lady turn with both hands 'round.
Opposite corners turn with both.
Head lady dos-a-dos (or back to back).
Opposite corners dos-a-dos.
Head couple join hands
Down the center and back.
Now hook right elbows
And turn once and a half around.
Now reel through the set.

(That is, alternately hook right elbows with your partner and left elbows with the next person in line, the lady, of course, turning the gentlemen, and the gentleman turning the ladies, until you have reached the foot of the set.)

Head couple swing each other
And march back to the head.
Cast off and lead the lines around.

(That is, the gentleman leads the gentlemen, and the lady leads the ladies, marching down the outside of the lines until partners meet at the foot and either join hands to form a bridge, or join hands and pass under.)

First two couples join hands in a bridge
And the rest pass under.
Separate your two lines.

(Repeat as many times as necessary.)

The chief trouble, as I said, with the Virginia Reel is the monotonous repetition and waiting for your turn on the corners. This can be obviated by a new form of the dance which is gradually growing in favor. In this form, instead of having corners bow, turn, etc., each gentleman, and all at once, crosses directly over and does all the moves with his own partner. Done carelessly, this leads to wild confusion (but fun). However, if the line of men all advance as a straight line, the ladies the same, and all return to places in straight lines it can be very effective. And everyone is active all the time up to the point when the head couple reels the set.

Of course, the call must be modified to:

Each gentleman salute the opposite lady.
Now turn her around with the right hand round,
etc.

or some similar call of your own improvisation.

If you would like a complete description of the *Virginia Reel* and of most of the other old American longways dances I can refer you to no better text than Elizabeth Burchenal's *American Country Dances* published by Schirmer. It not only has complete directions and music but diagrams which make everything clear.

Some of these old dances are also described in Ford's *Good Morning,* which also contains descriptions of the circle dances and the best descriptions I know of a large variety of round dances. But its chief value is for the New England Quadrilles and Lancers. To anyone who is taking up American dancing it is quite invaluable.

In our Western dancing we find a few New England dances with a sung call still surviving. And I think this call, which was sung, unquestionably had a great influence on the patter used by the Western caller. In the West where they had to do the best they could with whatever they had, it was inevitable that the fiddlers would be unfamiliar with some special tune and would have to substitute another, thereby killing the song, or the caller had forgotten the exact words and a patter grew up quite naturally, and the Western dance evolved as quite a distinct form.

There were several different types or patterns of dance that grew up in the West. And it would probably pay to discuss each type briefly. Before doing this we should mention one other New England contribution that became transplanted in the Western dance. There are two figures that regularly recur in the old New England dances. They are found over and over again in the Quadrilles, Longways dances, and Circle dances. They are the *right and left through* and the *ladies chain.* While they do not very often occur in the Western dance, the *ladies chain* being especially rare, they do merit a description; and, once learned, your group can widen the variety of its dances. Ford's *Novelty Two-Step,* for instance becomes great fun with a group who are familiar with these two simple figures.

In the *right and left through* two couples advance to each other, each lady, of course, being on the right side of her gentleman. Each dancer gives his right hand to the opposite (who, of course, is of the opposite sex as well) and passes beyond—the two couples passing through each other. Each gentleman then takes his lady's left hand in his left hand, and putting his right hand behind her waist, turns her around him to the left while he stands as a pivot. Then the two couples pass through each other again, giving opposites right hands as they do so. Then giving left hands to partners, the gentlemen again turn the ladies to place. Right hands to opposites and left hands to partners give it the name *right and left through.* Experts usually leave out the handshake, but beginners find it a help. This means that the dancers pass each other on the left side. Incidentally, in all passing, whether individuals, couples, or long lines, it is customary to pass on the left side of your opposite instead of on the right side as we are accustomed to do in modern American traffic. The old English custom of passing on the left prevails in our dancing as it still survives in modern London traffic. Perhaps it carries the roots of our dances back to the time when armed men passing in narrow lanes kept their sword arms toward each other for safety's sake and passed on the left.

In the *ladies chain* two couples face each other. Each gentleman passes his lady toward the other lady. The two ladies take right hands in passing each other and then give their left hands to the left hands of the opposite gentlemen. The gentlemen put their right hands behind the ladies' waists and turn them completely around to the left as they themselves pivot in position. Each gentleman now passes

1. Two couples advance to each other.

2. And taking right hands with opposites pass through each other.

RIGHT AND LEFT THROUGH

3. Partners now rejoin their left hands and—

4. Each lady pivots around her partner to the left.

RIGHT AND LEFT THROUGH

5. They advance to each other again taking right hands with opposites.

6. Pass through each other. Then joining left hands as above (in Fig. 3) will pivot left to place.

RIGHT AND LEFT THROUGH

his lady toward the other. The two ladies take right hands and pass again, giving their left hands to their partners this time, who again pivot and turn them to place. It is more graceful if the lady, when she gives her left hand to the gentleman, places her right hand well back on her hip, palm outward, so as to receive the gentleman's right hand when he turns her around.

When either of these figures is encountered I think it adds pleasure to the dance to recognize it as of the purest New England ancestry. And yet the *ladies chain* is so rare in the West that its commonest form modifies it from a two *ladies chain* to a *three ladies chain* in the dance of that name, and even sends the ladies *chaining* for the full length of the hall at times, giving right hands to each other and left hands to the fixed line of gentlemen, who stand dizzily pivoting to the left and passing the ladies on interminably.

Types of Western Squares

There are several distinct patterns or types of Western dances. If you understand the essential structure of each type you will fit any new call into its type immediately and only have to become acquainted with the variation. And so I believe it will pay to discuss the types in order that the whole general architecture of the dance may be kept in mind.

The Docey-Doe Type

The *docey-doe* type is perhaps the most typical form of the Western dance. The *docey-doe* serves as a subchorus, the *grand right and left* as the grand chorus. After an introduction, the first couple goes to the second, executes a special figure and a *docey-doe,* goes on to the third couple and does the same figure and the *docey-doe,* then on to the fourth, repeating the figure and the *docey-doe,* then balances home and they all do the *allemande left* and *grand right and left,* preceded usually with a swing, and ending always with a *promenade to place.* Then the second couple goes around the ring visiting each other couple in turn, third, fourth, and first, and does the figure and *docey-doe* with each and back home to join with all in the *grand right and left.* Then it is all repeated with the third couple visiting around the ring, then repeated for the fourth couple, and after the last *grand right and left* and last *promenade* the dance is over.

1. The ladies of two couples exchange places, taking right hands in passing.

2. They give their left hands to the opposite gentlemen and encircle them.

LADIES CHAIN

3. They pass back to their own partners, again touching right hands.

4. They give their left hands to their own partners.

LADIES CHAIN

5. The gentlemen put their right hands behind the ladies' backs.

6. And turn them around to place.

LADIES CHAIN

Variety may be added by using a variant of the *grand right and left*, or by using some other ending such as *Swing your opposite across the hall.* Good dancers sometimes add variety without the caller's help by letting the second couple do the figure and *docey-doe* with the third couple at the same time the first couple goes on to the fourth. This puts the whole set in action at once instead of having two couples standing inactive. Less often, and only with very expert dancers and very energetic ones, the whole set keeps in action all of the time. The third couple jumps out to the fourth and dances the figure with them while the first couple dances with the second. But the third must finish in time and be back home ready to receive the first when they advance to meet them. The fourth couple in the meantime swing more or less to the center of the set ready for the second couple, who advances to them and does the figure with them while the first and third are in action together. It is now the turn of the fourth to hurry and make sure they are home in time for the oncoming first. For, after all, the dance really belongs to the first couple, it is called for them, and the other couples must be in place to receive them when the caller sends them on. As the first and fourth do the figure the second meets the third with the same. Then they all balance home for the *grand right and left.* And so on through the four repetitions of the dance, they all keep active all of the time. Unless they are experts and sure of their timing, it only makes for confusion and sloppiness; even with experts there must be agreement as to who is the active couple, or it will lead to collisions. Of course, the first is active all three times, and perhaps it is best for the others to follow the order of third, fourth, and second couples being active each in turn on the off couple's figures. But any agreement as to this that any group arrives at will be satisfactory so long as it is an agreement that is always understood.

Sometimes the caller directs this double action, speeds things up, and shortens the dance with a call—*second couple follow up.* After the first couple has danced with the second couple and then with the third couple in the regular manner the caller says, *"On to the next and the second follow up."* The first couple then advances to the fourth and at the same time the second couple advances to the third, and the two groups of four are in action at the same time. Then on the call, "On to the next," the first couple goes back to their own position and remains there (since they have completed the circuit of the set) and the second couple advances to the fourth and dances with them. Then the caller says, *"On to the next and the third follow up."* The second couple now dances with the first couple, and the third couple at the same time dances with the fourth. In this way each couple goes around the set overlapping with the proceeding couple and stopping at their own home position and waiting for the couples behind them to catch up. As soon as the opportunity offers the *fourth follow up* and by the time the fourth couple gets back home, all will have been around the set. Thus three *grand right and lefts* will have been omitted, and they will all join now in a final *right and left.* It sounds complicated, but works out easily. Each couple follows up as soon as there is a couple free for them to dance with. In the figure it works out that all four couples are busy, then only two couples, then four again and so on alternately. It makes the dance more interesting and much shorter when called in this way.

Split-the-Ring Type

There are several dances built on a pattern in which the first couple goes down the center and splits the ring, *the lady goes right and the gent goes left.* In practically all of these dances, after the introduction, they begin by having:

The first couple balance;
The first couple swing,
And down the center,
And split the ring.

Aside from the direction *balance home* in which most dancers simply *go* home (though by rights they should balance even here) *balance* always means to step backward four steps and then forward four steps in our type of Western dance. So, if the first couple *balances* they face each other and each backs up four steps, then they come together four steps, and swing in the regular way. Then they march down the center and pass between the third couple and separate, the lady going around the outside of the ring to the right and the gentleman to the left, ready to do anything that the call directs them to do.

In most of the dances of this type whatever the figure may be, the man promenades with the corner girl, that is, with the girl on the left, and takes her to his home position. This means that each lady progresses one gentleman to the right each time. Thus, the first lady progresses to the position of the second couple, the second lady to the third, and so on. Usually the call continues *the same old gent* (that is, still the first gent) *and a brand new girl* (that is, the fourth girl) *down the center and away they whirl,* and they repeat the dance by splitting the ring and each circling around. The next time it is the same gentleman and still a new girl. On the fourth repetition the first gentleman finds his lady has progressed to the fourth position, and is now his *corner girl,* so he promenades with her and has her back home. Then usually a *left allemande and right and left grand* is used as a general chorus before the second couple is called out for the dance, and it all repeats itself.

Sometimes this is accomplished by each dancer executing a figure with the corner and being then directed to finish by promenading with the corner, which makes it all very simple to put the ladies through their progression. But more often the figure is done with the partner and then comes the call *all run away with the corner girl,* when each gentleman goes to the corner lady and leads her around the promenade to his home position. When the figure is executed with the corner, it is often followed with the call:

Allemande left just one,
And promenade the girl you swung.

This means that each man does an *allemande left* with the girl on his left and then returns to the corner girl with whom he just did the figure *(the girl he swung),* and promenades with her, thus effecting the necessary progression. This progression must be remembered as the essential feature of most of these *split the ring* dances.

In the *Waltz Quadrille,* an old favorite, we find a variation when the lady returns back center after the first couple has passed through the third couple; that is, she passes back through them again instead of circling around to the right, but the gentleman *stays outside* and circles in the regular manner. He meets her at their original position, but she has taken a short cut.

Symmetrical Type

This is a type of dance in which each couple does the same figure at the same time, giving a complete symmetry to the set. It is at its best in such dances as *Four Gents Lead out to the Right of the Ring* and *Ladies to the Center and Back to the Bar*. And in most of the dances of this type there is the same progression of ladies or gentlemen around the ring, so each will have a new partner for the four repetitions of the dance. This progression is achieved in one of the three ways described in the preceding section.

Another type of symmetrical dance starts with:

The first and third couple
Forward and back.

(This is suggestive of the New England Quadrille.) After taking four steps toward each other and four steps back and away from each other, the first and third couples move into a position that puts all four couples in action and in symmetry.

The Single Visitor Type

There are a few dances in which a single lady or a single gentleman visits around the ring, doing some figure with each couple or one dancer of each couple in turn. Usually this type of dance borrows its patterns from the Kentucky Running Set, and the single lady is followed by each of the other ladies in turn until they are all going around the ring, or the lady is followed by her partner. In one dance, *The Pokey Nine,* even the caller jumps into the set, or some ninth dancer comes in from the wall, and follows around always with the odd couple until the dance is completed. And in *Take Her Right Along* the gentleman leads his lady out to the second couple, but leaves her there and takes the second lady on to leave her with the third gentleman while he takes that lady on, and so on until, after twelve swaps and twelve swings, he has his own lady back home.

The characteristic, then, of this type of dance is for one or more dancers individually to visit around the ring.

Promenade the Outside Ring

There are a few dances in which the first couple starts the dance by promenading the outside ring, or the inside ring as the caller may direct. Then the dance can take any of several directions. In fact, these directions are so various that the dance may move into a sort of symmetry or take almost any form, and so I doubt whether this is a true type, although we often loosely call it a type.

For instance, in one case, after the first couple promenades the outside ring *the lady goes half way 'round again* (and by so doing gives the name to the dance). This leaves her in a line of three with the third couple, and leaves her gentleman standing alone. He now becomes a single visitor and swings each lady in turn making the dance distinctly of the single visitor type.

We will find the first dance of the next section *The Grand March Change,* which distinctly belongs in that section, starting with the *Promenade the inside ring,* so I doubt if this is a true type at all.

Intermingling Type

Some of our finest dances are here, but since all the sets intermingle with each other in one long line they are not dances for beginners. They are, however, packed with fun for those advanced enough to execute them. The *Grand March Change* is perhaps the best liked of all of them. If all your sets are arranged in one line down a narrow hall, the first couple of each set promenades the inside ring and faces the wall, that is, faces outward from the set and toward the head of the hall. The second couples then promenade and fall in behind them, the ends (or third couples who are already facing the head of the hall) move up behind them, and the *sides* (or the fourth couple) move into line behind the *thirds.* All the dancers on the floor are now in one double column, and the old-fashioned grand march is done by ones, twos, fours, and eights. To be sure, if your hall is wide and you have too many sets to form in one line down the middle of the hall, you may have to form a line down either side. In this case you will have two double columns facing the head of the hall. And each column will have to execute its own grand march without intermingling with the other, and by staying always on its own half of the floor.

After many possible variations of the Grand March you end with an *eight by eight,* or a *column eight,* and each set, of course, forms one of these groups of eight abreast. Now, if they are directed to *circle eight,* the two end dancers of each eight circle around and take hands so as to form a closed ring, and a *swing* and a *promenade* will put them all back in regular position on the floor as the sets were at the beginning of the dance. Or you can slip in as many complicated figures as you like before you promenade them to their home positions.

The other dances of this intermingling type can be danced either entirely within each set as a unit or intermingling with other sets for the length of the hall. Perhaps it will be best to get a picture of their structure within a single unit before complicating them with too much intermingling.

The essential pattern is achieved by moving the first couple to the second and calling for a *four and a half,* which means for them to join hands and *circle four* half way around. This leaves the first couple facing the center of the set, the second couple with their backs to the center and beyond them the fourth couple. This puts three couples in a row. If the first couple, with some such figure as a *right and left through* or an *arch,* passes through the second, they are facing the fourth. Now as they pass through the fourth with the same figure, the second couple can be turning around and again face the center of the set. The fourth, having passed through, is now in the middle facing the second. The fourth passes through the second while the first turns around, now leaving the second and first facing each other for another pass through. And so they could go on, shuttling back and forth forever.

Now, if there were another set, the two sets could shuttle across the hall with six couples passing through each other alternately, in which case each couple must remember to go clear to each wall and back before they are home and all straightened out. Or if the second couple leads out to the third on the first repetition of the dance, second, third, and first couples are in line in each set, and if there are many sets on the floor each couple can pass through to the ends of the hall and back.

If a half dozen sets intermingle in line to the two ends of the hall and back it will prove quite enough, and the odd couples will simply have to stand and await their turns. In a single set we often call only four passes, which leaves the active couple in the center, and the side couples each standing in the other's place on the wrong sides of the set. The active couple now *circles four with the odd couple oh, and around and around with a docey-doe,* which tends to pacify this odd couple, before the active couple goes on to the right with another *four and a half,* putting the three couples again in line. Now four more *passes* will put each couple back in its own place, the active couple in the center, and as soon as they balance home, a *left allemande* and a *grand right and left* can finish off that quarter of the dance, but with many sets intermingling the *odd couple* awaits their turn.

Irregular Types

There are a few dances that seem to fit into no classification or type. Sometimes you may have two that are alike enough to make a type, but two are hardly enough to merit a title. For instance, in the *Figure Eight* the dancers join hands in a line and parade around in single file. In the *Grapevine Twist* they do the same, turning in and out through each other as they march. But this is hardly enough to justify a type in our classification.

Therefore, in the second part of this book, where the calls are given, I shall lump all of these dances together in one irregular section. And there are some mighty fine dances to be found here. These dances are only irregular in the sense that they fit in no regular classification.

Now and then we do find a completely irregular dance, so irregular that it seems impossible. One night I was dancing with the Old Town Friendly Club (Old Town being the familiar name for Colorado City, the first territorial capitol of Colorado). A strange little man who had been dancing with us, though no one had ever seen him before, announced that he was a caller and asked permission to call a square. The whole party blew up when he called the first couple out to the left. There was not a person there who had ever seen the first couple go left, or what they called "backwards." But he stoutly insisted that as many dances went left as right, so they tried his dance. I wrote down the call which was as follows:

First couple out to the left
And face the wall.
Put on style and back to the hall,

And swing a little while.
Four hands 'round
And gents patter down.

But he couldn't make them understand what he wanted. On his *gents patter down* he insisted on a back-handed *docey-doe* which he called an *Allemande left with four*. Some of our old dancers had danced in squares for over sixty years, but they could make nothing out of his call. After their first try and hopeless confusion they stood laughing at him, and he went home in a huff, so very irregular that he could fit nowhere in our scheme of things.

Original Dances

Surely it is obvious that every dance in existence had to be done a first time by someone. Some, to be sure, are modifications of older dances, but each modification also had to be done for the first time. In dancing especially is it true that "there is nothing new under the sun." The arrangement of old elements in each dance, and its pattern, was original sometime with someone somewhere. Only the dead tree ceases to put out shoots. Surely it is a sign of vitality for each caller to experiment a little with some new call or new arrangement. I have only had time to do a little of this, but I simply could not help inventing a few new dances of my own, borrowing from European folk-dance figures, or from any figure that I thought might be used.

I have put a few of these original calls as my very last section. I have not separated them for distinction or for apology, but as a challenge to other groups to make their own. Since many readers will want to be able to distinguish the old and traditional from the new and brash, it seems only fair to admit that these are not old traditional dances of the Western pioneers. They are simply experiments on the old square frame done for pure fun.

Exhibition Dancing

If your group should become familiar with many of the old dances they are pretty sure to be called upon to exhibit them somewhere. If they do, there is one last suggestion that I should like to make. Keep them alive and up to tempo, and avoid as many repetitions as possible.

When many sets are dancing by themselves for the pure enjoyment of the dance (the only real justification, after all) they may prefer a slow and easy tempo. And they will, of course, want to do each dance completely, each couple taking its turn at leading each figure. But this is deadly to watch. The first time through is interesting; the second repetition may help you in your better understanding of the figure, but the third and fourth repetitions drag until from an audience's point of view they are almost unbearable. And if, as often happens in a contest, some other set uses the same call and drags through it all again for four more times, it is almost beyond audience endurance.

Often at a contest the judges are old dancers themselves, and they somehow feel that it isn't a real dance unless it repeats itself through the full four times, and in loyalty to the past they will sit through it even if it kills them. But I believe and have often urged, without much avail, that if each couple were called out on a brand-new call it would not only give the variety of four different changes but would be a much better test of the ability of both the caller and the dancers. The weight of tradition says, "No!" However, when you are exhibiting you wish to make the thing you exhibit as attractive as possible. There is no one to say you nay, and I feel you should speed it up and give as many samples of the square dance as your time will permit. A few old-timers, with a loyalty to their past, may object, but I believe even they will enjoy the program more in spite of (or perhaps because of) their objections.

Indeed, a group of young dancers in a private dance of their own enjoy and even beg for a change of call for each couple, even when there is no audience. I believe that it is good to indulge them now and then. It takes four times as much memory and four times as much ingenuity to carry a whole evening through that way, but the caller's job is to give the very maximum of enjoyment to the group he has before him on the floor.

Little Children

One last word! Please do not teach these dances to little children. Grade-school pupils may enjoy them but it will mark the dances forever in your community with the stigma of "kid stuff." Well-meaning gymnasium teachers have taught the splendid circle folk dances of the peasants of Europe to girls' gymnasium classes and to little children, until folk dancing is popularly thought of as "sissy stuff," and most manly chaps will have nothing to do with it without a deal of tactful educating.

Not only are the dances so vigorous and manly and strenuous that they are quite unsuited for girls' classes or children but they will thus be killed for everyone. If, in your community, you can start the dances with the manliest and most popular young fellows, with older men mixing in, the program will become a great joy. But if you see any well-meaning woman trying to teach them to children or to classes of girls, please rush to the nearest court and get out an injunction to keep her from robbing the adult public of a precious sport that really belongs to it. Also, the children who are incapable of getting more than half the fun out of them, will be robbing themselves of those adult pleasures which they have a right to when they grow up, and which they themselves will have destroyed as children. Even when you organize an adult group you may find children a problem. Some women whose husbands cannot or will not dance with them, will bring small sons, who can hardly reach to the waists of the partners they will have to *swing*. And small daughters will beg to come and make the dance equally impossible for the men. To be sure a full set of children would do no harm at all at an adult dance, unless they tried to take more than their share of the attention or of space; in fact, the old-time dances were community affairs. Children would form sets off in the corners and become quite expert. The whole family would be there. When I am invited to an old-time dance in this year of our Lord, I always know it's the real thing, if I see a few baskets on chairs around the edge of the hall with tiny babies sleeping in them, oblivious to all the noise and fun their parents are making. But that is an entirely different kettle of fish from making these adult dances into a "child activity program."

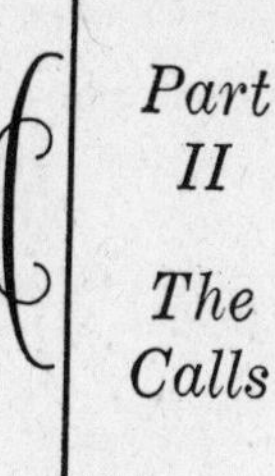

Part II

The Calls

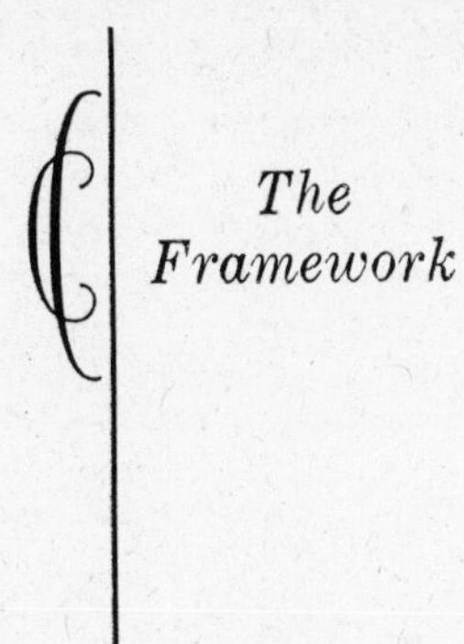

The Framework

Introductions

EACH square dance opens with an introductory figure. There are several standard introductions. Any one of these can be substituted for any other according to the fancy of the caller; in fact, he should use enough different introductions during the evening to assure variety.

There are also many different standard ways of calling the "grand chorus," or ending, for each section of the dance. These endings likewise should be shuffled and changed and chosen for the sake of variety.

The *docey-doe* "call" or the "subchorus" also has many variations, especially in the patter which fills it out. A good caller should make use of all these variations, shifting and changing them to suit his own fancy and to please his crowd.

For each of these dances given in the next section, there is given a standard introduction and a standard ending, chosen more or less at random. This will help the beginner and give him a complete call, as it will help the literary dilettante who may also want an example of a complete call. But for those given an experienced caller must substitute introductions and endings of his own choice.

In the following pages we have assembled some of these framework elements of the dance, so he will have them all in one place and be able more easily to make his choice and his own substitutions. In fact, he should get them all so well in mind that their use is instinctive.

See page 56 for description of square position. Each term will be described fully the first time it is used in this section. Refer back or turn to the glossary if the same term is used later without explanation.

A flourish!

Used sometimes instead of "All set" or "Ready now" before the dance figure begins.

Everybody in your places,
Straighten up your faces,
Loosen up your belly-bands
Tighten up your traces
For another long pull.

In Colorado I have always heard this given without the third line. But in Arizona this third line proved the favorite.

(1) INTRODUCTION:

Honors right and honors left,
All join hands and circle to the left,
Break and swing and promenade back.

(Explanation: The call is always for the men, with the ladies doing the complementary step. Therefore, the men bow to their partners, on their right, then to the ladies on their left. Then all eight join hands and circle around to the left until the call *break*. They then take a modified dance position (almost face to face with the man's right arm around the lady's waist, his left hand extended and supporting her right hand, and her left hand resting on his shoulder. It is best for them to stand a little off center with right hip against right hip.) They swing around or pivot twice to the right (in the direction each is facing). They then take the promenade position (side by side with the lady to the right and with hands grasped, right in right and left in left, and the man's right arm crossed over the lady's left) and in this position march back (counterclockwise) to their original positions, ready for the main part of the dance.

See pages 58-62 for more complete discussion and for illustrations.

(2) INTRODUCTION:

Salute your company and the lady on the left,
All join paddies and circle to the left,
Break and swing and promenade back.

(A variant in call of the same introductory figure described above.)

(3) INTRODUCTION:

Salute partners, salute corners,
Join hands and circle 'round,
Swing 'em hard and trot 'em home.

(A shorter variant of the same introductory figure.)

(4) INTRODUCTION:

All jump up and never come down,
Swing your honey around and around,
'Till the hollow of your foot makes a hole
in the ground.
And promenade, oh promenade!

(Explanation: With a "holler" all jump as high as they can. As they come down each couple takes the modified dance position and spins dizzily until the call directs them to take the promenade position. They then promenade once around the circle to the right, counterclockwise, and back to their own places.)

(5) INTRODUCTION:

One foot up and the other foot down,
Grab your honey in your arms
And turn her around,
And allemande left as you come down.
Now promenade your honey round.

(Explanation: Usually danced as in No. 3 with a jump into the air and then a vigorous swing with your partner. But sometimes it is danced literally by partners facing each other (or all facing center) and each raising the right knee as high as possible, in an exaggerated loosening-up exercise and then the left knee as high and the partners swing. Then each man turns to the lady on the left, and taking left hands with her turns once full around her and back to his partner with whom he promenades around the square and back to his own position.)

(6) INTRODUCTION:

One foot up and the other foot down,
Grab your little sage hens and swing 'em
around.
Left allemande and a right hand grand,
And promenade, oh promenade.

(Sometimes "little heifers" is substituted for "little sage hens.")

(Explanation: This is the same as No. 4, except that after the left allemande, when each man turns *the left hand girl with the left hand* he gives his right hand to his partner, and each passes by to the next, to whom they give a left hand, then the next with the right, etc., moving in a serpentine, all men circling to the right or counterclockwise and all the ladies circling to the left or clockwise. This, of course, is the *grand right and left.* When partners meet they take the promenade position and continue in the man's direction (counterclockwise) back to their places.)

See pages 47-53 for more complete discussion and illustrations of the allemande.

(7) INTRODUCTION:

Up and down and around and around,
Allemande left and allemande aye,
Ingo bingo, six penny high,
Big pig, little pig, root hog or die.

(Explanation: Danced exactly the same as No. 6, but put up in a more fancy and colorful call, which was first given to me by an officer on the Denver police force who had remembered it from his boyhood.)

(8) INTRODUCTION:

Everybody swing his prettiest gal.
Left allemande and a right hand grand,
And promenade, boys, promenade.

(Explanation: The same as No. 6 but without the preliminary jump or raised knee, it starts right in with the swing.)

(9) INTRODUCTION:

All eight balance, all eight swing.
A left allemande and a right hand grand.
Meet your partner and promenade eight
'Til you come straight.

(Explanation: Partners face each other, and each steps back four steps, then forward four steps and then they swing. From the swing it finishes exactly as No. 6.)

(10) INTRODUCTION:

Swing your partners don't be late.
Now swing on the corner like swingin' on
the gate.
Now your own and promenade eight.

(Explanation: Each gentleman swings his partner twice around, then he turns to the lady on his left, "his corner," and swings her twice around. Then he swings his partner again and promenades with her around the set and back to his own place.)

(11) INTRODUCTION:

Everybody swing his prettiest gal
And promenade, boys, promenade.

(Explanation: Each gentleman takes his partner in regular dance position and swings her twice around. He then promenades with her around the set in a counterclockwise direction and back to place.)

*Endings**

Used as a grand chorus after each couple has gone all around with a change.

(1) ENDING:

Swing, swing, everybody swing!

(Explanation: Usually used to precede most of the following endings, but occasionally used alone, without even a promenade.)

Note*—Quite often endings and introductions are used interchangeably. One may be substituted for the other.

Allemande Group

(2) ENDING:

Swing the left hand lady with your left hand,
Right hand to partner and right and left grand.
Meet your partner and promenade.

(Explanation: The simplest ending call for beginners since it specifically explains the "allemande" without using the word. Each gentleman takes the left hand lady's left hand in his own left hand and walks completely around her and back to place. This leaves partners now facing each other. They take right hands and pass each other giving left hands to the next lady or gentleman and so on around alternately right and left in a serpentine, the men moving counterclockwise, the column of women clockwise, until they meet their partners with whom they promenade (continuing in the men's direction or to the right) until they get back to their own positions.

See pages 47-53 for more complete discussion and for illustrations of the allemande.

(3) ENDING:

Allemande left with your left hand,
Right hand to partner,
And right and left grand.
Promenade eight when you come straight.

(Explanation: The commoner call and executed exactly the same as No. 2.)

(4) ENDING:

Swing your partners all around,
Allemande left as you come down,
Grand right and left and so on around,
Right foot up and left foot down,
Make that big foot jar the ground,
Now promenade your honey 'round.

(Explanation: No. 1 and No. 2 combined into one call which is expanded with "patter" to time more exactly. Execution same as No. 2 but with a preliminary swing.)

(5) ENDING:

Allemande left, oh a left hand swing,
Grand right and left around the ring,
Hand over hand with the dear little thing.
Promenade, boys, promenade.

(Explanation: Same as No. 2.)

(6) ENDING:

Left Allemande, and a right hand grand,
Plant your 'taters in a sandy land,
And promenade home!

(Explanation: Same as No. 2.)

(7) ENDING:

Allemande left
And grand right and left.
Meet your partner and turn right back.

(Explanation: Same as No. 2, except that when partners meet in the *grand right and left* they take right hands and turn completely around each other, so they are facing in the opposite directions. Then they do a right and left in reverse direction until they meet their partners. They then promenade in the regular direction.)

(This "turn right back" can be used with any *right and left ending.* It is sometimes called *Meet your partner and take the back track.)*

(8) ENDING:

Allemande ho, Right hand up,
Around we go!
Promenade!

(Explanation: The same as No. 2 but reduced to the shortest call I have heard for this common ending.)

(9) ENDING:

Balance home and swing 'em all 'round,
Allemande left as you come down,
Grand right and left, and so on around.
Meet your honey and promenade.

(Explanation: The same as No. 2 but preceded by a balance and swing, that is, the partners step back from each other four steps, then together and swing.)

(10) ENDING:

All eight balance and all eight swing.
A left allemande
And a right hand grand,
Meet your partner
And promenade eight
'Til you come straight.

(Explanation: Same as No. 9.)

(11) ENDING:

Balance home and swing 'em all night,
Allemande left—go left and right.
Oh some'll go right and some'll go le-e-e-ft.
Now promenade.

(Explanation: Same as No. 9. The caller usually drags out the final "left" in a long nasal chant.)

(12) ENDING:

Balance home and swing 'em all day,
Allemande left in the same old way;
Hand over hand and right and left grand,
Oh, some'll go right and some'll go le-e-ft.
Now promenade.

(Explanation: Same as No. 9 or No. 11.)

(13) ENDING:

Swing on the corner, and have some fun,
Allemande left with the one you swung.
Right hand to partner and trot right along.

(Explanation: Each gentleman first swings the corner girl (his left hand girl) then does an *allemande left* with her, then a *grand right and left.)*

(14) ENDING:

Swing on the corner like swingin' on a gate.
Now your own if it ain't too late.
Now allemande left with your left hand,
Right hand to partner and right and left grand.

(Explanation: Each gentleman first swings his corner lady, then he swings his partner, and then proceeds as in No. 2.)

(15) ENDING:

Now you're home and all eight swing,
Swing on the corners,
Swing your own.
Swing the opposite,
Now your own.
Left allemande, a right hand grand.
Meet your partner and promenade.

(Explanation: After partners swing, each gentleman swings his left hand lady, and then his partner again. He now crosses the set and swings the lady of the opposite couple, and then back to swing his partner again. Then finishes by executing the same as ending No. 2.)

(16) ENDING:

Swing your opposite across the hall,
Now the lady on your right,
Now your opposite across the hall,
Now your own and promenade all.

(Explanation: In this ending the ladies stand in position and wait for the men to come to them. When all four men cross the set to their *opposites* at one time it makes a traffic jam in the center. If they all touch right hands as they pass each other, it makes a neat figure. But they usually prefer to collide and make a knot of it.

Each gentleman crosses the set and swings the opposite lady. He then goes to the next lady around the set in a promenade direction and swings her, that is his *right hand lady* when he is facing the center of the set. He then crosses again to the opposite lady from her and after swinging her, he returns to his partner, swings her and they all promenade. The second line is sometimes called "Now your right hand ladies all."

This is a common and delightful ending. To make it clearer let us illustrate for the first gentleman. He swings the third lady, then the fourth, then the second, and then his own.)

(17) ENDING:

Swing your opposite across the hall,
Now swing your corners,
Now your partners,
And promenade all.

(Explanation: A shorter version of No. 16 in which the gentlemen only cross the set once. By *corners* the gentlemen's original corners are meant, not the new corner counting from the opposite; that is, the first gentleman, for instance, swings the third lady, then the fourth lady and then his own.)

(18) ENDING:

Balance one and balance all.
Swing your opposite across the hall.
Now your own if she ain't too small.
And promenade, boys, promenade.

(Explanation: After a preliminary balance, this is a yet shorter version of No. 16, in which the gentleman swings the opposite lady and then right back to his partner. It sometimes ends with an *allemande left and right and left grand* before the promenade. The third line is sometimes called *Now your own if you're not too tall.)*

(19) ENDING:

Now swing your opposite across the hall,
You haven't swung her since last fall.
Now trot home and swing your own,
And thank your stars the bird ain't flown.
Now promenade.

(Explanation: The same as No. 18 but with a little patter to fill out the call.)

(20) ENDING:

Hurry up, boys, and don't be slow,
Meet your pard' with a double elbow.

(Explanation: This is an additional call, only given when they are finishing the *grand right and left* of any of the preceding calls. It adds a more complicated figure.

As each gentleman meets his partner, instead of promenading, they hook right elbows and swing around to the right for two counts, then hook left elbows and go to the left for four counts, usually with a high springing step. Each man then advances to the next girl and hooks right elbows with her and then left elbows. Then to the next lady whom he "double elbows" and so on back to his own lady with whom he promenades.

To count it carefully and keep everyone together in their changes it is necessary to allow two extra counts, one while changing from the right elbow to the left elbow with each girl and the other while changing from one girl to the next. The count then becomes one, two, change (elbows), one, two, three, four, change (girls). Once this pattern is established it is easier to do it all to the count of eight for each girl.

In some communities they count four with the right elbow, four with the left elbow, two for the change. This unfortunately gets the whole count off of the four bar basis. It is sometimes called:

Change your pards and don't be slow,
Swing 'em all with the double elbow.

(21) ENDING:

Watch your honey and watch her close,
Treat your honey to a double dose!
Swing 'em high and swing 'em low.
Keep on swingin' that calico!
Right foot up and left foot down,
Whirligig, Whirligig, Whirligig 'round!
Rope your cow and brand your calf,
Swing your honey an hour and a half!
Here I come with the old mess wagon,
Hind wheel broke and the axle draggin'.
Meet your honey and pat 'er on the head,
If she don't like biscuit give her cornbread!
Promenade, boys, promenade!

(Explanation: Just the same as No. 20 but with continuous patter to fill out the call. In No. 20 the caller has to stay quiet for a long while as the double elbow is being done. This call gives him something to amuse himself with.)

(22) ENDING:

It's once and a half, boys,
Meet your partner and once and a half.
Sold my cow and vealed my calf,
Swing the reel with a once and a half!
Winnow the wheat and blow the chaff.
And swing the next one once and a half!
Make 'em chuckle and make 'em laugh,
Swing the next one a half and the other half too.
When you meet your pard, you know what to do!
It's promenade, boys, promenade!

(Explanation: Since this usually follows a *grand right and left* the first line is a warning line, and the second line starts the swing. There is enough patter to fill in most of the dance.

This dance must never be danced as in No. 21, *the double elbow,* although unfortunately and all too often it is carelessly so danced. *A once and a half,* which is a common figure in European folk dances, must be the origin of the dance, and the call has retained the phrase, but too often it is executed incorrectly as a *double elbow.* In a true *once and a half* which we should do for this call each gentleman swings his girl with his right elbow, completely around once and then continues for another half, which puts him beyond her. (That is, if he stands facing a girl, he hooks elbows, and swings her once around he will be back just where he started from. But if he continues a half swing more, he will be on the other side of her.) He then goes on to the next girl and hooks left elbows with her, swings once and a half and advances to the next. He hooks rights with her and swings once and a half with her, then on to the next with his left elbow. It is really *grand right and left* done without a reverse, swinging each girl once and a half around, the first girl entirely with the right elbow, the second girl only with the left, the next girl with the right, and the last one with the left. The next to last line of the call *Swing her the half and the other half too* indicates to me, alas, that it is all too often done as a *double elbow*. But it shouldn't be.

(23) ENDING:

Promenade in single file,
And just let me remind you,
To turn right back on the same old track
And swing that girl behind you.

(Explanation: The entire group promenades around the set in single file, with each lady preceding her partner. On the call *turn right back* each gentleman turns around (right face or toward the outside of the circle) and swings the girl behind him, twice around. He then puts her down in front of him and they promenade in single file again. Thus each time he turns back and swings a new girl. This call has to be repeated three times (four times in all) until each gentleman gets his own lady back. The caller usually then adds:

Promenade to places now.

and they all promenade in couples back to their own positions.

A slight variant of this call that is sometimes heard is:

Now single promenade with the lady in the lead.
Turn right back in the very same track,
And swing that girl behind you.

(24) ENDING:

Promenade in single file
Lady in the lead and Indian style,
Turn right back and swing 'em awhile.

(Explanation: The same as No. 23 except on the word "Indian style" the dancers usually crouch and with hands over mouths give an Indian war whoop.)

A variant of this call is:

Break that circle with the lady in the lead,
Single file, Indian style,
Stop and swing her once in a while.

Finish Phrases

At the end of the first "tip," when the first dance is finished and the dancers remain in their sets ready for the second tip, you may hear such phrases as the following:

1) *Swing your honey,*
   And there you stand.
2) *There you stand!*
3) *That's it!*
4) *You're done!*

When the second "tip" is finished and the dancers are to return to their seats the following finish phrases may be heard:

1) *Keno! Promenade to your seats!*
2) *Promenade! You know where and I don't care,*
   Take your honey to a nice soft chair!
3) *Lead her out and give her air!*
4) *Meet your partner and promenade there.*
   Take your honey to a rocking chair!
5) *Hurry up girls and don't be slow,*
   Kiss that caller before you go!

Docey-Doe Calls

All *docey-does* are essentially the same in execution, but a great variety of calls can be used, especially in the way of nonsensical patter, which fills in while the figure is being executed. In the following variants no notes will be given if the execution is standard.

(1)

Circle four and docey-doe.

(Explanation: Two couples join hands in a circle of four with each lady on the right side of her partner and opposite the other lady. The four circle to the left or clockwise. Each gentleman then passes his lady's left hand from his right hand to his left, in such a way that at the moment of break she passes beyond the opposite lady or between the opposite couple. She now makes a left turn, taking his left hand with her left hand. And the two gentlemen remain facing each other, while each passes his lady behind him (letting go her hand as soon as necessary) and reaches out with his right hand and takes the opposite lady, who is coming around from behind the opposite man, by her right hand, and without turning away from facing the opposite man, passes her around behind him. He now reaches out with his left hand and takes his partner, who has just passed around the opposite gentleman, by her left hand. Still holding her left hand in his left, he puts his right hand behind her waist and turns her to whatever new position the dance calls for. For a complete discussion of the *docey-doe* see page 108.)

(2)

Four hands up and here we go,
Around and around and a docey-doe.

(Explanation for this and the following variations of the call is the same as No. 1.)

(3)

Docey-doe with the gent you know,
Ladies go C and the gents go doe!

(4)

Four hands round, and round you go.
The ladies go C and the gents go doe!

(5)

Four hands round,
Gents patter down,
Ladies step out,
And go to town.

(6)

Four hands up and around you go,
Docey ladies and gents solo.

(7)

Four hands up and around we go,
Ladies docey—docey-doe!

(8)

Break and circle four in a ring,
With a docey-doe and a docey-ding!

(9)

Four hands up and here we go
Around and around and a docey-doe.
Doe and a dough and a little more dough,
Chicken in a bread-tray pickin' up the dough,
One more change and on we go.

(10)

Circle four—ladies doe and the gents say "no."
Chicken in a bread-tray pickin' up the dough,
Some use a shovel and some grab a hoe,
One more change and on we go.

(11)

Four hands up and here we go,
Around and around and a docey-doe.
Hurry up boys and don't be slow,
You'll never get to heaven if you don't do so.
One more change and on you go.

(or the last two lines are sometimes heard)

You'll never kiss your uncle if you don't do so.
One more change and home you go.

(12)

Circle four in the middle of the floor,
Half way round as you did before.
Ladies doe and the gents you know,
Hurry up boys and roll your dough!

(13)

Docey lady and docey gent,
Docey lady and on you went,
Docey lady and a docey-doe,
Docey lady and on you go!

(14)

The ladies doe and the gents you know,
By gosh! You ought to know,
With a million doses of docey-doe.
One more change and on you go!

(15)

Up the river and around the bend,
Four hands half and goin' again.
Ladies doe and the gents you know.
One more change and home you go!

(Though I have often heard this call, the first line of its patter seems contradictory to the figure. And I have an uncorroborated feeling that *up the river and around the bend* was a southern phrase for the *allemande left.)*

(16)

Ladies doe and the gents you know,
Four hands up and around you go!
Around and around and a docey-doe.

(In older groups when a *docey-doe* call begins this way, the two ladies do a *dos-a-dos* or back to back, each lady advancing to the opposite, passing right shoulders, stepping sideways back to back, and still facing the same direction walk backward to place (passing left shoulders in going back). The two men then do a *dos-a-dos.* And then they all *circle four* and do the standard *docey-doe* described above.)

(17)

Circle four
And swing your opposite with your right,
Now your partner with the left,
And on to the next.

(This simpler call is sometimes substituted for the *docey-doe* with a group of beginners. You will note that it is actually the last half of the *docey-doe* and does not begin by the gentlemen passing the partner from right to left hand and around behind, then to the left, but takes up the figure from that point. Incidentally some groups do this twice, in place of a *docey-doe.* See page 117.)

(18)

Four hands half,
A right and left thru,
And on to the next.

(This is sometimes heard as a substitute for the *docey-doe.* The two couples join hands and circle left halfway around. The two couples then pass between each other, with the ladies passing between the opposite couple, and the gentlemen on the outside. Each gentleman should give his right hand to the opposite lady as he passes through, then take his partner's left hand in his left and with his right hand around her waist lead her to the next position.)

(19)

Circle four,
Now ladies chain.
And chain right back!
On to the next.

(Another substitute that is sometimes used for the *docey-doe* to add variety to a dance. After circling, each lady takes the opposite lady by the right hand, passes her and gives her left to the opposite man, circles him, and crosses again giving her right to the opposite lady, and then her left to her partner who turns her around and leads her on to the next figure.)

(20)

Circle four,
Ladies change with the right hand cross,
Now back with the right to the same old hoss!

(Same figure as No. 19.)

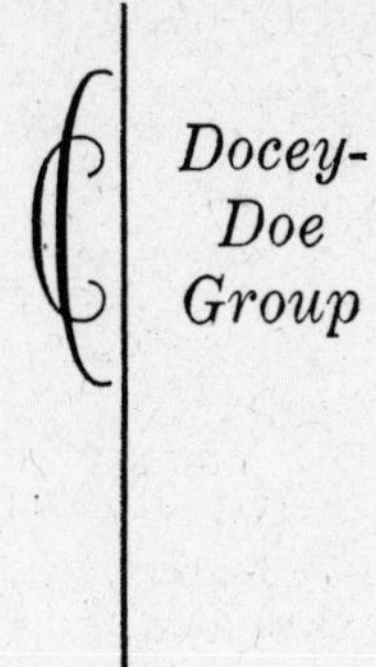

Docey-
Doe
Group

In which each couple visits around the set, doing a simple change and then a *docey-doe* with each couple they visit. See page 108 for a discussion of the *docey-doe*, and the pages immediately preceding for a variety of calls for this figure.

EXPLANATION OF DIAGRAMS

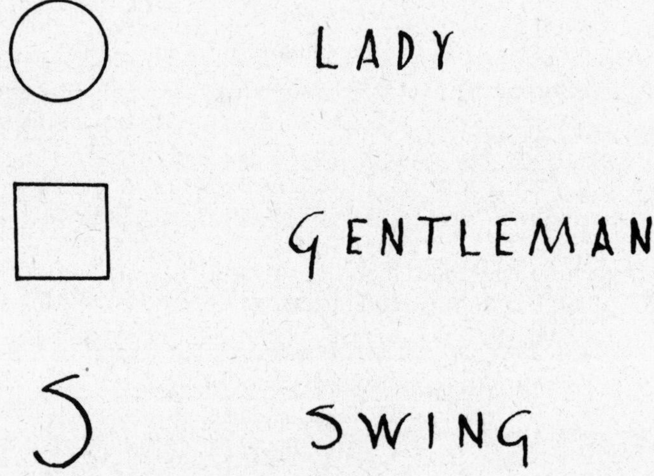

The squares represent the gentlemen (think of square shoulders) and the circles represent the ladies (think of curves). The letter *S* shows the position of the swing.

When there is more than one swing, they are numbered with subscripts to show the order of the swings. Occasionally the tracks of action are also numbered to show the order in which they are followed.

Dotted and solid lines have no significance except to keep different tracks from being confused with each other.

The portion of the action which a diagram represents is indicated by the letters under it. "B" and "C" would indicate that it represents that section of the call numbered "b" and "c."

The number in the circle or the square indicates whether it is the first, second, third, or fourth lady or gentleman.

By noting the crook or bend of the arm in some diagrams you can determine which direction a figure is facing.

Star by the Right

(A very simple dance for beginners, in which only the last half of the *docey-doe* is used.)

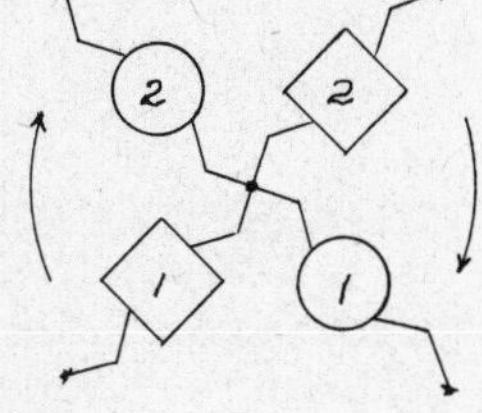

THE CALL:

1. *Honors right and honors left;*
   All join hands and circle to the left;
   Break and swing and promenade back.

2. a) *First couple out*
   To the couple on the right.
   b) *Form a star with the right hand cross*
   c) *Back with the left and don't get lost.*
   d) *Swing your opposite with your right;*
   e) *Now your partner with your left,*
   f) *And on to the next.*

   Repeat 2 as written beginning with (b).
   Repeat again, changing last line to:

   g) *Balance home.*

3. *And everybody swing*
   Now swing the left hand lady
   With your left hand.

Back with the left and don't get lost.

Right hand to partner
And right and left grand.
Promenade eight when you come straight.

Repeat 2 and 3 entire for second, third, and fourth couples.

THE EXPLANATION:

1. See page 148 for directions, or substitute any other introduction described there.
2. a) First couple join hands and walk to second couple.
   b) All four turn left face and join right hands held high and march around for four steps, still holding hands.
   c) Break holds, and each does a rightabout-face, and they all join left hands and march back.
   d) Break holds; first gentleman takes second lady by the right hand and swings her around behind him and releases hold. Second gentleman does the same thing with the first lady.
   e) Each gentleman takes partner by left hand and swings her around behind him to place.
   f) First gentleman takes partner's left hand in his right and advances to the third couple, being sure his partner is on the right side when he faces the new couple with whom they repeat *b* through *f*. On next repetition he advances to the fourth couple.
   g) After the last repetition he walks back to place with his partner, and all four couples do a balance by separating four steps then coming together again.
3. See page 152 for directions or substitute any other ending described there.

VARIATIONS:

The figures (b) and (c) are sometimes called as follows:

1) *Star by the right*
And how do you do?
Back with the left,
And how are you?

or 2) *Form a four hand cross*
And how do you do?
Now cross with your left,
And how are you?

These variations can be alternated with the regular call in repetitions of the figure. Or sometimes a caller will make up a long string of variations such as:

Star by the right; did you get a letter?
Back with the left; yeh, the folks are better.

☼ ☼ ☼

Star by the right; and how are you hittin'?
Back with the left; let's do some sittin'.

☼ ☼ ☼

Star by the right; its warmish weather.
Back with the left; keep stompin' leather.

VARIATION: Right Hand Back to the Lady's Left

This very simple dance can be made fun for experienced dancers by using the following substitution for d), e), and f).

Right hand back to the lady left,
Break with the left and pull her through,
Shuffle along with the old choo-choo,
Now you're doing the docey-doe,
A little bit of heel and a little bit of toe,
One more change and on you go.

But don't attempt this until you are familiar with the movements of the *docey-doe* in the dances that follow. Then you will find that if the gentlemen put their *right hands back* over their left shoulders and join right hands with this *lady on the left,* while still continuing with left-hand star, they will instinctively pull the lady through and around behind them when they *break with their left hands.* Thus your lady also will have passed through and will now be coming around from behind your opposite, and if you take her with the left hand and behind you, you will find you are now starting a regular *docey-doe.* And it's very good fun.

Lady Round the Lady

THE CALL:

1. *Honors right and honors left.*
   All join hands and circle to the left.
   Break and swing and promenade back.

GENT STOPS HERE

2. a) *First couple out*
   To the couple on the right.
   b) *The lady round the lady*
   c) *And the gent so low.*
   d) *The lady round the gent*
   e) *And the gent don't go.*
   f) *Four hands up and here we go*
   'Round and around and a docey-doe.
   g) *On to the next.*

   Repeat 2 as written, beginning with (b).
   Repeat again changing last line to:

   h) *Balance home.*

Lady round the lady and the gent so low.

3. *And everybody swing*
Now allemande left with your left hand.
Right hand to partner and right and left grand.
Meet your partner and promenade!

Repeat 2 and 3 entire three more times (for second, third, and fourth couples).

THE EXPLANATION:

1. See page 148 for directions or substitute any other introduction described there.

2. a) First couple join nearest hands and advance to second couple.
   b) The first lady passes between second couple (who must separate a few steps) and walks to the left around the second lady either still holding her partnear's hand or independently of him.
   c) The first gentleman follows her around the second lady one step behind her.
   d) The first lady passes between the second couple again and turning right encircles the second gentleman; that is, she completes a figure eight around the second gentleman.
   e) The first gentleman does not follow but stands facing the second gentleman with the second lady on his left hand.
   f) Finishing her circle, the first lady comes between the first and second gentlemen, and all four join hands and circle to the left.

   See page 160 for directions for *docey-doe* or substitute any other of its call variations.
   g) First couple advances to the third couple, the lady slightly in advance and repeats (b) to (g). On the next repetition they advance to the fourth couple and repeat (b) to (g). After the last repetition:
   h) They return to their own position in the square, and all four couples balance.

3. See page 152 for directions, or substitute any other ending found there.

Two Gents Swing with the Elbow Swing

THE CALL:

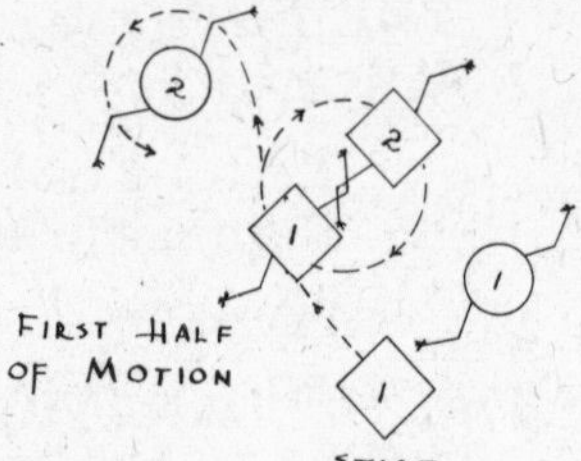

1. *All jump up and never come down,*
   Swing your honey around and around,
   'Til the hollow of your foot
   Makes a hole in the ground,
   And promenade, boys, promenade!

2. a) *First couple out to the right.*
   b) *Two gents swing with the elbow swing.*
   c) *Now opposite partners elbow swing,*
   d) *And now two gents with the same old thing,*
   e) *And now your partners elbow swing.*
   f) *Now circle four, oh, circle four*
   And docey-doe with the gent you know.
   The ladies go si and the gents go do.
   g) *And on to the next.*

Repeat 2 as written, beginning with (b).
Repeat again changing the last line to:

Balance home.

Two gents swing with the elbow swing.

3. *And everybody swing.*
Now swing your opposite across the hall,
Now the lady on your right,
Now your opposite across the hall,
And now your own,
And promenade all!

Repeat 2 and 3 for second, third, and fourth couples.

THE EXPLANATION:

1. See page 149 for directions or substitute any other introduction given there.
2. a) First couple advances to second couple.
   b) The two gentlemen hook right elbows and swing around once and a half.
   c) Each gentleman hooks left elbows with the opposite lady (first gentleman with second lady and second gentleman with first lady) and swings once around.
   d) Two gentlemen again hook right elbows and swing once and a half around.
   e) Each gentleman hooks left elbows with his partner and swings her once around. He releases her so that she is standing on his right as he faces the opposite gentleman.
   f) See page 160 for directions for *docey-doe* or for possible substitute calls.
   g) First couple with the lady on the right advances to the third couple and repeats from (b). On the next repetition they advance to fourth couple and repeat from (b) and finish by returning to their places in the square, where each couple balances.
3. See page 155 for directions or substitute any other ending given there.

Step Right Up and Swing Her Awhile

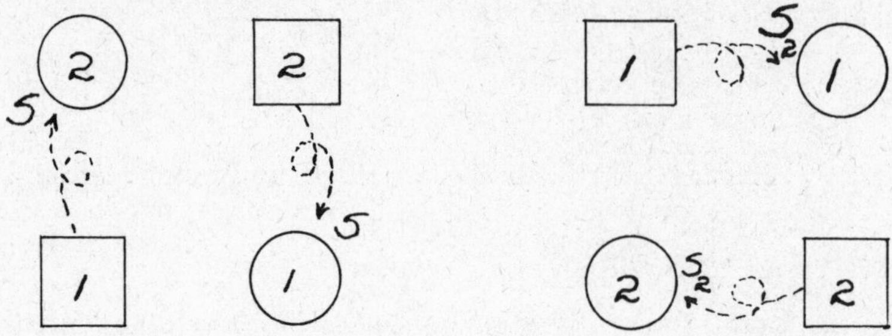

FIRST HALF SECOND HALF

THE CALL:

1. *Everybody swing his prettiest gal,*
   And promenade, boys, promenade!

2. a) *First couple out to the couple on the right*
   b) *And honors all!*
   c) *Step right back and watch her smile*
   Step right up and swing her awhile.

Step right back and watch 'em grin.

d) *Step right back and watch 'em grin*
Grab your own and swing her again.
e) *Four hands up and here we go*
'Round and around and a docey-doe.
f) *On to the next.*

Repeat 2 as written, beginning with (b).
Repeat again changing last line to:

Balance home.

3. *And swing 'em all day.*
Allemande left in the same old way.
Now hand over hand with the dear little things.
Promenade eight when you come straight.

Note: (See page 234 for longer and commoner arrangement of what is apparently the same call.)

THE EXPLANATION:

1. See page 151 for directions or substitute any other introduction described there.

2. a) First couple joins near hands and advances to second couple.
   b) First gentleman and second lady bow deeply to each other while the first lady and second gentleman bow.
   c) Each gentleman steps back a few steps from the lady to whom he bowed, advances again, and swings her twice around in regular dance position, and puts her down on his right as he faces the opposite gentleman.
   d) Each gentleman now faces his partner, steps back a few steps, advances again and swings her, and puts her down on his right.
   e) See page 160 for directions or substitute other calls for *docey-doe*.
   f) First couple, with lady on the right, advances to third couple and repeats from (b). They next repeat with the fourth couple and then return to places in square.

3. See page 154 for directions or substitute any other ending described there.

I'll Swing Your Girl; You Swing Mine

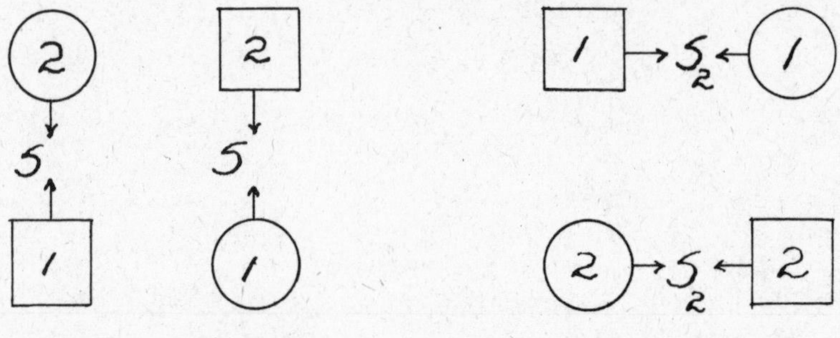

THE CALL:

1. *Honors right and honors left,*
   All join hands and circle to the left.
   Break and swing and promenade back.

2. a) *First couple out to the couple on the right.*
   b) *I'll swing your girl; you swing mine.*
   By golly! Ain't that fine!
   c) *You swing your girl; I'll swing mine,*
   I'll swing my girl every time.
   d) *Four hands up and here we go*
   'Round and around and a docey-doe.

I'll swing your girl, you swing mine.

e) *And on to the next.*
Repeat 2 as written, beginning with (b).
Repeat again changing last line to:
Balance home.

3. *And swing 'em all night.*
Allemande left,
Go left and right.
Some'll go right
And some'll go le-e-eft! (With a long drawl.)
Meet your partner and promenade.
Repeat 2 and 3 for second, third, and fourth couples.

THE EXPLANATION:

1. See page 148 for directions, or substitute any other introduction described there.

2. a) First couple advances to second couple.
   b) First gentleman, taking regular dance position, swings second lady, and the second gentleman swings first lady, putting them down to the right.
   c) Each gentleman swings his own partner and puts her down on his right.
   d) See page 160 for directions and for variations of the *docey-doe* call.
   e) First couple with lady on the right advances to third couple and repeats from (b). Then they advance to fourth couple, and repeat from (b). Then they return to their places in the square and all four couples balance.

3. See page 154 for directions, or substitute any other ending found there.

Note: Some of the variations of this call, especially the last couplet, are:

Your gal's pretty, so is mine,
I'll swing my gal every time.

Or—

An even swap, an even trade,
Your pretty gal for my old maid.
(or vice versa)

Or simply—

Opposites swing,
Partners swing

Swing at the Wall

THE CALL:

1. *Honors right and honors left,*
   All join hands and circle to the left.
   Break and swing and promenade back.

2. a) *First couple out to the couple on the right,*
   b) *Around that couple*
   And swing at the wall.
   c) *Through that couple*
   And swing in the hall.
   d) *Circle four, oh, circle four.*
   Docey-doe with the gent you know,
   The lady goes si and the gent goes do.
   e) *And on to the next.*

   Repeat 2 as written, beginning with (b).
   Repeat again and change last line to:

   Balance home.

3. *And everybody swing.*
   A left allemande
   And a right hand grand.
   Promenade eight when you come straight.

   Repeat 2 and 3 for second, third, and fourth couples.

Through that couple and swing in the hall.

THE EXPLANATION:

1. See page 148 for directions or substitute any other introduction given there.

2. a) First couple advances to second couple.
   b) The first couple separates and passes around the second couple, lady to the right and gentleman to the left. They meet beyond the second couple and, taking a regular dance position, swing twice around.
   c) The second couple separates by taking a step backward from each other, and the first couple passes between them. It is best for the second couple to take a step or two in the opposite direction (toward the outside of the square) so they pass around the first couple while the first passes between them. Each gentleman takes his own partner in dance position and both couples swing.
   d) See page 160 for directions or for possible variations of the call.
   e) First couple passes on to the third couple and repeats from (b). Then they go on and repeat with the fourth couple and finally return to their places, when each couple does a *balance*.

3. See page 153 for directions, or substitute any other ending given there.

   Repeat 2 and 3 entire for second, third, and fourth couples.

Go Round and Through

(Very similar to the preceding dance.)

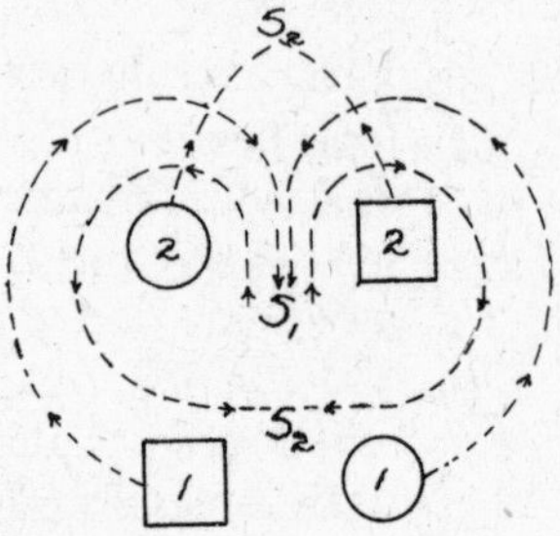

THE CALL:

1. *Everybody swing his prettiest gal,*
   And promenade, boys, promenade!

2. a) *First couple out to the right.*
   b) *Go round and through*
   And the center couple swing.
   c) *Go through and around*
   And both couples swing.
   d) *Four hands up, around we go,*
   Around and around and a docey-doe.
   e) *Then on to the next.*
   Repeat 2 as written, beginning with (b).
   Repeat again changing last line to:
   Balance home.

3. *Balance one and balance all!*
   Swing your opposite across the hall.
   Now your own if she's not too small.
   And promenade, boys, promenade.
   Repeat 2 and 3 for second, third, and fourth couples.

Go through and around and both couples swing.

THE EXPLANATION:

1. See page 151 for directions or substitute any other introduction found there.

2. a) First couple advances to second couple.
   b) First couple separates and passes around outside of second couple, meet each other, and pass back between second couple (second couple taking what steps are necessary to make this easier). First couple swings twice around in regular dance position.
   c) First couple now passes between second couple, separates, and returns to place by passing around and outside second couple (second couple by a few steps in either direction making this as easy as possible). Each gentleman takes partner in dance position and swings her twice around.
   d) See page 160 for directions or variations.
   e) First couple passes on to third couple and repeats from (b), next time to fourth couple, and then back to own position.

3. See page 156 for descriptions or substitute any ending given there.

☼ ☼ ☼

Very similar to the previous dance, this call is heard much less frequently.

Him and Her

THE CALL:

1. *Everybody swing his prettiest gal,*
   And promenade.

2. a) *First couple out to the right.*
   b) *The lady round the lady*
   And the gent around the gent.
   c) *The gent around the lady*
   And the lady round the gent.
   d) *Circle four and docey-doe.*
   e) *On to the next.*

   b) *The her around the her*
   And the him around the him.
   c) *The him around the her*
   And the her around the him.
   d) *Circle four and docey-doe.*
   e) *And on to the next.*

   b) *The she around the she*
   And the he around the he.
   c) *The he around the she*
   And the she around the he.

The gent around the lady, and the lady round the gent.

d) *Circle four and a docey-doe.*
g) *And balance home.*

3. *And everybody swing.*
Now allemande ho!
Right hand up and here we go!
Meet your partner and promenade.

Repeat 2 and 3 for second, third, and fourth couples.

THE EXPLANATION:

1. See page 151 for directions or substitute any other introduction given there.

2. a) First couple advances to second couple.
   b) The first lady a little in advance of the first gentleman passes between the opposite couple and encircles the lady. The gentleman follows her between the opposite couple, but he encircles the gentleman.
   c) The first lady still in advance passes between the second couple again and encircles the gentleman. The first gentleman follows her through the opposite couple but encircles the second lady. (They each do a figure eight in the opposite direction from the other.)
   d) See page 160 for directions and a longer call for the *docey-doe.*
   e) The first couple advances to the third.
   f) The first couple advances to the fourth.
   g) The first couple returns to own position in the square and all couples balance.

3. See page 153 for directions or substitute any ending given there.

☼ ☼ ☼

There are many variations for this call, such as the following:

The shoe around the shoe
And the boot around the boot.
The boot around the shoe
And the shoe around the boot.

Or—

The sheep around the sheep
And the goat around the goat.
The goat around the sheep
And the sheep around the goat.

The possibilities are endless.

In the dance as given the first couple goes through and around the opposites. It is sometimes called in reverse order, in which case they go around and through the opposites, and on the last time through, the first lady crosses over in front of the first gentleman in order to be in the right position for the *docey-doe.* This is a little more awkward than the regular arrangement in which the crossover comes at the beginning. The call in reverse would be:

The gent around the lady
And the lady 'round the gent.
The lady 'round the lady
And the gent around the gent.

The Girl I Left Behind Me

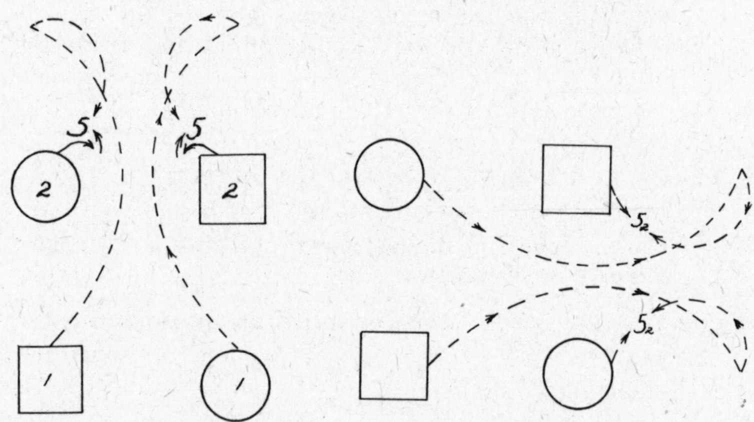

THE CALL:

1. *Honors right and honors left,*
   All join hands and circle to the left.
   Break and swing and promenade back.

2. a) *First couple out to the couple on the right;*

   b) *Pass right through and balance too*
   And swing that girl behind you.

   c) *Pass right back on the same old track*
   And swing that girl behind you.

   d) *Now four hands up and here we go*
   Around and around and a docey-doe.

   e) *And on to the next.*

   Repeat 2 as written, beginning with (b).
   Repeat again changing last line to:
   Balance home.

3. *And everybody swing.*
   Now promenade in single file
   And just let me remind you
   To turn right back in the same old track
   And swing that girl behind you.

   Repeat 3 three more times, or until each gentleman swings his own partner again.

All promenade to places now.

Repeat 2 and 3 for second, third, and fourth couples.

Promenade in single file.

Some callers so time this call that they manage to insert the line:

Swing that girl, that pretty little girl,
Oh, swing that girl behind you.

THE EXPLANATION:

1. See page 148 for directions or substitute any introduction given there.
2. a) First couple advances to second couple.
   b) Who separate so that the first couple can pass between them. Each dancer balances by taking a step backward and making a deep bow to his partner, and then turns back to face the opposite. The first gentleman swings the second lady and the second gentleman swings the first lady.
   c) The first gentleman and second lady now pass between the second gentleman and the first lady. Each of these pairs bow and turn and each gentleman then swings his own partner.
   d) See page 160 for directions or for variations of this call.
   e) First couple advances to third couple and repeats from (b); next to fourth couple; and at last return to places.
3. See page 159 for directions and for other calls of this type which can be alternated in the repetitions if desired.

Birdie in a Cage

THE CALL:

1. *Up and down and around and around,*
Allemande left and allemande aye.
Ingo, bingo, six penny high,
Big pig, little pig, root hog or die.

2. a) *First couple a balance-swing,*
Lead right out to the right of the ring

b) *With a birdie in a cage*
And three hands round.

c) *The bird hop out and the crow hop in.*

d) *The crow hop out and circle again.*

e) *Docey-doe with the gent you know.*
Ladies go si and the gents go do.

f) *On to the next—*

Repeat 2 as written beginning with (b).
Repeat again, changing last line to:

Balance home.

With a birdie in a cage and three hands round.

3. *Swing, swing, and swing 'em high.*
Allemande left and allemande aye,
Ingo, bingo, six penny high,
Big pig, little pig, root hog or die.

Repeat 2 and 3 for second, third, and fourth couples.

This is sometimes called:

The bird hop out and the crow hop in,
All join paddies and go around again,
The crow hop out and circle four.
Docey-doe, etc.

THE EXPLANATION:

1. See page 150 for directions or substitute any introduction given there.
2. a) First lady and gentleman step backwards from each other for four steps, then forward and take regular dance position and swing twice around. They then advance to second couple.
   b) First lady steps to the middle of the ring formed by the first gentleman and the second couple who join hands. As the three circle to the left, she turns to the right.
   c) The first lady steps out of the ring and takes the first gentleman's place as he steps in to the middle. The new three circle left while he turns to the right.
   d) The first gentleman steps out and takes his place in the ring between the two ladies. All four continue circling to the left.
   e) See page 160 for directions.
   f) First couple go on and repeat the figure with the third couple, then with the fourth couple, and return to their original place in the square.
3. See page 150 for directions or substitute any other ending. The one used is listed as an introduction, but serves just as well as an ending.

The Lady Walks Round

THE CALL:

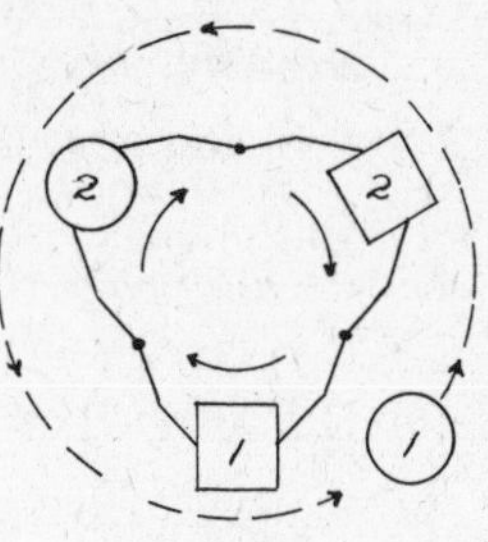

1. *Honors right and honors left.*
   All join hands and circle to the left.
   Break and swing and promenade home.

2. a) *First couple balance and swing.*
   Lead right out to the right of the ring,

   b) *Turn a three hand set*
   And the lady ballonet.

   c) *Go four hands round*
   And round you go.
   The ladies go si and the gents go do.

   d) *And on to the next.*

   Repeat 2 as written beginning with (b).
   Repeat again changing last line to:

   Now balance home.

Turn a three hand set and the lady ballonet.

3. *And everybody swing,*
Allemande left with your left hand.
Right hand to partner and right and left grand.
Meet your partner and turn right back,
Meet her again and promenade.

Repeat 2 and 3 for second, third, and fourth couples.

Ballonet is pronounced to rhyme with set.

THE EXPLANATION:

1. See page 148 for directions, or substitute any introduction given there.
2. a) First couple each step back from one another four steps, then together and swing. They then advance to the second couple.
   b) The first gentleman and the second couple take hands and circle left, while the first lady walks around them to the right. The second time her partner passes her she steps into the ring on his right and they circle four.
   c) See page 160 for directions and a longer call if desired.
   d) They advance to the third couple and repeat, then to the fourth, and return home.
3. See page 153 for directions or substitute any other ending given there.

VARIATION:

Where a Southern influence enters the following substitute is heard for b):

Three hands round and the lady go seek,
Swing your partners when you meet.

The Dollar Whirl

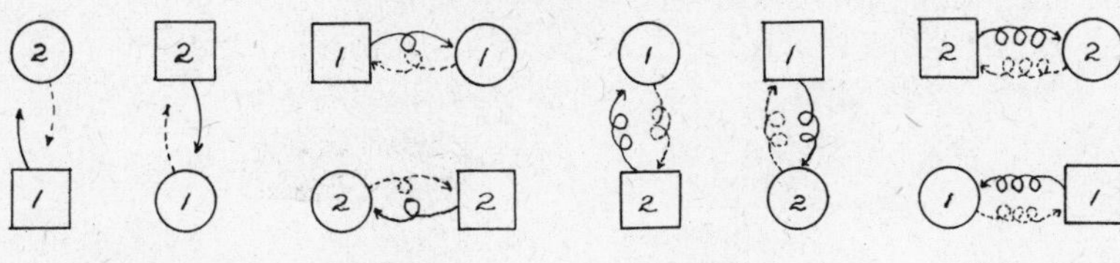

THE CALL:

1. *Everybody swing his prettiest gal*
   And promenade.

2. a) *First couple out to the couple on the right.*
   b) *Change and swing with the quarter whirl.*
   c) *Change again and swing her the half.*
   d) *Change again and swing her six bits.*
   e) *Change again—swing the dollar whirl.*
   f) *Four hands up and around we go,*
   'Round and around and a docey-doe.
   g) *On to the next.*

   Repeat 2 beginning with (b).
   Repeat again changing last line to:

   Balance home.

Change again and swing her six bits.

3. *And everybody swing.*
Now allemande left with your left hand.
Right hand to partner and right and left grand.
Meet your partner and promenade.

Repeat 2 and 3 for second, third, and fourth couples.

THE EXPLANATION:

1. See page 151 for directions or substitute any other introduction given there.

2. a) First couple advances to second couple.
   b) First and second gentlemen each take the opposite lady and swing her half around, that is, each exchanges places with her. (The swing can either be in dance position or a two-handed swing.)
   c) Each gentleman takes his own partner and swings once full around with her, each returning to his own position.
   d) Each gentleman again takes the opposite lady and swings with her once and a half around, again changing positions with her.
   e) Each gentleman takes his partner again and swings twice around with her, and putting her down to his right, they all join hands in a circle of four. The gentleman always returns to his own place when swinging his partners. He always changes places with the opposite, since it is a one half swing and a once and a half swing.)
   f) See page 160 for directions or for a longer call.
   g) First couple advances and repeats with the third couple, then with fourth, and returns to their home position.

3. See page 152 for directions, or substitute any other ending given there.

The Butterfly Whirl

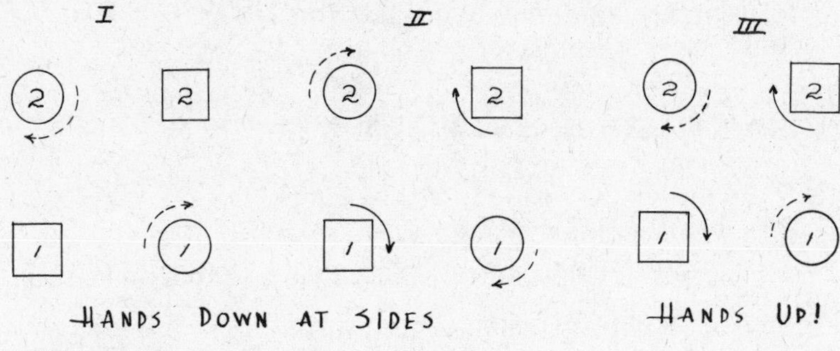

THE CALL:

1. *All jump up and never come down.*
   Swing your honey around and around,
   'Til the hollow of your foot makes a hole in the ground,
   And promenade, oh, promenade!

2. a) *First couple out to the right*
   And circle four.
   b) *The two ladies whirl;*
   c) *The two gents whirl;*
   d) *And don't forget the Butterfly whirl.*
   e) *Four hands up and around we go,*
   The ladies go si and the gents go do.

And don't forget the Butterfly whirl.

f) *And on to the next.*
Repeat 2 beginning with (b).
Repeat again changing last line to:
Balance home.

3. *And swing 'em all night,*
Allemande left, go left and right,
Hand over hand around the ring.
Hand over hand with the dear little thing,
Promenade eight when you come straight.

Repeat 2 and 3 for second, third, and fourth couples.

This is sometimes called simply:

Four hands up in a great big ring,
Don't forget the Butterfly Swing.

THE EXPLANATION:

1. See page 149 for directions or substitute any other introduction given there.
2. a) First couple advances to second couple and joins hands with them and all circle to the left.
   b) All drop hands and the two ladies, with their hands at their sides, whirl in position once around to the right.
   c) The two gentlemen in the same manner whirl to the right while the ladies continue whirling.
   d) All four lift their hands above their heads, ostensibly like butterfly wings, and whirl twice more around to the right.
   e) All join hands again and circle to the left. For directions for the *docey-doe* see page 160.
   f) First couple repeats with the third couple, then the fourth couple, and returns to place.
3. See page 154 for directions, or substitute any other ending given there.

☼ ☼ ☼

This dance is usually introduced for a laugh. There is nothing to the dance, but it is silly enough to set everyone laughing.

The Lady Round Two

THE CALL:

1. *Honors right and left,*
   All circle left—
   Couples swing and promenade to place.

2. a) *First couple balance-swing*
   And lead right out to the right of the ring.

   b) *The lady round two*

   c) *And the gent fall through,*

   d) *The gent around two,*

   e) *And the lady fall through.*

   f) *Four hands up and here we go*
   Around and around and a docey-doe.

   g) *And on to the next.*

   Repeat 2 beginning with (b).
   Repeat again changing last line to:

   And now go home.

The lady round two and the gent fall through.

3. *And swing 'em all day.*
Allemande left in the same old way.
Now right and left grand around the ring,
Hand over hand with the dear little thing.
Meet your partner and promenade.

Repeat 2 and 3 entire for second, third, and fourth couples.

☼ ☼ ☼

Another form of the call for this figure is:

First couple out to the couple on the right,
Around that couple with the lady in the lead,
The gent fall through and take the lead;
The lady fall through and circle four.
Docey-doe, etc.

THE EXPLANATION:

1. See page 148 for directions or substitute any introduction found there.

2. a) First couple separates four steps, each from the other, then they step together and swing. They then advance to the second couple with the lady slightly in the lead.
   b) The lady walks to the right of the second couple and circles around them to her left, and the first gentleman follows her.
   c) As the gentleman passes behind (or outside of) the second couple, he passes between them, cutting corners as it were, and is now in advance of his lady.
   d) He continues circling to the left and walks once more around the second couple.
   e) But as the first lady passes behind them she now drops between them, which puts her between the two gentlemen ready for the *docey-doe.*
   f) See page 160 for directions or for an alternate call.
   g) The first couple advance to the third couple, then the fourth couple, repeating 2 with each of them in turn, and then return to their place in the square.

3. See page 154 for directions or substitute any other ending given there.

Dive for the Oyster

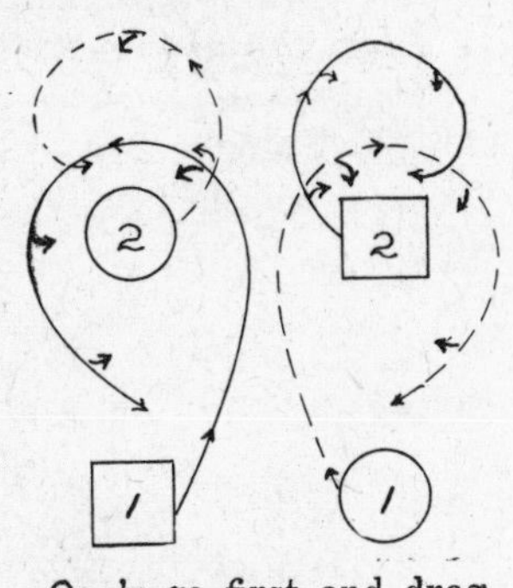

One's go first and drag two's after them. Arrows indicate direction each dancer faces.

THE CALL:

1. *All jump up and never come down,*
   Swing your honey around and around
   'Til the hollow of your foot makes a hole in the ground.
   And promenade, boys, promenade.

2. a) *First couple out to the couple on the right,*
   b) *And dive for the oyster,*
   c) *Dive for the clam,*
   d) *Dive for the sardine,*
   And take a full can.
   e) *Four hands up and here we go,*
   'Round and around and a docey-doe.
   f) *And on to the next.*

   Repeat 2 beginning with (b).
   Repeat again changing last line to:

   Balance home.

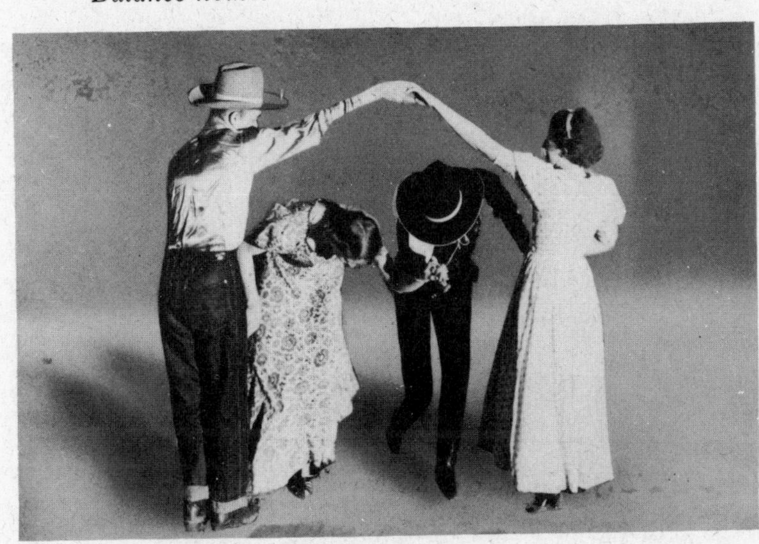

Dive for the oyster.

3. *And everybody swing.*
Now allemande left with your left hand,
Right hand to partner and right and left grand,
Promenade eight when you come straight.

Repeat 2 and 3 entire for second, third, and fourth couples.

☼ ☼ ☼

I am told there is a slight variation of this call which is heard on Cape Cod and goes:

Dig for the oyster,
Delve for the clam,
Take them all home,
In an old tin can.

This is logical enough in a clam-digging country. But the call as I first heard it came from Arizona, where they have to dig through the canned goods in the commissary and take sardines perforce.

THE EXPLANATION:

1. See page 149 for directions or substitute any other introduction given there.
2. a) First couple advances to the second couple, joins hands with them, and the four circle to the left.
   b) The first couple dives in under the raised arms of the second couple, and then steps back to place, all four still holding hands.
   d) The second couple dives in under the arms of the first couple and back to place, all four still holding hands.
   d) The first couple dives again under the arms of the second couple, this time passing through to the other side, all still holding hands. The first couple now raise their leading and joined hands and pass under this self-made arch in the old childhood figure, of "wringing the dishrag." In passing under their own joined hands, each turns to the outside or away from his partner (the gentleman pivoting left and the lady pivoting right). They now pull the second couple through after them under their still raised hands. The

second couple finds their outside and still join hands under which the first couple passes now above their other arms which have been pulled through and under. This pulls them face to face; then as the pulling arms continues it brings them shoulder to shoulder (the shoulders of the pulled arms, of course) then back to back. By this time they have been pulled through, and marvelous! they too have "wrung a dishrag" and are back in the original circle of four.

e) See page 160 for directions or substitute a longer call.

f) First couple advances to third couple and repeats with them. Then to fourth couple and finally back to place.

3. See page 152 for directions or substitute any other ending given there.

VARIATION:

LITTLE BROWN JUG

This figure can be complicated by substituting the following call; for b), c), d), and e):

Roll that jug along the floor,
Keep on rolling and roll some more.
Now roll it back, till your back gets sore,
Keep on rolling, and couple up four.
Now docey-doe with the gent you know,
The lady goes see and the gent goes doe.

In this case there is no preliminary diving under the arms and back, but the first couple go directly under the arched arms of the second couple and with a *dishrag* continue straight on until they have pulled the second couple through under their arms. The second couple now go back under the first couple's arms and with a *dishrag* continue until they have pulled the first back through to their original position. Then the four join hands, circle left, and do a *docey-doe.*

Eight Hands Over

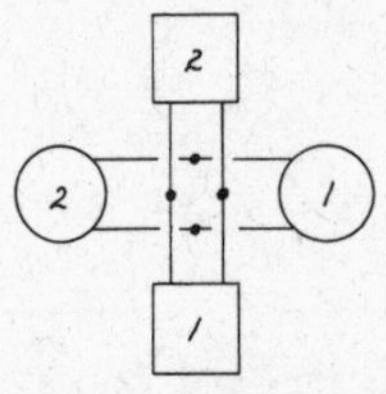

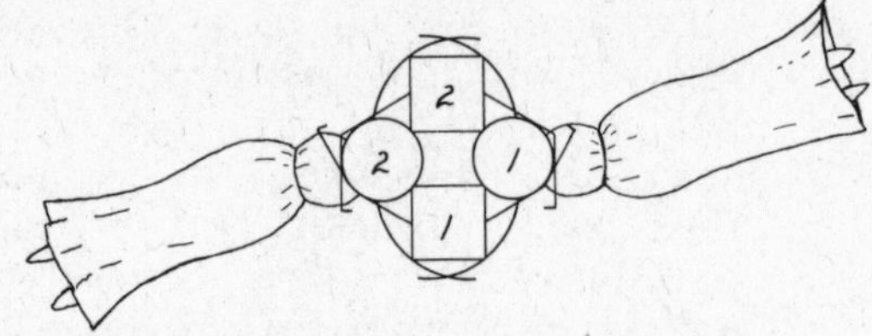

THE CALL:

1. *Honors right and honors left,*
   All join hands and circle to the left,
   Break and swing and promenade back.

2. a) *First couple out to the right*
   b) *And eight hands over.*
   c) *Ladies bow and the gents bow under,*
   d) *Round you go and go like thunder.*
   e) *Break and circle four in a ring,*
   Docey-doe and a docey-ding.
   f) *On to the next—*

   Repeat 2 beginning with (b).
   Repeat again changing last line to:
   Balance home.

Flap those girls and flap like thunder.

3. *And everybody swing.*
Allemande left with your left hand,
Right to your partner and right and left grand,
Promenade eight when you come straight!

Repeat 2 and 3 entire for second, third, and fourth couples.

☼ ☼ ☼

The last line of the figure is often called differently:

Hug those girls and go like thunder!

Or—

Hold your holds and go like thunder!

Or—

Squeeze 'em tight and go like thunder!

It is best, perhaps, to keep changing the last line, as you call, for the sake of variety.

THE EXPLANATION:

1. See page 148 for directions or substitute any introduction given there.

2. a) First couple advances to second couple.
   b) The two ladies join both hands across rights to lefts, and the two gentlemen likewise join their hands together over the ladies' hands.
   c) The two ladies bow low and pass in under the gentlemen's joined arms which are raised and swung back so as to rest around the ladies' shoulders. The gentlemen then bow and pass their heads under the ladies' joined hands, which now rest behind the gentlemen's necks.
   d) The ladies break their holds and crook their elbows tightly around the gentlemen's necks. (This is very important, or there may be an accident.) The gentlemen also let go of each other, and with their arms crossed over the ladies' shoulders, each takes a hold as securely as possible under the ladies' armpits. They all four throw their heads back as far as possible and circle to the left, the gentlemen lifting the ladies. The

centrifugal force is so great that if the gentlemen spin fast with short steps and their feet close together, or even sometimes interlaced through each other, the ladies' feet will come off the floor and they will spin around flattened out at a level with the men's shoulders. The men often dip slightly as they spin them, raising and lifting so that the ladies' bodies swing up and down like the wings of a butterfly, their feet often almost touching above the gentlemen's heads.

This last should not be attempted until the hold is completely mastered and they know what they are doing. I have seen an improperly held lady hurled clear across the room and against the wall. I have seen arms broken from falls in this dance. And the whirling feet of the ladies may do much damage if they hit anyone, or be severely hurt themselves if they hit any hard object

e) The four dancers break holds, and separating, join hands in a regular circle of four. See page 160 for directions for the *docey-doe*.

f) First couple advances to third couple and repeats, then to fourth couple, and returns to place in square.

3. See page 152 for directions or substitute any other ending given there.

☼ ☼ ☼

Most dancers prefer avoiding the dangers and being less strenuous. They execute this figure in the old form of the California Show Basket. Both the ladies' and gentlemen's joined arms are lowered in part (d) to the others' waists. All four lean back as far as possible, held at the waist, and form a basketlike group, flaring wide at the top. In this position they turn very slowly to the left. This can be very graceful and beautiful, although the footwork feels awkward to the dancers.

In order to make the footwork neat and co-ordinated a *buzz* step should be used. When circling to the left each dancer crosses his right foot over in front of his left and keeps it there through all the circling. The full weight is put on the right foot which steps flat on the floor, but the left foot (which is crossed behind), takes the weight only with a light step on the toe. With the four dancers stepping in unison with their right feet and touching their left toes in unison, a lovely smooth waving motion is given to the circle.

If the caller wishes to indicate this form; he can call:

Eight hands over,
Ladies bow and gents bow under.
California Show Basket. What a wonder!

Then if he wishes an intermediate form that is full of good comedy, he can call:

Eight hands over,
Ladies bow and gents bow under.
Set 'em up! And spin like thunder!

The men in this case sweep their arms down below the ladies' knees and literally lift them up, so that the ladies are sitting on these intertwined arms at the height of the men's shoulders. If they lean back and out they can form an awkward-looking Etruscan-vase effect, but I laugh more when they lean over and pound the men on the head and squeal, "Let me down! Let me down!"

Now if the caller wants the real MacKoy with lots of action he calls:

Flap them, boys, and flap like thunder!

Right and Left Group

Making use of the old figure, *right and left through and right and left back* in combination with any other change. For a discussion of *right and left through* see page 127.

Promenade the Outside Ring and Docey-Doe

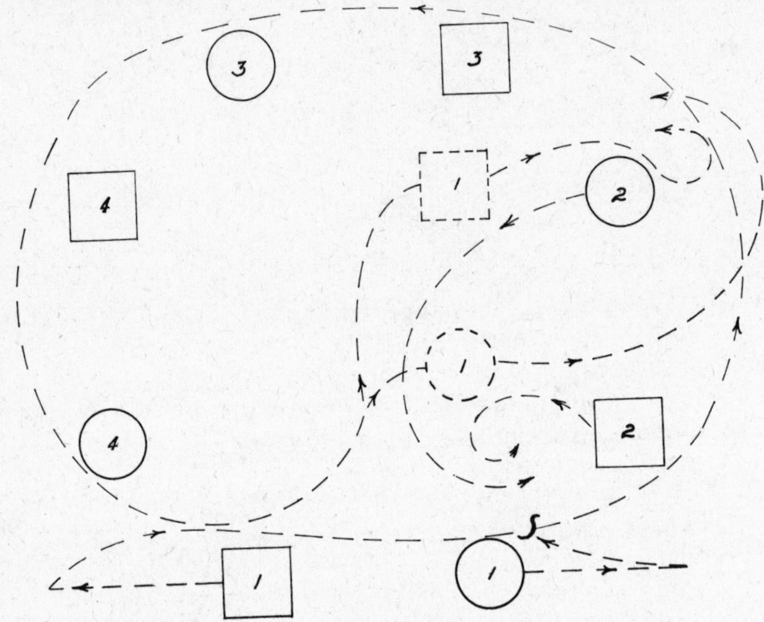

THE CALL:

1. *One foot up and the other foot down,*
   Grab your honey in your arms,
   And turn her around,
   And allemande left as you come down,
   Now promenade your honey 'round.

2. a) *First couple balance,*
   First couple swing.
   b) *First couple promenade the outside ring.*
   c) *Right and left with the couple you meet,*
   And right and left back.
   d) *The two ladies change,*
   And change right back.
   e) *Four hands up and here we go*
   Around and around with a docey-doe.
   f) *And a right and left through to the next.*
   Repeat 2 beginning with (c).
   Repeat again changing last line to:
   A right and left home.

3. *And everybody swing,*
   Allemande ho!
   Right hands up and here we go,
   Promenade!

Repeat 2 and 3 for second, third, and fourth couples.

THE EXPLANATION:

1. See page 149 for directions or variations.
2. a) First couple divide, and each takes four steps back from the other, then advancing together, take the dance position and swing.
   b) Then in promenade position (side by side, lady on the right, holding hands with arms crossed in front) they march around the outside of the square and passing their own place advance to the second couple.
   c) The first and second couples pass through each other, the ladies passing between the opposite couple (see page 127 for full directions.) Each couple turns left about and passes back through the other.

Right and left with the couple you meet.

d) The two ladies advance to each other touching right hands and pass on to the opposite gentleman to whom they give their left hands, turn around the gentleman (to the left) while the gentlemen pivot with the ladies, who return to their places touching right hands as they pass each other.

e) See page 160 for directions and variations of the *docey-doe.*

f) The couples pass through each other as before, the second couple turning to place, while the first couple advances to the third couple, and repeats 2 from (c), then they advance to the fourth couple, and finish by passing through them to their home position.

3. See page 153 for directions or variations.

Promenade the Inside Ring

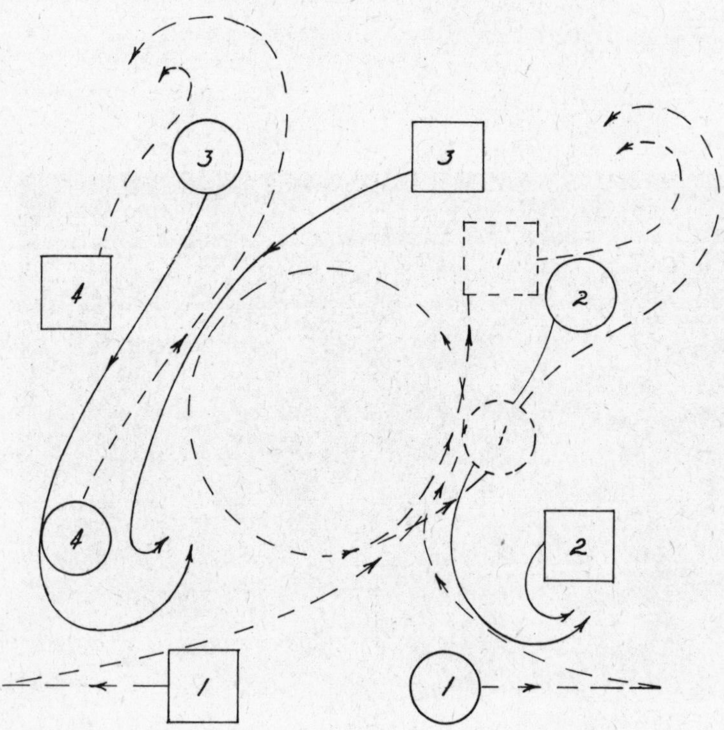

THE CALL:

1. *Salute your company and the lady on the left,*
   All join paddies and circle to the left.
   Break and swing and promenade back.

2. a) *First couple balance, first couple swing,*
   b) *First couple promenade the inside ring,*
   While the roosters crow and the birdies sing,
   And the geese overhead are on the wing.
   c) *Right and left with the couple you meet*
   d) *And the sides the same.*
   Now a right and left back.
   e) *Now the two ladies change.*
   And change right back.
   Form two rings and make 'em go.
   Four ladies break with a docey-doe.
   f) *Now a half promenade.*
   g) *And a right and left home.*

3. *Now balance home and everybody swing.*
   Now swing on the corner like swingin' on the gate,
   And now your own if you're not too late.
   Allemande left with your left hand

Two ladies change.

Right hand to partner and right and left grand.
Meet your honey and promenade.

Repeat 2 and 3 entire for second, third, and fourth couples.

☼ ☼ ☼

Often called *Promenade the outside ring,* and instead of *sides the same* sometimes called *two off couples the same.*

THE EXPLANATION:

1. See page 148 for directions or substitutions.
2. a) First lady and gentleman step back from each other four steps, then advance to each other and swing twice around.
   b) They take the promenade position and march around inside of the square, passing their own position, and advance to the second couple.
   c) First and second couple pass through each other. (See preceding page.)
   d) At the same time, couples three and four pass through each other in the same manner. All couples pass back to place.
   e) The first and second ladies change places as in the preceding dance and the third and fourth ladies change over and back at the same time.
   f) All couples take promenade position and first and second couples pass each other to the opposite's place (men passing left shoulders), make a left-about turn and again face each other. At the same time the third and fourth couples do the same with each other.
   g) Each couple passes through the opposite couple and back to place in the square.
   h) Each group now joins hands in a circle of four and does a docey-doe. (See page 160 for directions.)
3. See page 155 for directions for this ending.

VARIATION:

This dance can be speeded up with more dancers in action if the first and third couples are called out at the same time. They *promenade* at the same time on opposite sides of the *inside ring.* In this case the call *and the sides the same* is of course omitted. For the repetition of the dance the second and fourth couples are called out at the same time.

Right and Left

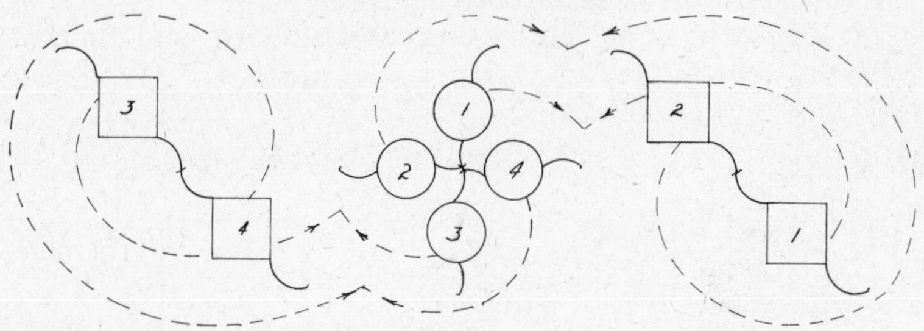

THE CALL:

1. *Everybody swing his prettiest gal.*
   Left allemande and right hand grand,
   And promenade, oh, promenade.

2. a) *First and third couples lead to the right,*
   b) *With a right and left through,*
   And a right and left back.
   c) *Two ladies change*
   And change right back.
   d) *Ladies star by the right in the center of the set,*
   e) *Two gents turn in a little side bet.*
   f) *Now grab your own—you're not through yet*
   g) *And circle four with the couple you met.*
   Docey-doe with the gent you know
   The ladies go si and the gents go do.
   Balance home and everybody swing.

Ladies circle four in the center of the set,
Gents turn left in a little side bet.

3. *Left allemande and a right hand grand.*
Plant your taters in a sandy land,
And promenade back to the same old stand.

Repeat 2 and 3 with "*second and fourth couples out to right.*"

THE EXPLANATION:

1. See page 150 for directions.

2. a) First couple advances to second couple while the third couple advances to the fourth couple. And throughout the dance the third and fourth couples execute the same movements as described for the first and second at the same time.
   b) First and second couples pass through each other and back. (See page 127 for directions.)
   c) First and second ladies change places with each other and back. (See page 127 for directions.)
   d) All four ladies join right hands and circle once around to the left in the center of the set.
   e) First and second gentlemen join left hands and circle twice around. (Third and fourth gentlemen, of course, do the same thing.)
   f) Timing the three circles (the four-hand mill of ladies with a two-hand mill of men on either side) so each dancer is back to original position at the same moment, each gentleman takes his partner's left hand in his right so they face the opposite couple. Each group of four joins hands in a ring and circles to the left.
   g) First and second couples do the *docey-doe* (see page 160), and the third and fourth couples the same. Each couple returns to own place in the square.

3. See page 153 for directions.

Swing Your Opposite All Alone

THE CALL:

1. *Everybody swing his prettiest gal,*
   Left allemande and a right hand
   grand,
   And promenade, oh, promenade.

2. a) *First couple out to the right,*
   b) *Swing your opposite all alone,*
   c) *Now the one you call your own.*
   d) *Now your opposite; don't be afraid.*
   e) *Now your own and half promenade,*
   f) *And right and left through to the next.*

   Repeat 2 beginning with (b).
   Repeat again changing last line to:

   And right and left home.

Half promenade.

3. *All eight balance and all eight swing,*
A left allemande,
And a right hand grand,
Meet your partner and promenade.

Repeat 2 and 3 for second, third, and fourth couples.

THE EXPLANATION:

1. See page 150 for directions or substitutions.
2. a) First couple advances to second couple.
   b) First gentleman swings the second lady and second gentleman swings the first lady once around. The two gentlemen face each other and put the ladies down on the right.
   c) Each gentleman swings his partner once around, putting her down to the right.
   d) Each gentleman again swings the opposite lady.
   e) Each gentleman again swings his partner, putting her on his right. He takes the promenade position and walks with her past the opposite couple (gentlemen passing left shoulders), and makes a left turn, again facing the opposite couple.
   f) Each couple passes through the opposite couple (see page 127) and the first couple passes on to the third couple while the second couple turns to their own place. After repeating with the third couple, the first couple advances to the fourth couple, repeats with them and then back to their own positions.
3. See page 154 for directions.

Change and Swing Half

THE CALL:

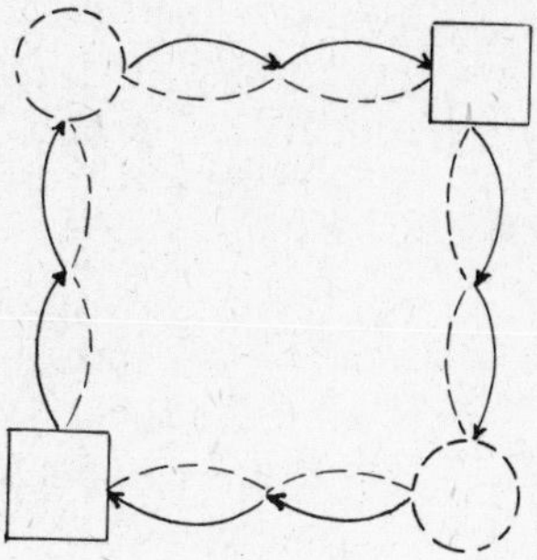

1. *Salute partners, salute corners,*
   Join hands and circle round,
   Swing 'em hard and trot 'em home.

2. a) *First couple out to the right,*
   b) *Change and swing half,*
   c) *Change and swing half,*
   d) *Change and swing half,*
   And don't be afraid,
   e) *Change and swing half*
   And a half promenade.
   f) *Right and left through*
   And on to the next.
   Repeat 2 beginning with (b).
   Repeat again changing (f) to:
   Now right and left home.

3. *Swing, swing, everybody swing!*
   Allemande ho!
   Right hand up and around we go,
   Meet your partner and promenade home.

Repeat 2 and 3 for second, third, and fourth couples.

Change and swing half.

THE EXPLANATION:

1. See page 149 for directions or substitutions.

2. a) First couple advances to second couple.
   b) First gentleman takes second lady by both hands and turns her half around to the right, so that he stands in her position and she in his. The second gentleman turns the first lady in the same manner.
   c) Each gentleman turns to his partner and taking her by both hands turns her in the same manner, so that he changes positions with her.
   d) Now each gentleman takes the opposite lady and turns her again.
   e) Each gentleman turns his partner again, and it brings everyone back to the position from which they started. Each gentleman takes his partner at his right side, holding with hands crossed in front, and promenades past the opposite couple, gentlemen passing left shoulders, and each gentleman pivots and turns himself and his partner left about so they face the opposites.
   f) Couples advance to each other, and each gentleman takes the opposite lady by the right hand, and the couples pass through each other (ladies going between the opposite couple). As soon as they pass through, each gentleman takes the left hand of his partner with his left and puts his right hand behind her waist. In this position the second couple turn to their original place and the first couple advance to the third and repeat the figure. Then they advance to the fourth couple and on the last repetition they return to their places in the square.

3. See page 153 for directions, or substitute any other ending given there.

Right and Left Four and Six

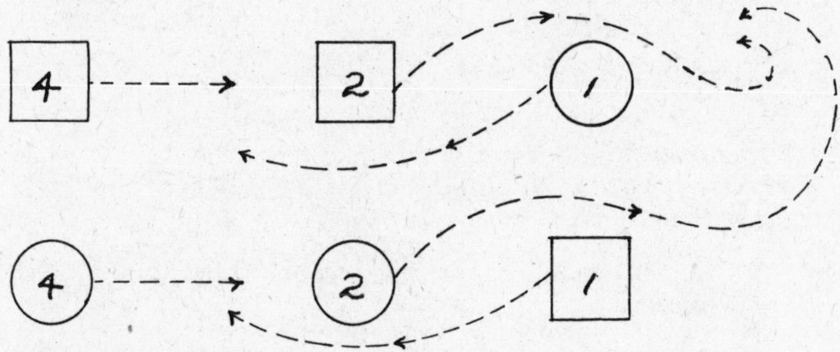

THE CALL:

1. *Honors right and honors left,*
   All join hands and circle to the left,
   Break and swing and promenade back.

2. a) *First couple out to the couple on the right,*
   b) *With a four and a half.*
   c) *Right and left four,*
   And a right and left six.
   Right and left on,
   And a right and left back.

Right and left six.

d) *On to the next and circle four.*
Docey-doe with the gent you know.
The lady goes si, the gent goes doe.

e) *On to the next with a four and a half.*
Right and left four,
And a right and left six.
Right and left on,
And a right and left back.

f) *Balance home and everybody swing.*

3. *A left allemande and a right hand grand.*
Hand over hand around the ring.
Hand over the hand with the dear little thing.
Meet your partner and promenade.

Repeat 2 and 3 for the second, third, and fourth couples.

THE EXPLANATION:

1. See page 148 for directions or substitutions.

2. a) First couple advances to second couple and joining hands they circle half around so that the first couple is on the outside and the second couple toward the center.

b) First couple then do a right and left through (see page 127) and, while the second couple turns around, the first couple continues on with a right and left through with the fourth. As the first couple turns around in place, the fourth continues on with a right and left through with the second couple. The fourth couple turns and stands in the second couple's place while the second couple continues on with a right and left through with the first. This leaves the first couple in the center, the second couple standing in the fourth couple's place and the fourth couple standing in the second couple's place.

c) First couple advances to third couple, and joining hands they circle full around to the left, finishing with a *docey-doe* (see page 160).

d) First couple advances to fourth couple's place, where the second couple are still standing. They repeat (b) which puts the fourth and second couples each back in their own places.

f) First couple, who is again in center, balances home and all swing.

3. See page 153 for directions or substitutions.

Right and Left Four
And the Center Couple Swing

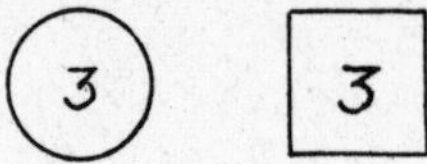

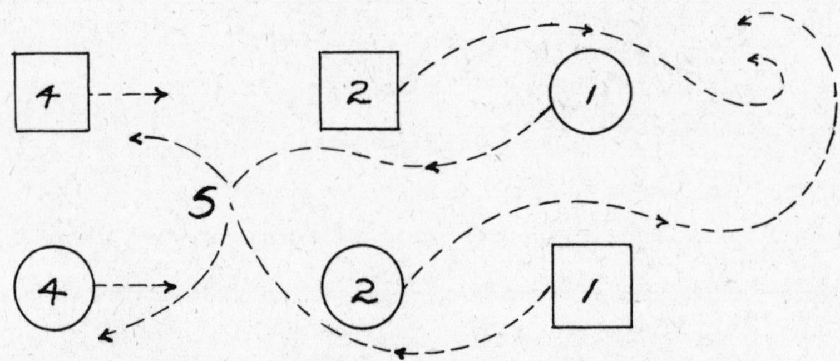

THE CALL:

1. *Everybody swing his prettiest gal*
   And promenade, boys, promenade.

2. a) *First couple out to the couple on the right*
   b) *And a four and a half.*
   c) *Right and left four*
   And the center couple swing.
   d) *Right and left six*
   And the center couple swing.
   e) *Right and left on*
   And the center couple swing.
   f) *Right and left back*
   And the center couple swing.
   g) *Now circle four with the odd couple oh,*
   Around and around and a docey-doe.
   h) *Now on to the next.*
   Repeat 2 from (b) changing (g) and (h) to:
   Balance home.

3. *And swing 'em all day.*
   Allemande left in the same old way.
   Hand over hand and a right and left grand.
   Meet your partner and promenade.
   Repeat 2 and 3 for second, third, and fourth couples.

This is sometimes called as follows:

Right and left through and center two swing,
Right and left through and center two swing,
Right and left through and center two swing,
Right and left through and center two swing,
Now lead to the foot
With a circle four and a docey-doe.

THE EXPLANATION:

1. See page 151 for directions or substitutions.

2. a) First couple advances to second couple.
   b) They all join hands and circle half around so as to change places.
   c) They pass through each other with a *right and left* (see page 127) leaving the first couple in the center of the set. First couple takes regular dance position and swings, while the second couple turns facing set.

Right and left four and the center couple swing.

d) First couple then passes through fourth couple with a right and left. The fourth couple, now in the center, swings, while the first couple turns around.

e) The fourth couple goes on and does a right and left with the second. The second is now in the center and swings.

f) The second couple now does a *right and left* with first couple. This puts the first couple back in the center where they swing again. And it leaves the second couple standing in the fourth couple's place and the fourth couple standing in the second couple's place.

g) The first couple now advances to the third couple, who have stood idle so far, and joining hands with them circles and does a *docey-doe* (see page 160).

h) They now advance to the fourth position where the second couple is standing and by repeating from (b) through (f) they get the second and fourth couples back in their own positions, and they balance home from the center of the set.

3. See page 154 for directions or substitute any other ending given there.

Right and Left Back and Both Couples Swing

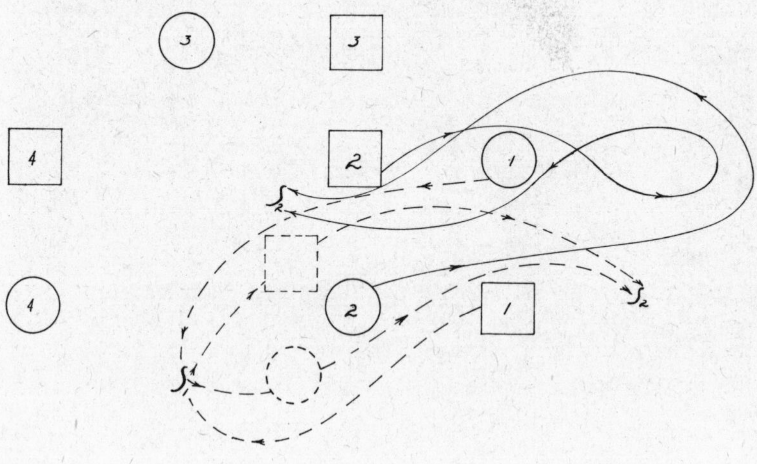

THE CALL:

1. *All jump up and never come down.*
   Swing your honey around and around
   'Til the hollow of your foot
   Makes a hole in the ground,
   And promenade, boys, promenade.
2. a) *First couple out to the couple on the right.*
   b) *Right and left through*
   And the center couple swing.
   c) *Right and left back*
   And both couples swing.
   d) *Now four hands up and here we go,*
   Round and around and a docey-doe.
   f) *On to the next.*
   Repeat 2 beginning with (b)
   Repeat again changing last line to:
   Balance home.
3. *And everybody swing.*
   Swing your opposite across the hall.
   Now the lady on your right.
   Now your opposite across the hall.
   Now your own and promenade all.
   Repeat 2 and 3 for second, third, and fourth couples

Right and left back and both couples swing.

THE EXPLANATION:

1. See page 149 for directions or substitute any introduction given there.
2. a) First couple advances to second couple.
   b) Two couples pass through each other with a right and left (see page 127). As the first couple turns around to face the set the second couple (who is in the center) takes dance position and swings.
   c) They pass back through each other with a right and left and both couples now take dance position and swing.
   d) The four join hands and circle and then do a *docey-doe* (see page 160).
   f) The first couple now advances to the third couple.
3. See page 155 for directions or substitute any other ending given there.

Right and Left Through and Swing That Girl Behind You

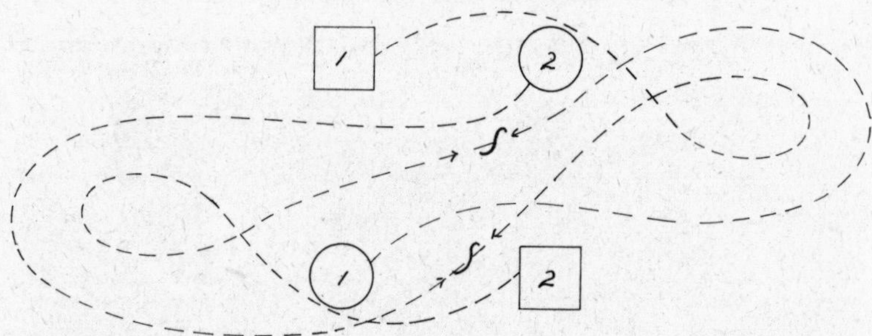

THE CALL:

1. *Honors right and honors left.*
   All join hands and circle to the left,
   Break and swing and promenade back.
2. a) *First couple balance-swing,*
   Lead right out to the right of the ring.
   b) *Right and left through*
   And swing that girl behind you.

c) *On to the next*
With a right and left through
And swing that girl behind you.

Repeat (c).

3. *Now single promenade*
With the lady in the lead.
Now turn right back
You're all agreed,
And swing that girl, that pretty little girl,
Swing that girl behind you.
Promenade to places now.

Repeat two more times, until straight.
Repeat 2 and 3 for second, third, and fourth couples.

☼ ☼ ☼

Some callers prefer the variation:

Circle four hands half,
Now right and left through
And swing that girl behind you.
Now right and left through to the next.

Then repeat with another:

Circle four hands half.

And swing that girl behind you.

THE EXPLANATION:

1. See page 148 for directions or substitutions.
2. a) First couple step back from each other four steps, then forward and take dance position and swing. They then advance to second couple.

   b) They pass through the second couple with a *right and left* (see page 127) and then each man turns back (partners turning back to back) and swings the opposite lady.

   c) The first gentleman and the second lady go on to the third couple and pass through them with a right and left, and each man turning back swings the opposite lady.

   The first gentleman with the third lady now goes on and repeats with the fourth couple.
3. Each gentleman now places his lady in front of him, and they promenade in single file. Then each gentleman turns back and swings the girl behind him. He now places her in front of him, and they promenade again and so continue until each has his own partner. They then take regular promenade position and continue around to their own places.

In which either the gentleman or the lady of one couple visits around the set alone.

Adam and Eve

THE CALL:

1. *One foot up and the other foot down.*
   Grab your honey in your arms
   And turn her around.
   Now allemande left as you come down.
   And promenade your partner round.

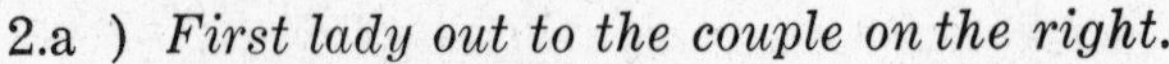

2.a) *First lady out to the couple on the right.*
   b) *Swing Mr. Adam,*
   c) *And swing Miss Eve,*
   d) *Now swing old Adam before you leave;*
   e) *And don't forget your own.*
   f) *On to the next.*

   Repeat 2 beginning with (b).
   Repeat again omitting the last line.

3. *Now everybody swing.*
   And swing 'em all day.
   Now allemande left in the same old way.

And swing Miss Eve.

Now hand over hand with a right and left grand.
Oh, some'll go right and some'll go left.
Now Promenade!

Repeat 2 and 3 complete for the second, third, and fourth couples.

THE EXPLANATION:

1. See page 149 for explanations or substitute any other introduction given there.
2. a) First lady advances to the second couple while the first gentleman remains in his place.
   b) She joins right hands with the second gentleman and swings him once around.
   c) She now joins left hands with the second lady and swings her once around.
   d) She swings the second gentleman again with a right hand swing.
   e) She skips back to her partner and joining left hands with him swings him once around.
   f) She now skips on to the third couple and swings them in the same way—always swinging the other men with her right hand and her partner and the ladies with her left hand.
3. See page 154 for explanation or substitute any other ending given there.

¤ ¤ ¤

Some dancers prefer using regular swing position, instead of single hands. When the two ladies swing together it is best for them to stand with right hips together, and each lady grasp the other's arms just below the shoulders. However, the swing position is more often used for the next call and the one hand swing for this one.

NOTE: This and the following dance are found in an infinite variety of forms and variations in different parts of the country.

Old Arkansaw

THE CALL:

1. *Salute your company*
And the lady on your left.
All join paddies
And circle to the left.
Break and swing and promenade back.

2. a) *First lady out to the couple on the right,*
b) *Swing your paw,*
c) *Swing your maw,*
d) *And don't forget old Arkansaw.*
e) *On to the next—*
Repeat 2 from (b).
Repeat again, omitting last line.

3. *Balance home and swing 'em all night,*
Allemande left—go left and right.
Meet your partner and promenade.

Swing your paw. (When a gentleman is called out.)

Repeat 2 and 3 entire for second, third, and fourth ladies.

☼ ☼ ☼

This call is sometimes heard:

Swing that Indian,
Swing that squaw,
And now that boy from Arkansaw.

Or when it is wished to send the gentlemen around instead of single ladies, it is:

First gent out to the couple on the right,
Swing your maw,
Swing your paw,
And don't forget your mother-in-law.

Or—

Don't forget to swing grandmaw.

THE EXPLANATION: This is a dance used for the sake of its comedy.

1. See page 148 for explanation or substitute any other introduction given there.
2. a) First lady advances to the second couple.
   b) She takes regular swing position with the second man and they swing once around.
   c) She takes regular swing position with the second lady (which is a bit confusing and provocative of laughter since neither lady knows which will take the man's position) and they swing once around.
   d) She returns to her partner and swings with him.
   e) She goes on to the third couple and does the same with them, then on to the fourth couple.
3. See page 154 for explanation or substitute any other ending given there.

Note: When lady swings with lady or man swings with man, this awkwardness can be avoided if each grasps the arms of the other just below the shoulders, thus making their holds identical.

Cheat and Swing

THE CALL:

1. *Everybody swing his prettiest gal,*
   A left allemande and a right hand grand,
   And promenade, oh, promenade.

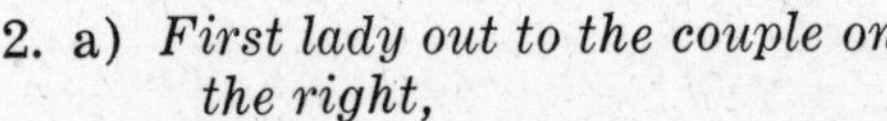

2. a) *First lady out to the couple on the right,*
   b) *Cheat or swing or do as you like,*
   c) *And don't forget your own.*
   d) *On to the next—*
   Repeat (b), (c), and (d).
   Repeat (b) and (c).

3. *Now you're home and everybody swing.*
   Swing your opposite across the hall,
   Now swing your corners,
   Now your partners,
   And promenade all.

Repeat 2 and 3 entire for second, third, and fourth ladies.

Cheat or swing.

THE EXPLANATION:

1. See page 150 for explanation or substitute any other introduction given there.
2. a) First lady leaves her partner and advances to second couple.
   b) She attempts to swing with the second man—he either swings with her, or rejects her and swings with his partner. It gives rise to much laughter if the man is a good tease and keeps them both guessing, and if the girls are clever in cheating for the swing and do their best to leave the other in the lurch.
   c) She returns to her partner and swings with him often in consolation for having been left at her last attempt). If the second man has swung with her he usually now gives his partner a consolation swing while the first couple are swinging.
   d) She now advances and repeats (b) with the third couple and so on around.
3. For explanation see page 156 or substitute any other ending given there.

¤ ¤ ¤

This dance is used for the sake of comedy.

VARIATION:

This dance is sometimes called:

First couple out to the couple on the right,
Cheat and swing and do as you like,
Now circle four and docey-doe
And lead right on to the next.

This can become so complicated that the following rules had better be established.

The active couple (that is, the couple called out) may either swing each other or either of them may swing any other dancer in the set.

The inactive dancers may only swing their own partners or swing with an active dancer if so chosen.

After the mixup you must get back with your own lady in your right hand for the circle four.

From the ending in 3, the caller may now and then substitute *cheat and swing* for *swing,* when anyone may grab anyone else anywhere on the floor for the *swing,* then scurry back for the call *go back home,* and for a regular ending.

Bow and Kneel to That Lady

THE CALL:

1. *Honors right and honors left.*
   All join hands and circle to the left,
   Break and swing and promenade back.

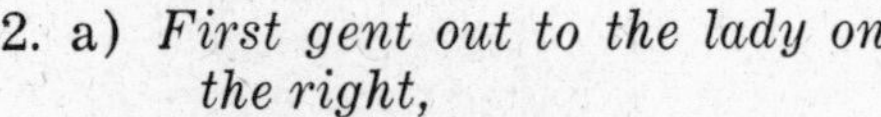

2. a) *First gent out to the lady on the right,*
   b) *Honor that lady,*
   c) *Bow to that lady,*
   d) *Kneel to that lady.*
   e) *Now step right back and watch her smile,*
   Step right up and swing her awhile.
   f) *Step right back and watch her grin,*
   Step right up and swing her again.
   g) *And on to the next—*
   Repeat 2 from (b) as written.
   Repeat again changing last line to:
   Balance home.

Kneel to that lady!

3. *And everybody swing.*
Now allemande left with your left hand,
Right hand to partner and right and left grand.
Promenade eight when you come straight.

Repeat 2 and 3 entire for second, third, and fourth gentlemen.

THE EXPLANATION:

1. See page 148 for explanation or substitute any introduction given there.
2. a) First gentleman leaves his partner and advances to the second lady.
   b) He gives her a slight curtsy, a slight nod of the head.
   c) He now gives her a very deep bow, with left hand on heart and right hand sweeping the floor.
   d) He now kneels before her with left hand on heart and right hand extended to her.
   e) He steps back from her four steps then advances to her and swings her once around.
   f) He steps back again, advances again, and swings her twice around.
   g) He goes on to the third lady and repeats it all with her and then to the fourth lady.
3. See page 152 for explanation or substitute any other endings given there.

☼ ☼ ☼

This dance, which should be done with exaggerated earnestness, is considered very tedious and uninteresting by my group except in exhibition, when a good clown has a fine opportunity.

Honor That Lady

THE CALL:

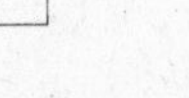

1. *Honors right and honors left.*
All join paddies and circle left.
Break and swing and promenade back.

2. a) *First gent out to the lady on the right.*
b) *Honor that lady,*
c) *Honor her again.*
d) *You honored her so nice,*
Now honor her again.
e) *Swing that lady,*
f) *Swing her again.*
g) *You swung her so nice,*
Now swing her again.
h) *Balance to the next—*

Repeat 2 from (b) as written.
Repeat again changing last line to:

Balance home.

Honor that lady.

3. *And everybody swing,*
Now allemande left with your left hand.
Right hand to partner and right and left grand.
And promenade, oh, promenade!

Repeat 2 and 3 entire for second, third, and fourth gentlemen.

THE EXPLANATION:

1. See page 148 for directions or substitute any other introduction given there.
2. a) The first gentleman leaves his partner and advances to the second lady.
   b) He bows to her politely.
   c) He bows to her with any exaggerated piece of clowning he can think of.
   d) He goes down, perhaps on both knees to her, with a deep salaam to her or perpetrates any extreme nonsense that occurs to him.
   e) He swings her once around.
   f) He swings her faster and twice around.
   g) He swings her furiously several times around.
   h) He advances to third lady and repeats all with her and then on to the fourth.
3. See page 152 for explanation or substitute any other ending given there.

¤ ¤ ¤

This silly dance is used to raise a laugh and lighten the spirits if a program is bogging down. It must be done with mock chivalry and a great deal of clowning. It is a favorite with one of my caller friends, but he prefers to use it with a new group who are not acquainted with it. In this case the man does not try for accumulative comedy as in the directions above, but is surprised and embarrassed at having to bow again and then again, and then having to swing again and again. The comedy arises from his discomfiture.

Docey Out As She Comes In

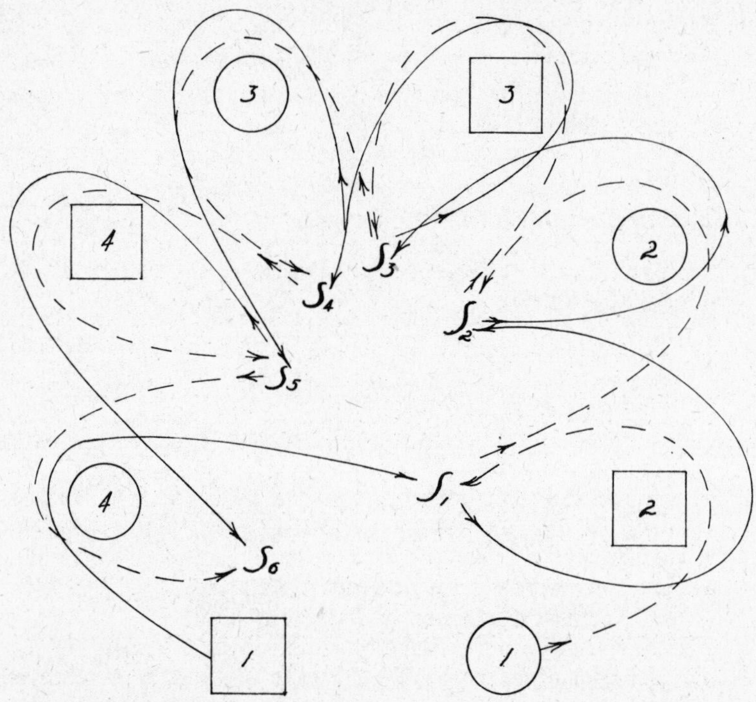

THE CALL:

1. *Up and down and around and around,*
   Allemande left and allemande aye,
   Ingo, bingo, six penny high,
   Big pig, little pig, root hog or die.

2. a) *First couple, docey corners right and left,*
   Meet and swing in the center of the set.
   b) *Now docey out as she comes in,*
   Meet in the center and swing her again.
   c) *Now docey in as she goes out,*
   And meet her again and swing her about;
   d) *Then docey out as she comes in,*
   And flop your wings and swing her ag'in.
   e) *Then docey in as she goes out,*
   And swing her ag'in and give a little shout.
   f) *And docey out as she goes in,*
   Yip and holler and everybody swing.

3. *Allemande left as you come down,*
Grand right and left and so on around,
Meet your partner and promenade.

Repeat 2 and 3 entire for the second, third, and fourth couples.

☼ ☼ ☼

The simpler and commoner call which is used for this dance is:

First lady out,
And docey round the right hand gent,
And swing your partner.
Now docey out as she comes in.
Meet her in the center and swing her again.

And the last two lines are repeated four more times or until they are around the set.

Allemande left and allemande aye,
Ingo bingo six penny high.

THE EXPLANATION:

1. See page 150 for directions or substitute any introduction given there.
2. a) The first couple separates, and the lady walks around the second gentleman, while the first gentleman walks around the fourth lady. This is not a *dos-a-dos*, walking back to back, but, while the corners stand still, the first lady and gentleman walk to each and, passing to the right, encircle them. They then meet in the center of the set and swing.

   b) The lady now walks around the second lady (by passing through the second couple and turning left) in the same way while the gentleman walks around the second gentleman. They meet in the center and again swing.

   c) The lady now walks around the third gentleman (by passing between him and the second lady and turning left) while the man walks around the second lady. They meet in the center and swing again.

   Please note that to go *out* is to pass between two couples, to go *in* is to pass between the partners of one couple. The lady will go alternately in and out in order to encircle each person in the set in regular order. The gentleman follows her, passing always around the person that she last circled. He, of course, will therefore have to go out whenever she goes in and vice-versa.

   d) He now goes between the second and third couples and encircles the third man, while she splits the third couple and encircles the third lady. They meet and swing again in the center.

   e) He splits the third couple and encircles the third lady while she goes between the third and fourth couples and encircles the fourth man. They meet and swing again in the center.

   f) He goes out between the third and fourth couples and encircles the fourth man, while she splits in between the fourth partners and encircles the fourth lady. They meet at their home position, and all four couples swing.
3. See page 153 for explanation or substitute any ending given there.

Swing the Right Hand Gent with the Right Hand Round

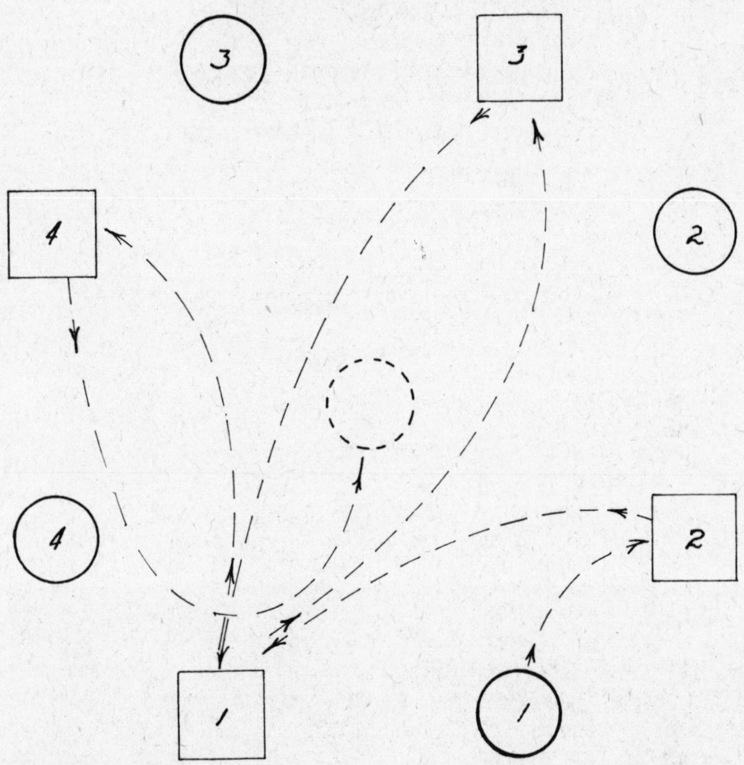

THE CALL:

1. *All eight balance, all eight swing.*
   A left allemande
   And a right hand grand.
   Meet your partner and promenade.

2. a) *First lady out to the right,*
   b) *Swing the right hand gent*
   With the right hand round,
   c) *Partner with your left*
   As you come down.
   d) *Swing the opposite gent with the*
   Right hand round,
   And left hand to partner as you come down.

e) *Swing the left hand gent with the*
Right hand round,
And left hand to partner as you come down.

f) *Now birdie in the center*
And seven hands round.

g) *The bird hops out and the crow hops in,*
All join paddies and go round ag'in.

h) *The crow hops out with a left allemande.*

3. *Right hands to partners*
And right and left grand.
Promenade eight
When you come straight.

Repeat 2 and 3 entire for second, third, and fourth ladies.

¤ ¤ ¤

The end of this dance is sometimes called:

Lady in the center and seven hands round,
Lady swing out and the gent swing in.
The gent swing out and everybody swing.
A left allemande and a right hand grand.

Birdie in the center and seven hands round.

THE EXPLANATION:

1. See page 151 for description or use any other introduction given there.
2. a) The first lady leaves her partner and advances to the second gentleman.
   b) Taking right hands they swing once around.
   c) She returns, usually with a light skipping step, to her partner and swings him once around with left hands joined.
   d) She skips on to the third gentleman and swings him with the right hand, and returns to her partner and swings with the left.
   e) She skips on to the fourth gentleman and swings him by the right hand, and returns to her partner and swings with the left.
   f) She now takes a position in the center of the set. The rest of the set, seven of them, join hands and circle to the left, while she turns slowly in the opposite direction.
   g) She steps out and takes her partner's place in the circle, while he steps in to the center. All the while the circle continues to the left.
   h) They all do an allemande left, the first gentleman stepping out to the fourth lady, of course, and turning her with a left allemande. (If the gentleman will always remember to break the circle as he comes out, at the only two ladies who are together, and do his allemande with the one who is not his partner, he can make no mistake.)
3. The allemande left completed, they continue as described on page 152.

¤ ¤ ¤

For a boisterous and spectacular ending of this dance see "Chase the Birds to the Top of the Tree" in the section of additional dances at the end of this book.

Don't You Touch Her

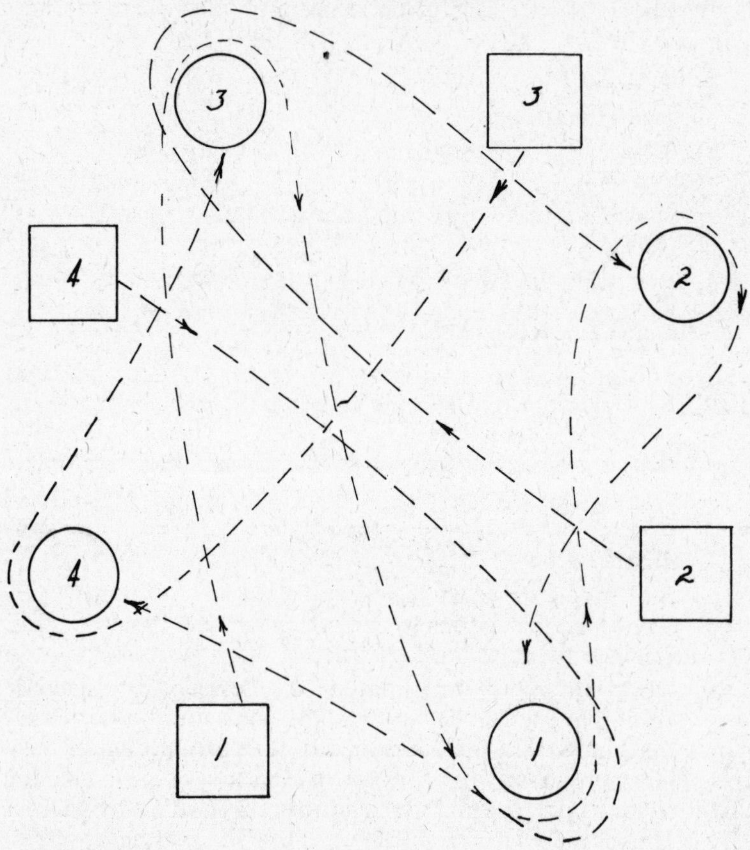

THE CALL:

1. *One foot up and the other foot down,*
   Take your honey in your arms,
   And turn her around.
   Promenade, boys, promenade.

2. a) *First gent out around the opposite lady,*
   And don't you touch her.

   b) *Now back around your own,*
   And don't you touch her.

   c) *All four gents around the right hand ladies,*
   And don't you touch 'em.

d) *Now promenade those ladies fair,*
But touch 'em? No sir, don't you dare!

Repeat 2 as written, for second, third, and fourth gentlemen.

3. *Now allemande left with your left hand,*
But don't you touch 'em.
Right hand to partners and right and left grand,
But don't you touch 'em.
Promenade, boys, and touch 'em if you like.

THE EXPLANATION:

1. See page 149 for explanation or substitute any introduction given there.

2. a) First gentleman leaves partner, and crosses to the third lady. He either does a *dos-a-dos* around her, or leans his shoulder toward her and with arms held behind him in a comedy position, goes round her without touching her.
   b) He now returns and encircles his own lady.
   c) Each gentleman now goes to the right behind his lady and encircles the next or right-hand lady with exaggerated comedy.

Right and left grand but don't you touch 'em.

d) They then promenade around with a lot of byplay of not touching each other. They return to the gentlemen's positions, which means that each lady has fallen back one place.

With three repetitions of (a) to (d) she is back in her own place.

3. A regular allemande left and grand right and left (see page 152) is now done, but with exaggerated and humorous care not to touch each other. The dancers often almost touch finger tips, but are careful not to really touch. At the final promenade they grab them firmly and joyously, as a relief from all the care not to touch them.

☼ ☼ ☼

A lot of comedy and fun can be had by this dance. In fact, the line "Don't you touch her" can be added to many of the different calls and thus adapt them to this pattern of fun. My dancers much prefer the preceding call "Swing the Right Hand Gent," so adapted, to the regular call here given.

Lady Go Halfway Round Again

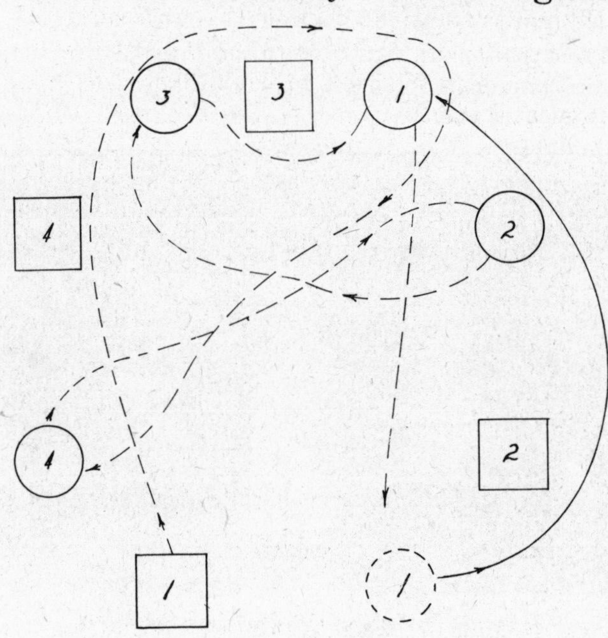

THE CALL:

1. *Honors right and honors left,*
   All join hands and circle to the left.
   Break and swing and promenade back.

2. a) *First couple balance, first couple swing,*
   First couple promenade the outside ring,
   b) *And the lady goes halfway round again.*
   c) *Forward three and three fall back,*
   d) *Forward three and three stand pat.*
   e) *The gent dos-ee around those three,*
   f) *And swing the left hand lady*
   With the right hand round,
   g) *Then the right hand lady*
   With the left hand round,
   h) *Then the opposite lady*
   With both hands round,
   j) *And now your own*
   With your arm around.
   k) *Balance home and everybody swing.*

3. *Now allemande left with your left hand,*
   Right hand to partner
   And right and left grand.
   Meet your partner
   And promenade.

Repeat 2 and 3 entire for second, third, and fourth couples.

The gent docey around these three.

THE EXPLANATION:

1. See page 148 for explanation or substitute any other introduction given there.

2. a) The first couple step back from each other with a bow, then step together and swing. They then promenade around the outside of the other three couples in the set.
   b) When they get back to their home position the first gentleman stands there alone, while his lady continues halfway on around the set and stops at the left side of the third gentleman.
   c) The third couple and the first lady take hands in a row with the gentleman in the middle and take four steps forward and four steps back to place.
   d) They then take four steps forward again and remain standing in a line in the middle of the set.
   e) The first gentleman now does a *dos-a-dos* around them, going to the left of the third lady, then, with his back to the three, sliding behind them to the right, he steps backward by the side of his partner and almost back to place.
   f) He now advances to the fourth lady and taking right hands with her swings once around.
   g) Crossing the set he joins left hands with the second lady and swings her once around.
   h) He now goes to the third lady and taking her with both hands swings her around.
   j) And now, taking regular swing or dance position with his partner, he swings her.
   k) Back to place while each of the other couples swing also.

3. See page 152 for explanation or substitute any other ending given there.

Promenade Your Corners Round

THE CALL:

1. *Salute your company and the lady on the left,*
   All join paddies and circle to the left,
   Break and swing and promenade back.

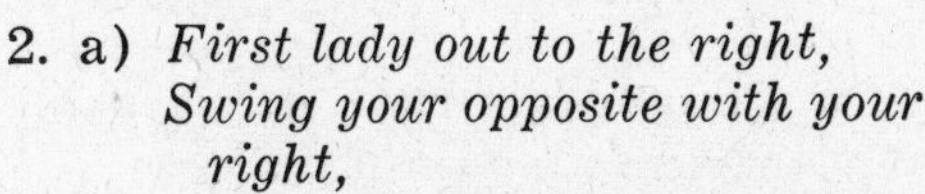

2. a) *First lady out to the right,*
   Swing your opposite with your right,

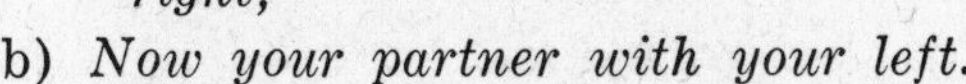

   b) *Now your partner with your left.*

   c) *All swing your corners*
   And promenade your corners round.

   Repeat (a), (b), and (c) three more times, substituting *same lady* for *first lady* in (a).

3. *Now allemande left with your left hand.*
   Right hand to partner and right and left grand.
   Promenade eight when you come straight.

Repeat 2 and 3 for second, third, and fourth ladies.

Promenade your corners round.

THE EXPLANATION:

1. See page 148 for explanations or substitute any introduction given there.

2. a) First lady leaves her partner and advances to second gentleman. She joins right hands with him and they swing once around.

   b) She returns to her partner and joining left hands with him swings once around (often, in this dance, all the other couples join left hands at the same time and swing around).

   c) Each gentleman now swings his corner or left hand lady in the regular dance or swing position.

   d) He promenades her around and back to his position. This means that each lady advances one place.

   On the repetition the first lady finds herself in second position and going to the right, in (a) she swings the third man with her right hand. She keeps advancing thus with each repetition until she is back in place.

3. See page 152 for explanation or substitute any ending given there.

Take Her Right Along

THE CALL:

1. *Everybody swing his prettiest gal,*
   And promenade, boys, promenade

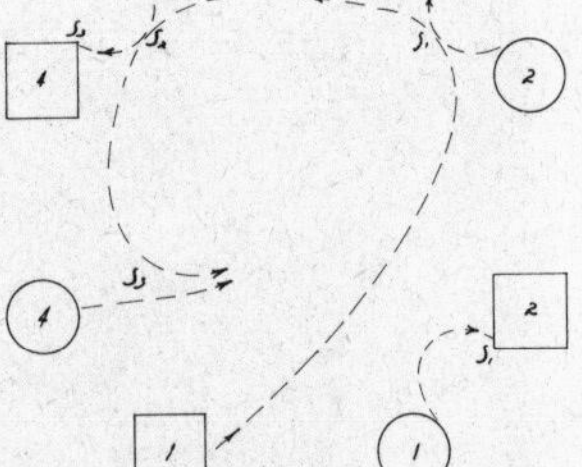

And on around for twelve swings.

2. a) *First couple out to the right,*
   b) *Change and swing*
   And take her right along.
   Repeat (b) eleven more times.

3. *Now you're home and everybody swing.*
   Now allemande left with your left hand.
   Right hand to partner and right and left grand.
   Promenade eight when you come straight.

Repeat 2 and 3 for second, third, and fourth couples.

For variety in the repetitions of (b) it is sometimes called:

Change and swing
With the carry-o swing.

or alternate between the two phrases.

THE EXPLANATION:

1. See page 151 for explanation or substitute any introduction given there.
2. a) First couple advances to second couple.
   b) The first gentleman swings the second lady while the second gentleman swings the first lady. The first gentleman with the second lady now advances to the third couple while the first lady remains with the second gentleman.

      On the next repetition the first gentleman swings the third lady and takes her on with him to the fourth couple.

      On the next repetition he swings the fourth lady and takes her across to the second couple.

      By constantly exchanging and swinging ladies and advancing them one position each time, on the twelfth time he swings his own lady back to her home position.

Change and swing and take her right along.

Of course, the standard swing is always twice around. But in this dance most men are contented to swing each girl just once. However, expert swingers swing each girl twice around, advancing to the next couple as they swing, and hardly losing a second as they change and swing the next girl with the intoxication of a whirling dervish.

3. See page 152 for explanation or substitute any ending given there.

¤ ¤ ¤

This is the "swingingest" dance there is. Some men get so dizzy that they cannot carry through to the end. Therefore it is sometimes wise to send the first man around once (three swings), then the second, third, and fourth men, each with three swings, which gets all the ladies safely home at last.

Yaller Gal

THE CALL:

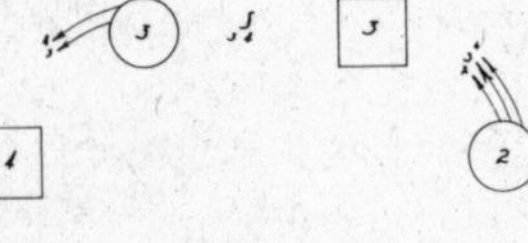

1. *All jump up and never come down*
Swing your honey around and around,
'Til the hollow of your foot makes a hole in the ground,
And promenade, oh, promenade.

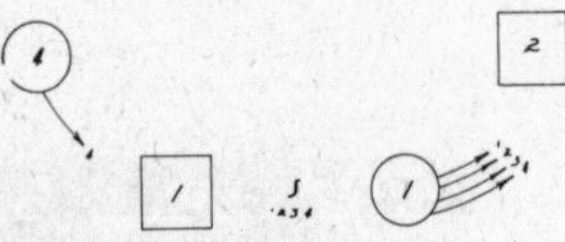

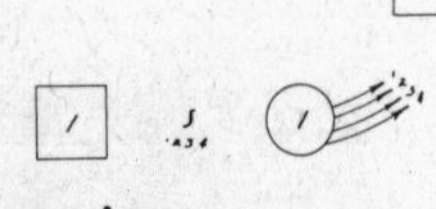

2. a) *First little yaller gal out around the ring*
Meet your partner, meet him with a swing.
b) *Two little yaller gals out around the ring,*
Meet your partners, meet 'em with a swing.
c) *Three little yaller gals out around the ring,*
Meet your partners, meet 'em with a swing.
d) *Four little yaller gals, out around the ring,*
Meet your partners and everybody swing.

3. *Allemande left as you come down,*
Right hand to partners and so on around,
Promenade eight, when you come straight.

Repeat 2 and 3 beginning with second, third, and fourth ladies.

If it is desired to send the men around the same way, *little yaller gal* is changed to *old alligator* in the call. Though some callers always have the ladies go round but use *alligator* or *yaller gal* indiscriminately for them, apparently only for the sake of variety.

THE EXPLANATION:

1. See page 149 for explanation or substitute any introduction given there.
2. a) The first lady leaves her partner and goes around the outside of the set, preferably with a skip step or a running step. When she gets back to her partner they swing.
   b) The first and second ladies both skip around the outside of the ring, the second, of course, ahead of the first as they circle, and both meet their partners and swing.
   c) The first, second, and third ladies all skip around the ring until they get back to their partners and swing.
   d) All four ladies now skip around the outside of the ring and all meet their partners and swing.
3. See page 152 for explanation or substitute any ending given there.

Four little yaller gals out around the ring.

Buffaloes and Injuns

(To be sung to the old tune of "Buffalo Gals Come Out Tonight")

THE CALL:

First little buffalo
Round the outside,
Round the outside,
Round the outside.
First little buffalo
round the outside
And everybody swing.

Two little buffaloes
Round the outside,
Etc., as above.
Three little buffaloes
Round the outside,
Etc.

Four little buffaloes
Round the outside,
Etc.

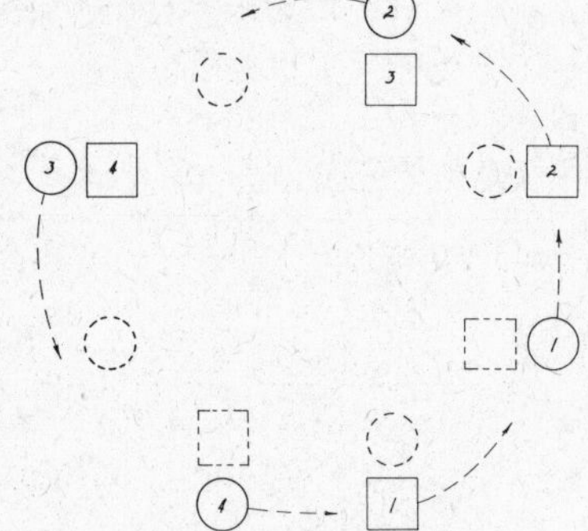

Four little buffaloes and two Indians around the outside.

Four little buffaloes and three Injuns out around the ring.

Four little buffaloes
And one Injun
Round the outside,
Round the outside,
Four little buffaloes and one Injun
And everybody swing.

Four little buffaloes
And two Injuns
Etc., as above.

Four little buffaloes
And three Injuns.
Etc.

Four little buffaloes
And four Injuns
Etc.
And everybody swing.
Now promenade to your seats.

Note: *Out around the ring* is often sung instead of the line, *Round the outside.*

THE EXPLANATION:

Almost the same dance as the preceding dance, *Yaller Gal,* except that since it is sung it has no regular Western dance introduction or ending. And after the four ladies go round the outside of the set, they are joined by the first gentleman, then the first and second gentlemen, etc., until all go around the outside.

The repetitions of *Round the outside* in each verse allow just time enough for the dancers to get around.

In the second half when the Injuns join in with the buffaloes, there are fewer and fewer dancers left standing in the set until, by the last repetition, when four buffaloes and four Injuns go round the outside, the set which they go around is purely imaginary.

The last line, *Promenade,* is spoken, of course, and not sung.

Since this dance is sung to a fixed tune it would argue that it is the older of the two. And since its use of "buffaloes" is the same as the word in the title of the tune, it suggests that it might be the original dance.

"Yaller Gal" and "Alligator" of course, suggest a Southern origin for the preceding dance. I wonder how much it was changed in coming West, and if it might be the original which in turn suggested the Western buffalo and Injun version.

Line Dances

In which the dancers usually form straight lines which advance and retire toward each other, or curving lines which progress in serpentine or circles.

Forward Up Six

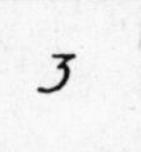

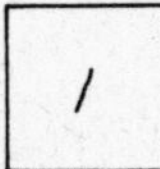

THE CALL:

1. *All eight balance, all eight swing,*
   A left allemande,
   A right hand grand,
   Meet your partner
   And promenade.

2. a) *First couple out to the right*
   And circle four.
   b) *Leave that gal, go on to the next,*
   And circle three.
   c) *Take that gal, go on to the next*
   And circle four.
   d) *Leave that gal and go home alone.*
   e) *Forward up six and fall back six,*
   f) *Forward up two and fall back two.*
   g) *Forward up six and pass right through,*
   h) *Forward up two and pass right through.*

   Repeat (e) to (h).

j) *Now swing on the corner*
Like swingin' on the gate.
Now your own if you're not too late.

3. *Now allemande ho, Right hands up*
And here we go! And promenade.

Repeat 2 and 3 entire for second, third, and fourth couples.

☼ ☼ ☼

Sometimes this dance is ended by substituting for (j):

Lone gents go right and circle four
Now docey-doe with the gents you know,
The ladies go si and the gents go do.
Now everybody swing.

THE EXPLANATION:

1. See page 151 for explanation or substitute any other introduction given there.

2. a) First couple advances to the second couple. They join hands and circle to the left.
   b) The first gentleman leaves the first lady with the second couple (she remains to the left of the second gentleman and the three join hands in a row). The

Forward up two and fall back two.

first gentleman goes on alone to the third couple and joins hands with them while they all three circle to the left.

c) The first gentleman takes the third lady on with him (leaving the third gentleman standing alone), and advances with her to the fourth couple. As he does so he changes her from his left hand to his right hand so that she is on his right side when they come to the fourth couple. They join hands with them and the four circle to the left.

d) He now leaves the third lady with the fourth couple (standing in a line of three with hands joined and the third lady on the left of the fourth gentleman) and returns to his place where he stands alone.

e) The six dancers standing in the side positions (the second and fourth men each with a lady on either side of him) advance four steps and retire four steps.

f) The two dancers standing alone (the first and third gentlemen) each advance and retire four steps.

g) The two threes now advance to each other and pass through so that each exchanges place with the other three. In passing through each gives his right hand to the opposite person, thus passing to the left of him (in most dances the old English traffic rule of passing to the left survives).

h) The two men advance to each other, touch right hands, and pass each other to the left. Each continues until he stands in the other's place. In repeating (e) to (h) they all pass back and stand in own positions.

j) Each gentleman now swings the girl on his left—that is, his corner girl on his left. He then returns to his partner and swings her back into home position.

3. See page 153 for explanation or substitute any other ending given there.

☼ ☼ ☼

If the second call is used the first and third gentlemen advance to and join hands with the three on their right. This makes two groups of four, who each circle to the left and then do a *docey-doe* (see page 160). After swinging to home position they are ready for any ending that may be called.

Forward Six and Fall Back Eight

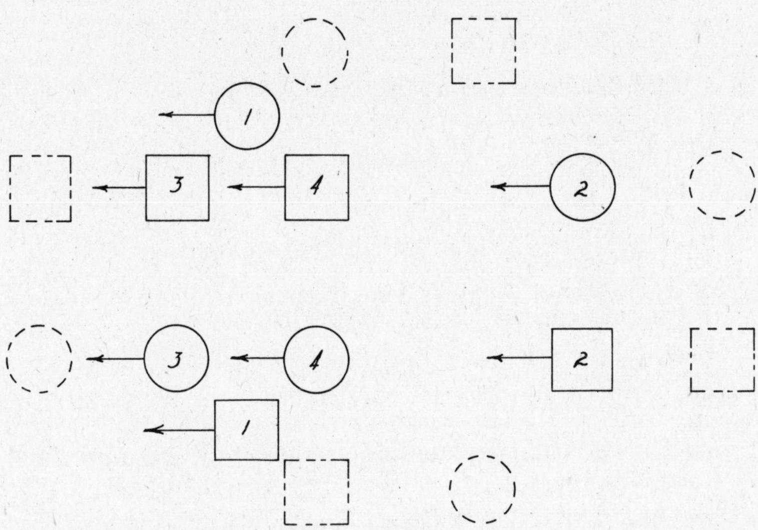

THE CALL:

1. *Swing your partners, don't be late.*
   Swing on the corner like swingin' on the gate.
   Now your own and promenade eight.

2. a) *First couple balance-swing.*
   Down the center and split the ring,
   The lady goes right and the gent goes left,
   And four in line you stand.

   b) *Forward four and fall back four.*
   Sashay four to the right.

   c) *Forward six and fall back eight.*
   Forward eight and fall back six.
   Sashay four to the right.

   d) *Forward four and fall back four.*
   Sashay four to the right.

   e) *Forward six, fall back eight.*
   Forward eight, fall back six.
   Sashay four to the right.

f) *Forward four and fall back four.*
Forward four and circle four.

g) *Ladies doe and the gents you know*
Circle again and docey-doe.

h) *Balance home and everybody swing.*

3. *A left allemande and a right hand grand.*
Meet your partner and promenade.

Repeat 2 and 3 for second, third, and fourth couples.

☼ ☼ ☼

With beginners it is often better to change (g) to:

Swing your opposite with your right,
Now your partner with your left.

THE EXPLANATION:

1. See page 151 for explanation or substitute any introduction given there.

2. a) First couple step back from each other, then advance to each other and swing. They go down the center of

Forward six and eight fall back.

the set and pass between the third couple. The lady turns to the right and stands at the left of the third gentleman. The first gentleman turns left and stands at the right of the third lady. They take hands four in a row.

b) The four advance in a straight line four steps to the center of the set, and fall back four steps to place. Then with gliding steps the line of four circles around to right (each individual still facing center) until the line of four stands directly behind the fourth couple.

c) Still holding hands in their row, the first lady gives her outside hand (left) to the fourth gentleman, and the first gentleman gives his outside hand (the right) to the fourth lady so that they form a very flattened circle of six, all facing center. This six advances to the center four steps and as they retire four steps, the second couple facing them goes with them. (This makes eight fall back.) Now the six advance again with the second couple who back up ahead of them to place. And the second couple stands in position, while the six retire to place. The four, still holding hands, slide around to the position of the first couple.

d) They advance and retire again and then slide step around to the right and behind the second couple.

e) Now they advance and retire as in (c) with the second couple, and the fourth couple following and preceding the six on the call of eight. They slide around to the right to the original position of the four.

f) They advance and retire again and then join hands and form a circle of four in the center of the set.

g) The two ladies do a *dos-a-dos* or back-to-back around each other. The two men *dos-a-dos,* and the four circle again to the left and finish with the regular *docey-doe* (see page 160 for directions).

h) The first couple returns home. All four couples balance with each other and then swing.

3. See page 153 for explanation or substitute any other ending given there.

With many sets on the floor, all advancing and retiring in perfect time, this is an impressive change to watch and a very simple dance to do.

In fact, it is so simple that it is a favorite with beginners, in which case it is best to use the substitute call for (g) on the opposite page. Then each gentleman gives his right hand to the opposite lady in the circle of four, swings her around behind him. He then takes his partner by the left hand and swings her to the home position.

Four in a Center Line

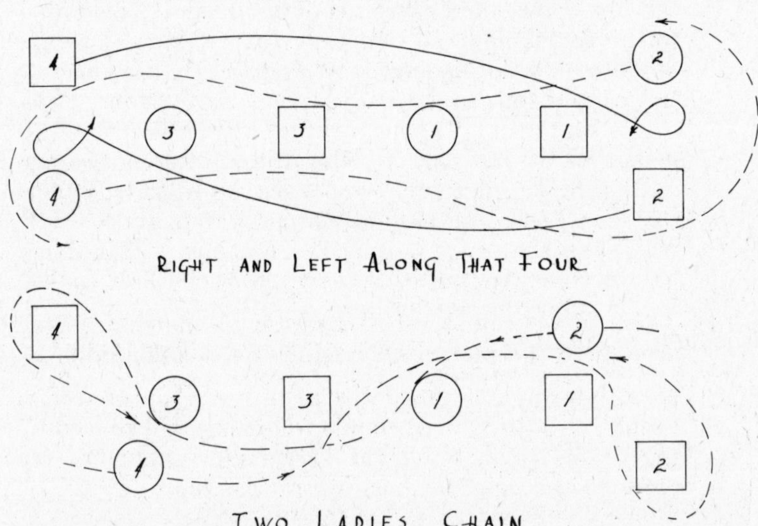

THE CALL:

1. *Salute your company and the lady on the left.*
   All join paddies and circle to the left.
   Break and swing and promenade back.

2. a) *First couple balance, first couple swing.*
   Promenade halfway round the ring.
   b) *Four hands in line to the center and back.*
   To the center again and there stand pat.
   c) *Side couples right and left along the four.*
   Right and left back as you were before.

d) *Side ladies change along the four*
And change right back as you were before.

e) *Center four with a circle four.*
Now docey-doe with the gents you know.
The lady go si and the gent go doe.

3. *Balance home and swing 'em all night.*
Allemande left, go left and right,
Hand over hand around the ring,
Hand over hand with the dear little thing.
Meet your own and promenade.

Repeat 2 and 3 for second, third, and fourth couples.

☼ ☼ ☼

For a more complicated figure (d) is called:

Side ladies change through the center of the four
And change right back as they were before.

For the most complicated form it is called:

All four ladies change on a woven track
And keep on changing 'til all change back.

THE EXPLANATION:

1. See page 148 for explanation or substitute any introduction given there.

2. a) The first couple step back from each other, then step together and swing. They promenade around behind

Side couples right and left along that four.

the second couple and stand to the left of the third couple, with whom they join hands in a line of four.

b) This line takes four steps to the center and then four steps back. They advance to the center again and remain there.

c) Each side couple separates and advances to the center with the lady going down one side of the line of four and the gentleman going down the other. Each gentleman takes the opposite lady by the right hand and passes her. As each couple advances beyond the line of four, the lady puts her left hand in her partner's left, and, with his right hand around her waist, he turns her around so as to face the set again. The two couples each separate and return to their places now in the same manner, along either side of the line of four.

d) Each lady advances along the line of four (the fourth lady in front and the second lady behind) to the opposite man. She gives her left hand to him and is turned around by him so that she returns down the opposite side of the four and her partner turns her to place by the left hand.

e) The line of four bends into a circle of four and executes a *docey-doe.* (See page 160.)

3. See page 154 for explanation or substitute any ending given there.

¤ ¤ ¤

If it is desired to make the figure a little more complicated the line of four separates in the middle and the two ladies give each other right hands and pass each other through this gap. Continuing down the other side, they meet and are turned by the men as before.

For the most complex form, each lady in the center line of four advances to the nearest side lady (it is necessary for the first man to pass his lady around in front of him to meet the second lady), the other ladies being already in position. The ladies give each other right hands and advance to the next men giving them left hands. The two men in the line do a half turn, each passing a lady to the center. The two side men do a full turn sending their ladies back into the line. They continue this until each lady has been around each end man and is back in place. All the while the two center men keep passing the string of ladies on, always with a half turn to the left.

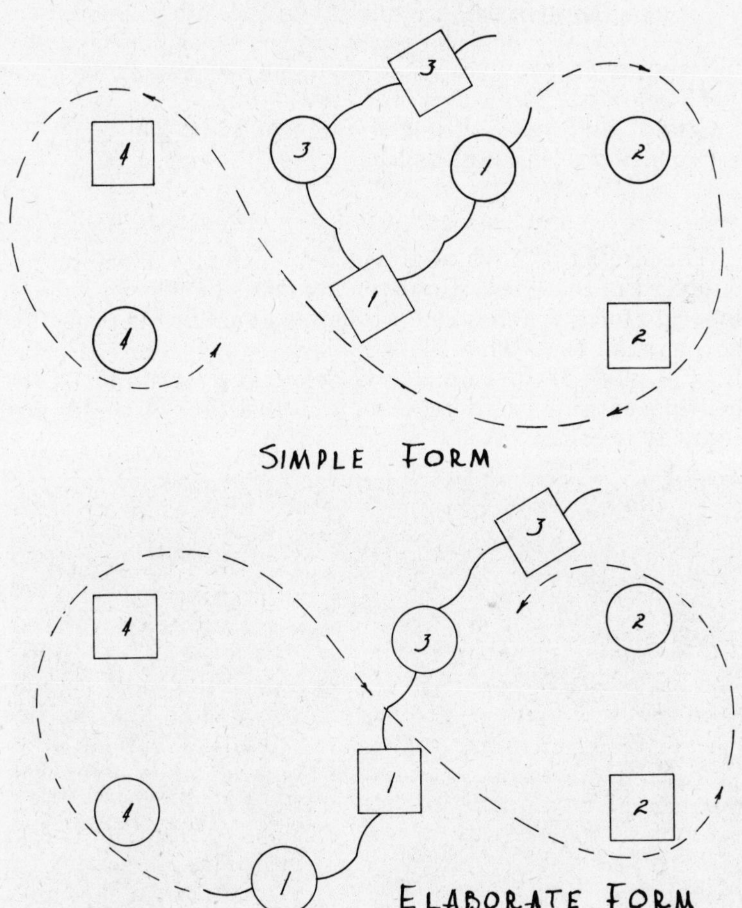

THE CALL:

1. *All eight balance, and all eight swing.*
   A left allemande and a right hand grand.
   Meet your partner and promenade.

2. a) *First and third couples forward and back,*
   Forward again and form a line
   With the ladies in the lead and the gents behind.
   b) *Cut a figure eight with the lady in the lead.*
   c) *Circle in the center and break to a line,*
   With the gent in the lead and the lady behind.
   d) *Cut a figure eight with the gent in the lead.*
   Then circle home.

3. *Swing your partners all around.*
   Allemande left as you come down.
   Grand right and left and so on around.
   Promenade, boys, promenade.

☼ ☼ ☼

This is the commonest form in which the dance is encountered in the West. However, we occasionally see a more elaborate form which is really a better dance and is probably the original one. This more elaborate figure has several steps in place of (a), numbered below (e), (f), and (g)—then in (h) and (j) it reverses the direction of the figure eight. It is called:

Cut a figure eight with the lady in the lead.

e) *First lady and opposite gent*
Right hands cross, left hand back.
f) *Join rights with partners and balance in a line.*
With a gee and a haw
And a gee and a haw.
g) *Break in the center and swing half around,*
h) *Cut a figure eight with the lady in the lead.*
j) *Break in the center and swing half around,*
Cut a figure eight with the gent in the lead.
Now circle four in the Kentucky way.
Swing your rights, now your lefts,
Now your own and balance home.

THE EXPLANATION:

1. See page 151 for explanation or substitute any introduction given there.

2. a) First and third couples, holding hands, advance four steps toward each other and then four steps back to place. They advance toward each other again and the first gentleman takes the third lady by the hand. This makes a curved line of four.
   b) The first lady now leads this line around behind the second couple by starting through the space between second and third positions and passing back to back around the second couple. Then she crosses the set diagonally and goes behind the fourth couple (between the third and fourth positions) completing her figure eight. The line of four faces the fourth couple in circling them.
   c) As the line reaches the center of the set the first lady and the third gentleman take hands and all circle four. The third lady and first gentleman break holds, again forming a line of four and thus putting the first gentleman in the lead.
   d) The first gentleman now leads them all in a figure eight around the same path that was taken by his lady. As they reach the center of the set they again circle four and break and swing home.

3. See page 152 for explanation or substitute any ending given there.

The more elaborate figure is danced as follows:

e) The first lady and third gentleman advance and join right hands and turn half around. They let go, reverse, join left hands, and turn half back. Still holding left hands, each takes his own partner with right hands. This makes a line of four, with the ladies facing second couple and the men facing fourth couple. All four balance by rocking forward on their right feet and closing with their left, then rocking backward on their right feet and closing with the left. They repeat this forward and back balance, the ladies and gentlemen going opposite directions and lightly swaying back and forth past each other (or if they prefer balancing together, they may all balance toward the fourth couple, then all toward the second).

g) The first lady and third gentleman let go each other's hands, and each couple pivots around their own clasped hands (individuals circling forward) and the first gentleman and third lady now take hands to reform a line of four.

h) The first lady marches directly forward leading the line behind and around the fourth couple (starting through the opening between first and fourth positions) and continues the figure eight by crossing the square diagonally and encircling the second couple (starting around them through the opening between second and first positions).

j) As the line of four crosses the diagonal of the square again, the first gentleman and third lady let go their holds. Each couple pivots around their own clasped hands. The first lady and third gentleman now take hands, reforming the line of four with the first gentleman in the lead. He now leads the line in a figure eight around the same path taken by his lady. As the circle of four closes the men are left back to back *(Kentucky way)*. They let go left hands, and then swing the right hand girl behind them (as in a *docey-doe)* then the opposite girl with the left hand, then their own with the right again, and so balance home.

Grapevine Twist

(As called by Mrs. Charlotte Coffman, Stone City, Colorado, who won the State Caller's Contest with this dance.)

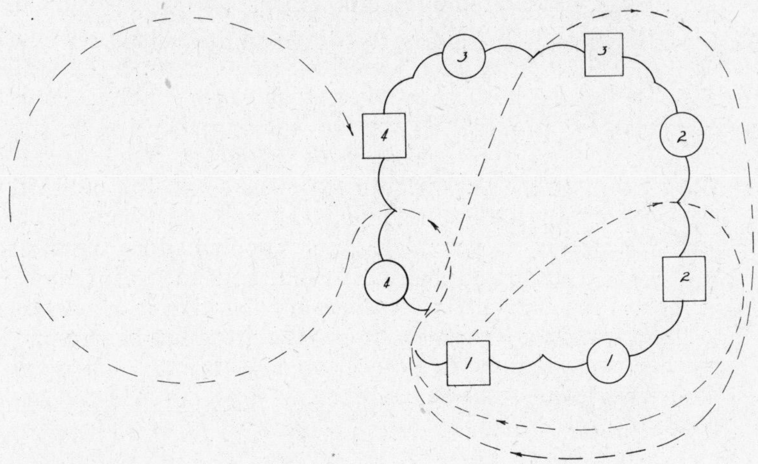

THE CALL:

1. (No introductory call.)

2. a) *First couple, just you two,*
Step right out and spin 'em a few;
b) *Now gather in four to the middle of the floor,*
And dance again as you did before.
c) *Now pick up six, and don't get mixed,*
And dance around 'til you all get fixed;
d) *Then simmer down eight, and don't be late.*
e) *Form the grapevine twist like the one on the gate.*
Here you twist and there you whirl
Right around that pretty girl.
f) *Here you duck and there you dive,*
Pep up boys, and act alive.
g) *Twist 'em right and twist 'em wrong.*
Straighten 'em out and trot right along.

3. a) *Now allemande left with your left hand,*
Right hand to partner and right and left grand.
Meet your partner and promenade.

Repeat 2 for second couple and finish with:

b) *Promenade, Indian style,*
Lady in the lead and single file,
Turn right back and swing 'em awhile.

Repeat 2 for third couple ending with 3 (a).
Repeat again for fourth couple ending with 3 (b).

THE EXPLANATION:

1. With no introductory call the dancers come skipping on the floor in single file, hands waving and everybody "hollering." Before they come in, they line up as first, second, third, and fourth couples with the men leading. If there is more than one set, it is necessary for the first man of each set to break from the line and skip around the circle where his set is to be in a direction contrary to the promenade direction; that is, clockwise, until he has all his couples in position.

2. a) The first gentleman takes his partner by both hands and skips once around in one spot with her near the center of the set.

Twist 'em right, now twist 'em wrong.

b) He lets go with his left hand and takes the second lady's hand while the first lady takes the second gentleman's hand and they all skip around once as a circle four.

c) The first gentleman again lets go with his left hand and takes the third lady's hand, while the second lady takes the third gentleman's hand making a circle of six. They skip once around.

d) Again the first gentleman lets go with his left hand and takes the fourth lady with it while the third lady takes the fourth gentleman, making a circle of eight which skips around for a few steps.

e) And then the first man lets go his left hand again and skips in under the raised arms of the second couple, leading his partner and the second gentleman with him. This makes it necessary for the second gentleman to "turn a dishrag" or turn in under his own right arm without breaking his hold.

The first gentleman turns to the right when he passes under and circles back again with the others following toward the middle of the original circle.

f) He now leads the line under the raised arms of the third couple (the third gentleman this time "turning a dishrag" under his own right arm) and turns right once more circling around to the line, all of whom are still skipping and following him.

g) He now leads them under the raised arms of the fourth couple and turns to the right as before for a few steps, then turns "wrong" or loops back to his left. He then "straightens them out" by turning right again and circling round until they have joined hands once more in a skipping circle of eight.

3. a and b) See pages 152 and 159 for explanation or substitutions.

Rattlesnake Twist

THE CALL:

1. *All jump up and never come down,*
And swing your honey around and around,
'Til the hollow of yóur foot
Makes a hole in the ground.
And promenade, oh, promenade.

2. a) *Now all join hands and circle to the left.*
The first couple break.
b) *The first gent lead down the rattlesnake's hole,*
In and out with a rattlesnake twist.
c) *The first lady lead back*
With a rattlesnake twist,
And circle eight.

3. *Now allemande left with your left hand.*
Right hand to partner and right and left grand.
Meet your partner and promenade.

Repeat 2 and 3 for second, third, and fourth couples.

First gent lead down the rattlesnake's hole.

This call, only partly remembered by him, was given me by an old-time caller up at Missouri Lake, Colorado.

THE EXPLANATION:

1. See page 149 for explanation or substitute any introduction given there.

2. a) After all joining hands and circling to the left, the first couple breaks the circle by letting go each other's hands.

   b) The first gentleman passes under the raised arms of the fourth couple behind the fourth gentleman, in front of the third lady, between the third couple and behind the third gentleman, and so on until he has woven in and around everyone in the line. The whole line is still holding hands and without a break passes in and out after him through the full set.

   As the fourth lady passes under, she has to pass under her own left hand, and, without breaking holds, pass this left hand down behind her head and out behind her. Each lady has to do this half dishrag as she passes under her own hand. But the gentlemen find that since the line passes behind them they have to do a complete right about face under their own left arms before they can follow on after the leader.

   c) As the line straightens out and everyone has passed under, the first lady turns back and leads the line in reverse under the raised hands of the second couple, around the lady and back between second and third couple, in under the raised arms of third couple, etc., in and out through the whole line.

   In this case, as the second gentleman follows in under his own right arm, he passes it down behind his head and out behind him. Each of the other gentlemen in turn have to do the same. But the ladies, this time have to do a complete left about face under their own right arms.

   When the line is straightened out the first couple rejoin hands and they all circle to the left.

3. See page 152 for explanation or substitute any other ending given there.

Grapevine Twist

(Garden Variety)

THE CALL:

1. *Honors right and honors left.*
All join hands and circle to the left,
Break and swing and promenade back.

2. a) *First gent lead his partner*
Through the couple on the right
And around that lady for a grapevine twist.
b) *Out to the center with a haw and gee,*
And around the gent with a twiddle-de-dee.
c) *Now circle four and lead to the next,*
d) *And around that lady with a grapevine twist,*
Out to the center and loop right back,
Around the gent on a crooked track,
Now circle six and lead to the next.
e) *And around that lady with a grapevine twist,*
Out to the center with a figure eight,
Then around the gent; he'll have to wait.
Then circle eight.

Out to the center with a haw and a gee.

3. *Now allemande left with your left hand,*
Right hand to partner and right and left grand.
Promenade eight when you are straight.

Repeat 2 and 3 for second, third, and fourth couples.

¤ ¤ ¤

This change is obviously derived from a New England Quadrille. And yet, it is the favorite square in Anson, Texas, where each circle is ended with a *do-pas-o.*

THE EXPLANATION:

1. See page 148 for explanation or substitute any introduction given there.

2. a) The first gentleman holding his partner by the hand leads her between the second couple and around and behind the second lady.

   b) To the center of the set, where he does a right turn and circles back over his own track and passes again between the second couple and around behind the second gentleman to the center of the set.

   c) All four join hands and circle once around to the left.

   d) The first gentleman and the second lady let go hands, and he leads the line of four between the third couple and around behind the third lady to the center of the set. He loops to the right and turns back over his own track where the second lady has just barely got by and leads the line around the third gentleman. The path he follows is an exact figure eight, except that the final upstroke continues on and bends around the third gentleman. He now circles around the center in such a way that the second lady can join hands with the third gentleman, and he takes the hand of the third lady, making a circle of six. After a few steps the circle is broken by his letting go the hand of the third lady, and he leads the line of six to the fourth couple.

   e) He leads them around behind the fourth lady to the center where the line loops back over its own track and then between the fourth couple again and around the fourth gentleman. It now circles until it picks up the fourth couple between the third lady and the first gentleman, and all eight circle to the left.

3. See page 152 or substitute any ending given there.

Bird in a Cage and Allemande Six

THE CALL:

1. *Up and down and around and around,*
Allemande left and allemande aye,
Ingo, bingo, six penny high,
Big pig, little pig, root hog or die.

2. a) *First couple out to the right,*
With a bird in the cage and circle three.

b) *Bird hop out and the crow hop in.*
All join paddies and go around again.

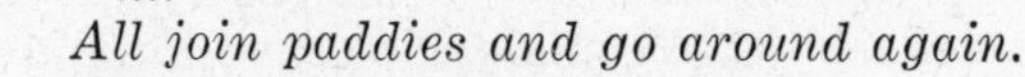

c) *The crow hop out and circle four,*
Now docey-doe with the gent you know,
The lady go C and the gent go doe.

d) *On to the next*
With a two, four, and six hands round,
Then birdie in a cage with five hands round,
The bird hop out and the crow hop in.
All join paddies and go around again.

DOTTED LINES SHOW LEFT ALLEMANDE

Birdie in a cage with five hands round.

e) *Crow hop out with a six allemande.*
Right hand to partner and right and left grand,
Meet your partner and promenade.

f) *Couples swing in and reverse promenade.*

g) *Now two, four, six, and eight hands round,*
Then birdie in a cage and seven hands round,
Bird hop out and the crow hop in.
All join paddies and go around again.
Crow hop out with a left allemande.
Right hand to partner and right and left grand,
Meet your honey and promenade.

Repeat 2 for second, third, and fourth couples.

☼ ☼ ☼

There are several variations of this call, but we find that this form works out the most smoothly.

THE EXPLANATION:

1. See page 150 or substitute any other introduction given there.

2. a) The first couple advances to the second couple and the first gentleman joins hands with this couple with the first lady standing alone in the circle of three. As they turn to the left she slowly pivots in the opposite direction.

   b) The first gentleman now steps in to the center while the first lady steps out and takes his place in the circle.

   c) The first gentleman now steps out, taking his place between the two ladies, and the four circle to the left and then do a *docey-doe* (see page 160).

   d) The first couple advances to the third couple, with the second couple following and they all join hands in a circle of six.

   The first lady steps to the center and the remaining five circle around her. The first gentleman then trades places with her again.

   e) Instead of taking his place in the circle between the two ladies who are together, the first gentleman gives his left hand to the one not his partner. At the same time each of the other two gentlemen do an *allemande left,* and they all do a *grand right and left* (see page 152).

f) As they promenade, each couple swings in to the center, pivoting around the gentleman, and promenades in the reverse direction. (Without this reversal it is confusing to get all four couples in the right order in the next step.)

g) They all join hands again and this time include the fourth couple (between the first gentleman and the third lady.) The first lady then steps to the center while the seven circle round her. The first gentleman steps in and trades places with her again. He steps out between the two adjacent ladies again giving his left hand to the one not his partner. And they all finish with an *allemande left,* and *right and left grand* (see page 152).

Four Leaf Clover

THE CALL:

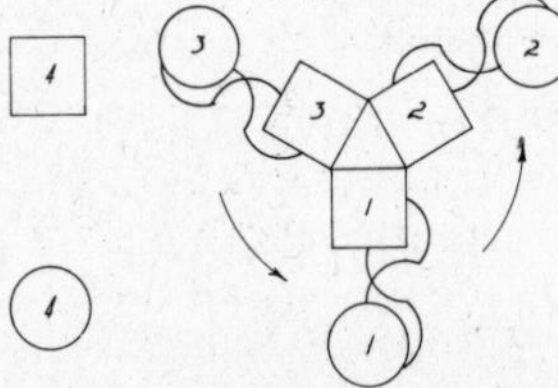

1. *Swing your partners, swing all eight,*
   Now swing on the corner like swingin' on the gate,
   Now swing your own and promenade eight.

2. a) *First couple out to the couple on the right*
   And circle four, oh, circle four,
   b) *Now swing your opposite with your right,*
   Now your partner with your left,
   c) *Now four promenade with shoulders over.*
   d) *Now a two and a four and a six hands round,*
   A left allemande and a right hand grand.
   And six promenade and gents shoulder over.
   Six promenade like a three-leaf clover.
   e) *Now two, four, six, and eight hands round,*
   A left allemande and a right hand grand.
   Promenade eight with shoulders over,
   Promenade close like a four-leaf clover.

3. *Now swing, swing and everybody swing,*
   Swing your opposite across the hall,
   Now the lady on your right,

Now your opposite across the hall,
Now your own and promenade all.

Repeat 2 and 3 for second, third, and fourth couples.

THE EXPLANATION:

1. See page 151 or substitute any introduction given there.
2. a) First couple advances to second couple and joins hands with them and all circle to the left.
   b) Each gentleman takes the opposite lady by the right hand and turns her once around, then his partner with the left and turns her around.
   c) Each couple then takes promenade position (side by side with hands held crossed in front) and the two gentlemen lean their left shoulders over and brace against each other as the line of four promenades once around.
   d) Each couple swings in and join hands again, this time including the third couple, between the second lady and the first gentleman. They all circle left and then six do a *left allemande* and a *right and left grand* (see

Promenade close like a four leaf clover.

page 152). As they promenade, each gentleman again leans his left shoulder over so that all three touch and promenade in this close three-leafed form.

e) They all swing in and join hands again, this time including the fourth couple between the third lady and the first man. They circle again and do an *allemande* and *right and left* (see page 152). When they promenade, they come close together, bend shoulders 'til the four gentlemen are leaning again and circle as a "four-leaf clover."

3. See page 155 for explanation or substitute any ending given there.

Indian Circle

THE CALL:

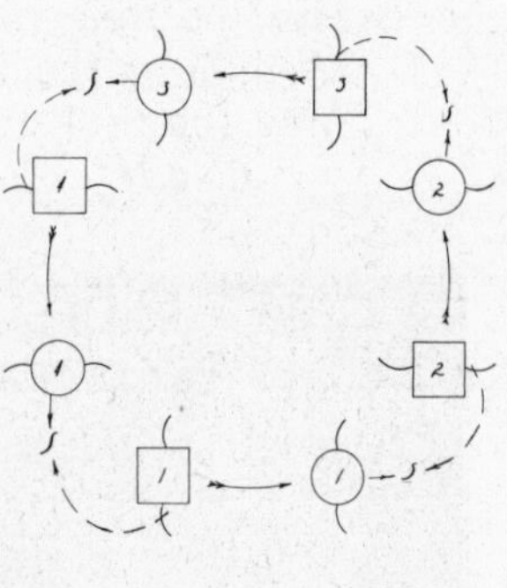

1. *War-whoop to center and war-*
   whoop back,
   Swing your little squaw 'til all her
   ribs crack,
   And promenade like you had
   feathers down your back.

2. a) *First couple out to the couple*
   on the right,
   Circle four in an Indian way,
   Hold your holds and re-sashay.

   b) *Then promenade in single file,*
   Lady in the lead and Indian style.
   Turn right back and swing 'em awhile.
   Repeat (b) once.

   c) *Now two, four, and six hands play,*
   Hold your holds and re-sashay.

   b) *Then promenade in single file*
   Lady in the lead and Indian style.
   Turn right back and swing 'em awhile.
   Repeat (b) twice.

   d) *Now a two, four, six, and eight hand play,*
   Hold your holds and re-sashay.

b) *Promenade in single file,*
Lady in the lead and Indian style.
Turn right back and swing 'em awhile.

Repeat (b) three more times.

3. *Now swing, swing, and everybody swing,*
And an allemande left with your left hand,
Right hand to partner and right and left grand
And promenade eight when you come straight.

Repeat 2 and 3 for second, third, and fourth couples.

THE EXPLANATION:

1. Bending low, all take four steps to center and back, giving a war-whoop with hands wavering over their mouths as they do so. Then each couple swings vigorously and promenades once around the set.
2. a) The first couple advances to the second couple and the four join hands and circle to the left. Without breaking holds they reverse and circle to the right.

   b) They let go their holds and continue walking in single file to the right. On the word "turn" each gentleman

Promenade in single file,
Lady in the lead and Indian style.

turns back (a right turn or to the outside of the circle) and swings the lady behind him.

On the repetition of this call he puts the lady he has just swung in front of him and they promenade again in single file, and when they turn back again each man swings his own partner.

c) The first and second couple again join hands and this time take in the third couple between the second lady and the first gentleman and all circle left. Without breaking holds the six circle to the right.

b) They break holds and promenade in single file, and each gentleman turns back and swings the girl behind him. They repeat this until each swings his own partner.

d) They take hands again and this time include the fourth couple between the third lady and the first gentleman. All eight circle to the left and reverse and circle to the right.

b) They break holds and promenade in single file again, turning back and swinging the lady behind until each gentleman gets his own partner.

3. See page 152 for explanation or substitute any other ending given there.

Divide-the-Ring Group

Dances in which the characteristic is for one couple to advance through the center of the set and between the opposite couple, thus dividing the ring. Usually the lady circles to the right and the gentleman to the left and all do some symmetrical figure.

Divide the Ring and Cut Away Four

THE CALL:

1. *Honors right and honors left,*
   All join hands and circle to the left,
   Break and swing and promenade back.

2. a) *First couple balance, first couple swing,*
   Down the center and divide the ring.
   The lady goes right and the gent goes left,

   b) *Swing when you meet*
   At the head and the feet.

   c) *Down the center and cut away four,*
   The lady goes right and the gent goes wrong.
   Swing when you meet,
   At the head and the feet.

   d) *Down the center and cut away two,*
   The lady goes gee and the gent goes haw,

   e) *And everybody swing.*

Down the center and cut away four.

3. *Now swing on the corner,*
Allemande left with the one you swung,
Right hand to partner and trot right along,
Promenade eight when you get straight.

Repeat 2 and 3 for second, third, and fourth couples.

☼ ☼ ☼

There are several variants of this call. Sometimes the foot couple does not swing, such as:

Swing when you meet as you did before,
Down the center and cast off four.
Swing your honey and she'll swing you,
Down the center and a-cast off two.

or when it is desired that all four couples swing, the (b) is changed to:

Swing at the head and the foot swing too
And the side four swing as you used to do.

THE EXPLANATION:

1. See page 148 for explanation or substitute any introduction given there.

2. a) First couple step back from each other four steps, then advance and swing together. With the gentleman holding the lady's hand they walk down the center of the set and pass through the third couple, who separate to let them pass. The lady turns right and walks around the outside of the set and back to place while the gentleman turns to the left and does the same.
   b) When they meet at their home position they swing again, and at the same time the third couple also swings.
   c) The first couple again goes down the center and separates so that the lady, turning right, passes between the second and third couple, while the gentleman turning left passes between the third and fourth couple. Each continues around the outside of the set and back to place. They thus cut away or walk

around four (that is, two on each side). When they get back to their own position, they swing again and the third couple again swings at the foot of the set.

d) Then first couple again advances to the center and cuts away two (one on each side) by the lady passing through the second couple and circling the second gentleman and back home; while the gentleman passes through the fourth couple, encircles the fourth lady and returns home.

e) All four couples swing.

3. See page 154 for explanation or substitute any ending given there.

Split the Ring and Allemande

THE CALL:

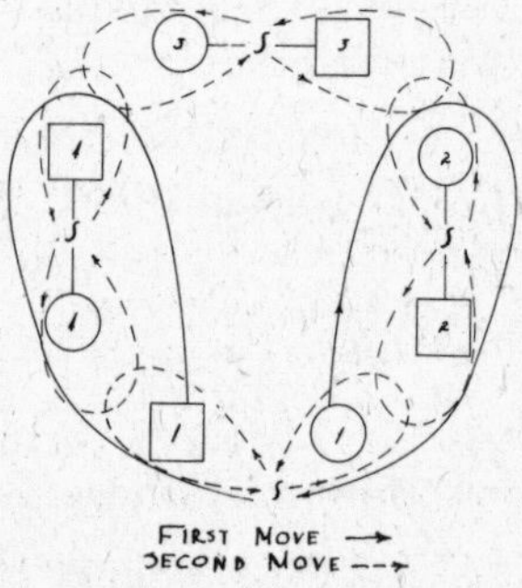

1. *Salute your company and the lady on the left,*
   All join hands and circle to the left.
   Break and swing and promenade back.

2. a) *First couple balance, first couple swing,*
   Go down the center and split the ring,

FIRST MOVE →
SECOND MOVE - - →

   b) *The lady goes right and the gent goes left,*
   c) *Swing when you meet both head and feet,*
   And the side four the same.
   d) *Left allemande the corner girl,*
   And swing your own with another whirl.
   Now down the center as you did before,
   e) *Down the center and cast of four,*
   Repeat (b), (c), and (d).
   Now down the center like you used to do,
   f) *Down the center and cast off two.*
   Repeat (b) and (d).

3. *Allemande left with your left hand,*
   Right hand to partner and right and left grand.
   Promenade eight when you come straight.

Repeat 2 and 3 for second, third, and fourth couples.

THE EXPLANATION:

1. See page 148 for explanation or substitute any introduction given there.

2. a) First couple step back from each other four steps, then come together and swing. They advance together through the center of the set and pass between the third couple who separate to let them through.

   b) The lady goes back to place around the outside of the set to the right and the gentleman does the same to the left.

   c) When they meet they swing and the other three couples swing at the same time.

   d) Each man gives his left hand to the left hand girl and turns her around, then returns to his partner and swings her again.

   e) The first couple now goes down the center and the lady turns right between the second lady and the third gentleman and returns to place around the outside, while the gentleman turns left between the third and fourth couples.

   Repeat (c) and (d) as above.

Swing when you meet both head and feet.

f) The first couple advances again to the middle of the set and the lady passes right between the second couple while the gentleman goes left between the fourth couple.

Repeat (b) and (c).

3. See page 152 for explanation.

Divide the Ring and Swing Corners

THE CALL:

1. *Up and down and around and around,*
Allemande left and allemande aye.
Ingo, bingo, six penny high,
Big pig, little pig, root hog or die.

2. a) *First couple balance, first couple swing.*
b) *Go down the center and divide the ring.*
The lady go right and the gent go left,
c) *Swing 'em on the corners as you come round,*
d) *Now allemande left just one*
And promenade the girl you swung.

Swing 'em on the corner as you come around.

e) *The same old gent and a brand new girl,*
Down the center and away they whirl.
The lady goes right and the gent goes wrong.
Repeat (c) and (d).

f) *The same old gent and a new little thing,*
Down the center and around the ring.
The lady goes gee and the gent goes haw.
Repeat (c) and (d).

g) *The same old gent and a brand new girl,*
Down the center and around the world,
The lady goes right and the gent goes wrong.
Repeat (c) and (d).

3. *Now swing, swing, and everybody swing,*
Allemande left as you come down.
Right hand to partner and so on around,
Promenade eight when you come straight.
Repeat 2 and 3 for second, third, and fourth couples.

THE EXPLANATION:

1. See page 150 or substitute any introduction given there.
2. a) First couple separate four steps, return to each other, and swing.
   b) Hand in hand they walk down the center of the ring and pass between the lady and gentleman of the third couple. The first lady turns to the right and returns around the outside of the ring, while the first gentleman does the same to the left.
   c) When she arrives at his position, the first lady swings the second gentleman. The first gentleman swings the fourth lady. At the same time the two stationary corners also swing.
   d) Each gentleman now gives the lady on his left his left hand and walks once around her. Then returns to the lady he has just swung and promenades with her around the ring and back to the gentleman's original position. (Note that the ladies have each advanced one position and are now with new partners.)
   e) (f) (g) The first gentleman having brought a new lady to his position takes her down the ring, divides as in (b) and then repeats (c) and (d).
3. See page 152 for explanation or substitute any other ending given there.

Divide the Ring and Docey Partners

THE CALL:

1. *Everybody swing his prettiest gal,*
   Left allemande and a right hand grand,
   And promenade, oh, promenade.

2. a) *First couple balance, first couple swing,*
   b) *Down the center and divide the ring,*
   The lady goes right and the gent goes left.

DOCEY PARTNERS ONE AND ALL

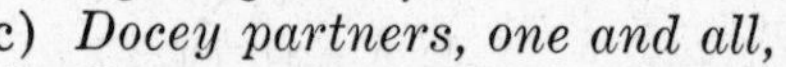

   c) *Docey partners, one and all,*
   d) *Docey corners, don't you fall.*
   e) *Swing your own with a pretty little whirl,*
   f) *And all run away with the corner girl.*
   g) *Same old gent and a new little thing*
   Down the center and divide the ring,
   The lady goes right and the gent goes wrong.
   Repeat (c) to (f).
   h) *Same old gent and a brand new dame*
   Down the center and turn the same
   The lady goes gee and the gent goes haw,
   Repeat (c) to (f).

Docey corners, don't you fall.

j) *Same old gent and a brand new date*
Down the center and through the gate
The lady goes right and the gent goes wrong.
Repeat (c) to (f).

3. *Now you're home and everybody swing,*
Allemande left with your left hand.
Right hand to partner and right and left grand.
Promenade eight when you come straight.
Repeat 2 and 3 for second, third, and fourth couples.

THE EXPLANATION:

1. See page 150 or substitute any other introduction given there.

2. a) First couple steps back from each other four steps, then together and swing.
   b) They walk hand in hand down the center of the circle and pass between the lady and the gentleman of the third couple. The lady turns right around the outside of the set and the gentleman turns left.
   c) As they meet each other at their home position they do a *dos-a-dos* or encircle each other back to back. At the same time the other three couples face each other and do a *dos-a-dos;* that is, they advance to each other, each gentleman passes his partner (passing right shoulders); then each moves to the right; they pass each other back to back, and, without changing the direction they are facing, return backward to place.
   d) Each now turns to the corner and does a *dos-a-dos* with the corner.
   e) Each returns to his partner, and partners swing twice around.
   f) Each gentleman returns to the corner lady and, with a preliminary *allemande left,* turns her to his side and promenades around the set with her and back to the gentleman's position. (Each lady has thus advanced one place.)
   g), (h), and (j) The first gentleman having brought a new girl to his position takes her down the ring, divides as in (b) and the whole set repeats (c) through (f).

3. See page 152 for explanation or substitute any other ending given there.

Divide the Ring and Corners Bow

THE CALL:

1. *Swing your partner, swing all eight.*
   Now swing on the corner like swingin' on a gate.
   Now swing your own and promenade eight.

CORNERS BOW AND PARTNERS WHIRL

2. a) *First couple balance, first couple swing.*
   Now down the center and divide the ring.
   The lady goes right and the gent goes left.
   b) *Now corners bow, and partners whirl,*
   c) *And all run away with the corner girl.*
   d) *Same old gent and a new little thing.*
   Down the center and divide the ring.
   The lady goes right and the gent goes wrong.
   Repeat (b) and (c).
   e) *Same old gent and a brand new girl,*
   Down the center and around the world,
   The lady goes gee and the gent goes haw—
   Repeat (b) and (c).

Corners bow!

f) *Same old gent and a new little dame,*
Down the center and turn the same,
The lady goes right and the gent goes left—
Repeat (b) and (c).

3. *Now you're home and everybody swing.*
A left allemande and a right hand grand.
And promenade.

THE EXPLANATION:

1. See page 151 for explanation or substitute any introduction given there.

2. a) First couple take four steps back from each other, four steps together and swing. They then cross hand in hand through the center of the ring, and pass between the third couple, the lady turning right around the set and back to place while the gentleman turns left to place.

   b) Each turns back to corner and makes a deep bow. At the same time the rest of the set bows to corners. Then each turns back to his partner and all four partners swing.

   c) Each gentleman again swings the corner lady, turns her to his side and promenades around the ring with her and back to his place (the ladies each advance one place).

   d), (e), and (f) The first gentleman having brought a new lady to his position takes her down the ring, divides as in the last half of (a) and then the whole set repeats (b) and (c). He finally gets his own lady back and they are ready for the ending.

3. See page 153 for explanation or substitute any ending given there.

Divide the Ring Combination

THE CALL:

1. *Honors right and honors left.*
   All join hands and circle to the left.
   Break and swing and promenade back.

2. a) *First couple balance, first couple swing,*
   Down the center and divide the ring.
   The lady goes right and the gent goes left.
   Swing on the corner like swingin' on the gate.
   Now allemande left just one
   And promenade the girl you swung.

   b) *The same old gent and a brand new girl*
   Down the center and away they whirl.
   The lady goes right and the gent goes wrong,
   Corners bow, partners whirl
   And all run away with the corner girl.

   c) *The same old gent and a new little thing*
   Down the center and around the ring,
   The lady goes gee and the gent goes haw.

All run away with the corner girl

Docey partners one and all.
Docey corners, don't you fall.
Swing your own with a pretty little whirl.
And all run away with the corner girl.

d) *The same old gent and a new little girl*
Down the center and around the world,
The lady goes east and the gent goes west.
Swing your corners with your left,
Now your partners with your right
Now your corners with your left
And promenade those corners round.

3. *Now swing, swing, and everybody swing,*
Allemande left with your left hand.
Right hand to partner and right and left grand.
Promenade eight when you come straight.

Repeat 2 and 3 for second, third, and fourth couples.

THE EXPLANATION:

1. See page 148 for explanation or substitute any introduction given there.
2. a) See page 290.
   b) See page 294.
   c) See page 292.
   a), (b), and (c) are repetitions of the three preceding dances.
   d) The first gentleman and his new partner divide the ring as above and as they return to place, all the corners turn once around with left hand holds. Each gentleman turns his own last partner with his right hand, then turns his corner with his left and promenades with her. (She, of course, will be his original partner.)
3. See page 152 or substitute any other ending given there.

☼ ☼ ☼

This combination form has more variety and is therefore more fun to dance with experienced dancers. For intermediate dancers it is sometimes well to let the first couple do a swing on the corner all the way round as in (a), then the second couple do (b) "corners bow" all the way round, the third couple do (c) "docey partners" all the way round, and the fourth couple either do (d) "swing with left and right" all the way round. Or better yet the fourth couple can summarize (adding the new figure (d)), by doing the whole combination dance as given in 2 above thus changing the figure for each couple, or repeat (a) for (d) in this combination.

Divide the Ring and Forward Up Six

THE CALL:

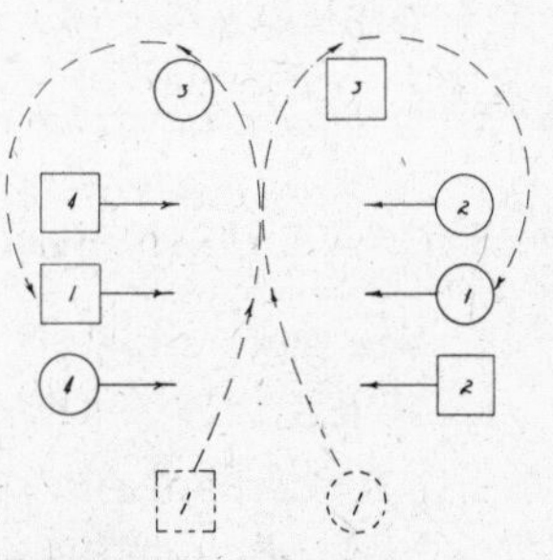

1. *One foot up and the other foot*
   down,
   Grab your little sage hens and
   swing 'em round.
   Allemande left as you come down,
   Grand right and left and so on
   around.
   Meet your partner and promenade.

2. a) *First couple balance, first couple swing,*
   Down the center and divide the ring.
   The lady go right and the gent go left,
   b) *And between side couples you stand.*
   c) *Forward up six and fall back six.*
   d) *Forward again and right and left through,*
   e) *Forward up six and fall back six,*
   Forward again and right and left through.
   f) *Same couple center and couple up foot,*
   Four hands round and round you go.
   And the lady go si and the gent go do.
   g) *Balance home and everybody swing.*

3. *Swing your opposite across the hall,*
   Now your own if she's not too small
   A left allemande and a right and left grand.
   And promenade.

Repeat 2 and 3 for second, third, and fourth couples.

THE EXPLANATION:

1. See page 149 or substitute any other introduction given there.
2. a) First couple step back from each other four steps, then step together and swing. Hand in hand they walk through the center of the set and between the third couple. The lady turns to the right and the gentleman to the left.
   b) The lady then stands between the second lady and the gentleman, and the man between the fourth lady and gentleman.
   c) The three on each side, holding hands in a line, advance four steps toward each other and then fall back four steps.
   d) They advance again four steps, and each gives the opposite person in the other line of three his right hand and passes beyond him. Each line thus reaches the other's position. The individuals turn around (rightabout-face) and take hands in the opposite direction.
   e) They advance, retire, advance and pass through again as in (c) and (d), and thus return to their own positions.

Down the center and divide the ring.
The lady go right and the gent go left.

f) The first lady and the first gentleman advance to each other in the center of the set and the third couple joins them. The four take hands and circle to the left and do a *docey-doe* (see page 160).

g) All return to positions, and all four couples swing.

3. See page 156 for explanation or substitute any other ending given there.

Divide the Ring and Waltz Corners

Must be danced to very fast waltz time.

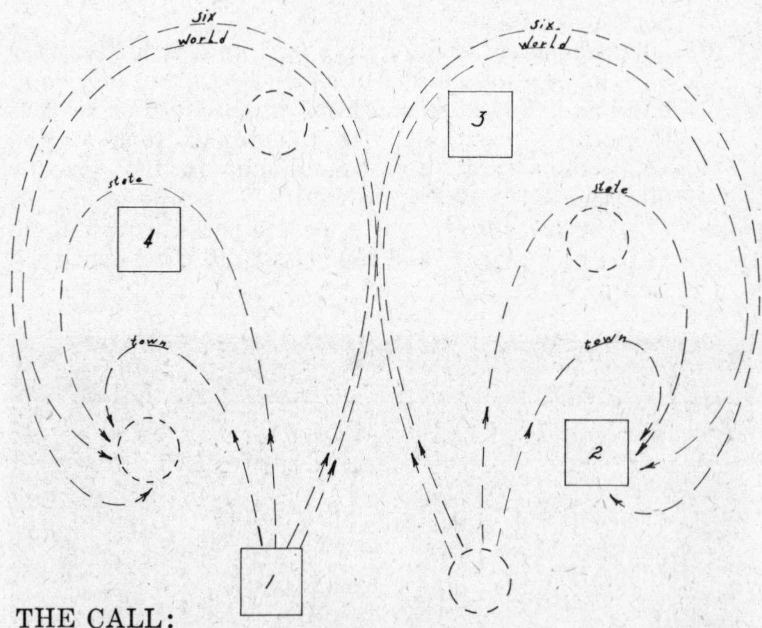

THE CALL:

1. *Honors right and honors left,*
All join hands and circle to the left,
Break and swing and promenade back.

2. a) *First couple balance and swing three licks,*
Down the center and cut away six,
Lady go right and the gent go left.

b) *Swing on the corner with a waltz promenade.*

c) *Same old gent with a brand new girl,*
Down the center and go round the world,
Lady go right and the gent go wrong.

b1) *Swing on the corner with a waltz promenade.*

d) *Same old gent if he ain't too late.*
Down the center and go round the state,
Lady go east and the gent go west.

b2) *Swing on the corner with a waltz promenade.*

e) *Same old gent, he's a doin' it brown.*
Down the center and go round the town.
The lady go gee and the gent go haw.

b3) *Swing on the corner with a waltz promenade.*

3. *Now you're home.*
All eight balance, all eight swing,
A left allemande and a right hand grand,
Promenade eight when you come straight.

Repeat 2 and 3 for second, third, and fourth couples.

☼ ☼ ☼

In calling the last line of (d), call the two points of the compass that square with hall and sets.

Swing on the corner with a waltz promenade.

THE EXPLANATION:

1. See page 148 or substitute any introduction given there.

2. a) First couple separate four steps, reunite and swing three times around. They then waltz down center and through the third couples, the lady turning back around outside to the right and the gentleman to the left.
   b) As they meet the corners (the second gentleman and the fourth lady), all take dance position with their corners and waltz once around the set.
   c) When the gentleman gets back to place with his new partner (the fourth lady) he goes down center with her and passes between the third couple again. (b1) They all swing on the corner and repeat the waltz.
   d) With his new partner (the third lady) he does the same except that this time he passes through the space between third and fourth couples and turns left, while the lady passes through the space between the second and third couples to the right. (b2) They all waltz corners again.
   e) With his new partner (the second lady) he goes to the center and while she turns right between the second couple he turns left between the fourth. (b3) They all waltz corners, this time getting their original partners back, with whom they waltz to their home positions.

3. See page 152 or substitute any other ending given there.

☼ ☼ ☼

At the beginning of the dance they "cut off six," on the first repetition, "the world," they again cut six. For "the state" they cut four, and for the "town" they cut two.

Both the introduction and the ending, as well as the dance, are waltzed throughout. This gives a quaint and delightful charm to familiar figures.

Waltz Quadrille

(A great favorite. Can be sung to the old tune "Sweet Evelina" or see special music. In some communities all four couples waltz once around the set as soon as music commences and without a call. Then when each returns to place the caller sings.)

THE CALL:

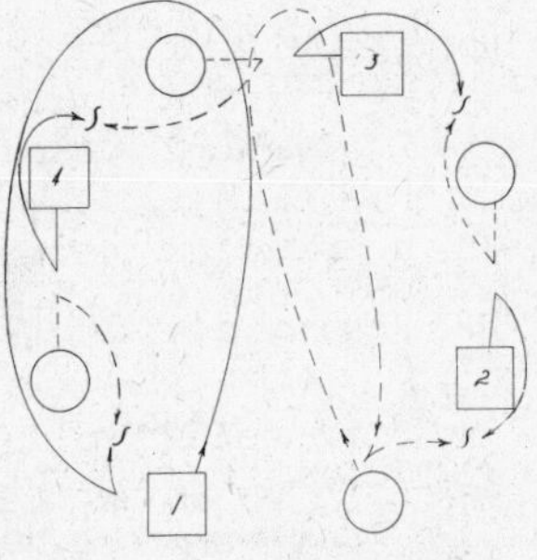

a) *First couple down center*
And there they divide
b) *The lady back center*
And the gent stay outside.
c) *Now honor your partners*
d) *And don't be afraid,*
e) *And swing on the corners with*
a waltz promenade.
a1) *Same couple down center*

(And it is all repeated three more times until each gentleman gets his own lady again and waltzes her back to place.)

Repeat entire for second, third, and fourth couples.

The lady back center and the gent stay outside.

WALTZ QUADRILLE

Younger sets who have danced this often get tired of the many repetitions. If the first couples dance twice, instead of four times, then the second couples twice, the ladies will be back in place; then the third couples only twice, and the fourth twice and they will be back again, and the dance will have been cut in half.

THE EXPLANATION:

a) The first couple waltzes down through the center of the set and between the third couple. As they separate it looks well for the man to turn the lady under his left arm with the flourish of a little whirl.

b) She waltzes back to position alone through the center

of the set, while the gentleman turns left and waltzes alone around the outside of the set and back to place.

c) As they meet each makes a deep bow to the other and at the same time the other couples bow low to each other.

d) Each turns and bows to the corner lady. (Don't hurry. Do not take dance position with corner until the words, "Swing on the corner.")

e) Then each man takes his corner lady in regular dance position, swings her once around, and waltzes her around the set. It is important that each couple keeps its relative position the same while waltzing and that each follows the exact path of a promenade around the set, rotating always to the right to keep from breaking the symmetry of this path. Each must be back in place in exact time for the call when it continues.

a1) Each gentleman now has a new lady beside him. The first couple (with a new lady) repeats the above entire. After dancing the whole dance four times (once with each lady) each gentleman has his partner back. And the call continues with "Second couple down center."

Note: Instead of calling *Swing on the corner* which is the standard form, some callers substitute *Dip to the corner and waltz promenade,* in which case the waltz starts with the balance step described on page 100 instead of with a swing.

In Illinois they usually call the first and third couples out at the some time. They waltz past each other across the center of the set. Each lady turns right around the outside of the set, and each gentleman to the left. As the gentlemen pass the opposite ladies behind the side couples they *pass to the outside* giving the ladies the shorter path. This cuts the dance in half and keeps more people in action all the time. After the head couples have danced four times and have their own ladies back the side couples do the same.

The call could be:

Head couples down center
And there they divide
The ladies go right
And the gents pass outside
Now honour your partners, etc.

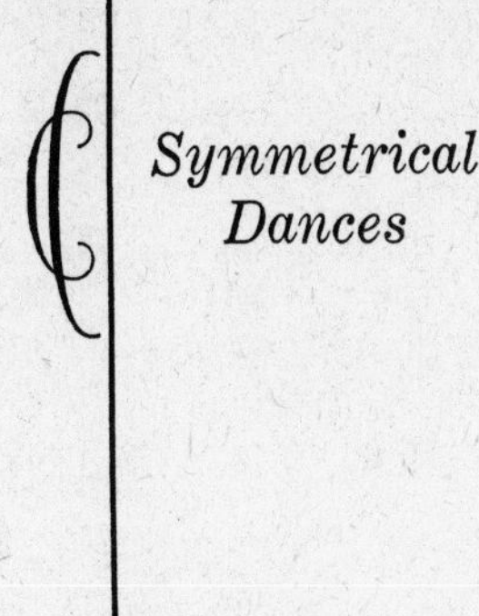

Symmetrical Dances

In which all four couples do the same thing at the same time, making a symmetrical figure, or opposite pairs do complementary figures leading to a symmetry.

Four Gents Lead Out

THE CALL:

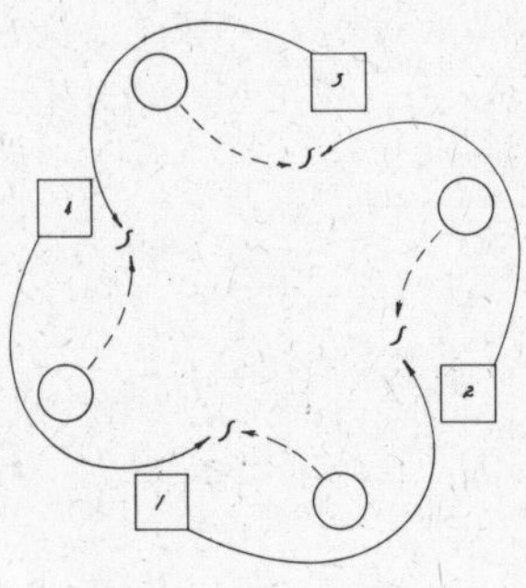

1. *All eight balance, all eight swing.*
   A left allemande and a right hand grand.
   Meet your partner and promenade.

2. a) *Four gents lead out*
   To the right of the ring.

   b) *And when you get there*
   Just give 'em a swing.
   And when you do that
   Remember my call—

   c) *It's allemande left*

   d) *And promenade all.*
   Repeat three more times.

   a1) *Four ladies lead out*
   To the left of the ring

Give 'em a swing. . . . It's allemande left. (Showing all stages of this transition.)

b1) *And when you get there*
Just give them a swing.
And when you do that
Remember my call—
c1) *It's allemande left*
d1) *And promenade all.*
Repeat three more times.

3. (Usually omitted or any ending can be used.)

¤ ¤ ¤

It is apparent that this call was originally sung to its own special music. Sometimes we hear it now sung to the Irish Washerwoman. But usually today it is called, not sung.

THE EXPLANATION:

1. See page 151 or substitute any other introduction given there.

2. a) Each gentleman steps behind his own lady and advances to the next lady on his right. (The first gentleman advances to the second lady.)
   b) He takes regular dance position with her and swings twice around.
   c) He then returns to his original lady and turns her once around with his left hand. (That is, the first gentleman does an allemande left with the first lady.)
   d) And then returns to the lady he has just swung (that is, the first gentleman returns to the second lady). And he promenades with her around the set and back to his own position. This means each lady has dropped back one position. After three more repetitions each lady is back home with her partner.
a1, b1) Each lady steps behind her partner and advances to the next man on her left and swings with him.
   c1) She does an allemande left with her original partner.
   d1) And returning to the man she swung, promenades with him around the set and back to his position. At each repetition she falls back one place until finally she is with her original partner once more.

3. After the final promenade the dance is usually ended, though any other ending may be used if so desired.

Texas Star

THE CALL:

1. *Salute your company and the lady on the left,*
   All join paddies and circle to the left.
   Break and swing and promenade back.

2. a) *Ladies to the center*
   And back to the bar.
   b) *Gents to the center*
   For a Texas Star,
   With the right hand cross.
   c) *Back with left and don't get lost.*
   d) *Pass your gal and take the next.*
   e) *Ladies swing in and the gents swing out.*
   f) *Break in the center and everybody swing.*
   g) *Now allemande left just one,*
   h) *And promenade the girl you swung.*

(Just after) *Ladies swing in and the gents swing out.*

Repeat three more times, on the first and second repetition saying:

Pass that gal and take the next.

And the last time saying:

Pass that gal and take your own.

3. *Now you're home and everybody swing,*
   Allemande left with your left hand
   Right hand to partner and right and left grand,
   Meet your partner and promenade.

☼ ☼ ☼

The whole call, sometimes, is repeated in reverse by calling:

Four gents to the center and back to the bar.

THE EXPLANATION:

1. See page 148 for explanation or substitute any introduction given there.
2. a) The four ladies advance to the center of the set and each makes a rightabout turn so they stand momentarily back to back. (It is really more of a turn and a dip than a turn and a pause.) And then each returns to her own place.
   b) The four gentlemen advance to the center of the set and join their right hands and circle to the left.
   c) Each reverses and they join left hands and circle back to the right.
   d) Each continues circling past his own partner, and, still holding left hands in the center, each man offers his right arm to the next lady. She hooks on to his arm and circles with him in a double mill.
   e) The gentlemen let go in the center and each pivots his lady so they all swing in together and the ladies join right hands in the center. The mill now reverses and they all circle to the left, the ladies still holding right hands in the center and the men's arms hooked to their left arms.
   f) The ladies let go in the center and each man swings into dance position with his lady and they swing twice around.

g) Each gentleman then swings the lady on his left once around with his left hand.

h) And returns to the lady with whom he just swung and with whom he had circled in the mill, and they promenade around the set until the ladies are again called to the center. Each time the ladies advance in position to the next man until finally they come back to their own.

3. See page 152 or substitute any other ending.

Swing at the Center and Swing at the Sides

THE CALL:

1. *All jump up and never come down,*
Swing your honey around and around,
'Til the hollow of your foot
Makes a hole in the ground.
And promenade, oh, promenade!

2. a) *First and third couples forward and back,*
b) *Forward again and the sides divide.*
c) *Swing at the center and swing at the sides.*

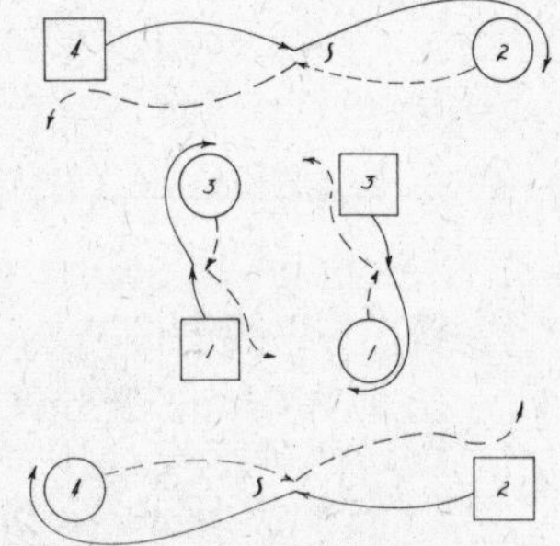

The start, each walks completely around his square in direction indicated.

Swing at the center and swing at the sides.

Swing at the center and swing at the sides.
Swing at the center and swing at the sides.
Swing at the center and swing at the sides.

d) *Now allemande left with your left hand.*
Right hand to partner and right and left grand.
And promenade, oh, promenade.
Second and fourth couples forward and back
Repeat (a), (b), (c), and (d).
Third and first couples forward and back.
Repeat the whole dance again.
Fourth and second couples forward and back.
Repeat the whole dance again.

3. Any further ending usually omitted.

THE EXPLANATION:

1. See page 149 or substitute any other introduction given there.

2. a) The first and third couples each advance four steps to the center of the set, curtsy to each other and return with four steps to places.

   b) They advance again to the center and stand facing each other while the side couples separate from each other, and stand individually at the four corners of a larger square outside the set.

   c) The first gentleman takes the third lady by both hands and swings around with her so that they exchange places and the third gentleman does the same with the first lady. At the same time, as the center couples swing in this way, the side couples also swing. The second gentleman advances to the fourth lady. They meet (at the home position of couple number one), take both hands and swing around exchanging positions, and they walk backward to the other's original position. At the same time the second lady advances to the fourth gentleman (meeting him in the original position of the third couple) they take hands, turn, and go to each other's corners.

   On each repetition each continues around this square in the direction he is going, the individuals of the second and fourth couples going from corner to corner of the larger outer square, and the individuals of the first and third couples to the corners of the smaller inner square, always taking both hands of the person they meet in the middle of the sides, releasing and continuing on to the next corner, until each is back in his original corner.

☼ ☼ ☼

In both the outer and inner square the gentlemen go around the square from corner to corner in a clockwise direction, while the ladies go in a counterclockwise direction.

d) Each gentleman does an *allemande left* (turns the left hand lady with his left hand) with his corner. It happens that this is always the person on the same corner of the other square. That is, each person in the inner square does an *allemande* with the person on the nearest or identical corner of the larger square. Then they give right hands to their partners and do a *right and left grand* around the set. When they meet their partners again, they promenade back to position.

In the first repetition the dance is the same, but the sides come to the center and the head couples separate. The second repetition is identical with the dance described above, and in the last repetition the sides again come to the center square.

Sides Divide

THE CALL:

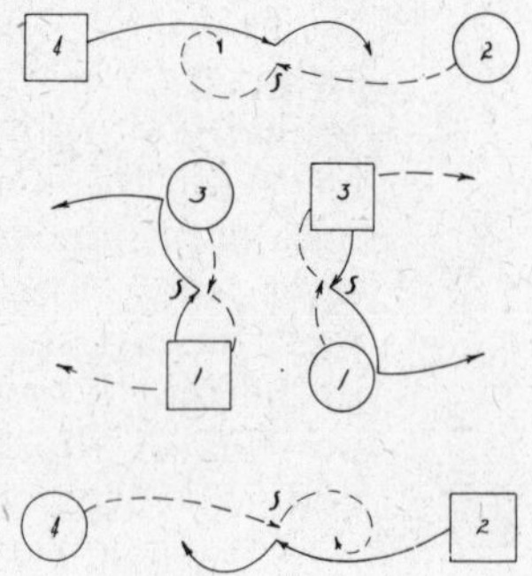

1. *Honors right and honors left,*
   All join hands and circle to the left,
   Break and swing and promenade back.
2. a) *First and third forward*
   And the sides divide.

   b) *Change at the center*
   And swing the sides

   c) *First and third forward*
   And the sides divide
   Change at the center
   And swing the sides.

d) *First and third forward and the sides divide.*
Change at the center
And swing the sides.

e) *First and third forward*
And the sides divide.
Change at the center
And swing the sides.

3. *Now you're home and everybody swing.*
With a left allemande and a right hand grand,
Meet your partners and promenade.

THE EXPLANATION:

1. See page 148 for explanation or substitute any introduction given there.

2. a) First and third couples advance to each other. As they do so the individuals of the second and fourth couples separate from each other and stand at the outside corners of the set.

   b) The first gentleman takes the third lady by both hands

Change and swing the center and swing the sides.

and exchanges places with her, and these two back up into the fourth couple's position. The third gentleman does the same with the first lady and finishes in second couple's position. At the same time the second gentleman and the fourth lady meet, swing (two hands) and remain at the first position—while the second lady and the fourth gentleman do the same at the third position.

c) Those occupying first and third position advance to center and those in second and fourth position separate, and they all swing and change position and partners as in (b).

d) Those standing in first and third position now advance to center, and the others proceed as in (c).

e) This repetition (same as (c)) brings each dancer to his own partner and back to his own position.

3. See page 153 or substitute any other ending given there.

☼ ☼ ☼

This can be danced by having the regular swing (twice around in dance position) each time instead of the two-hand swing.

Run Away to Alabam'

THE CALL:

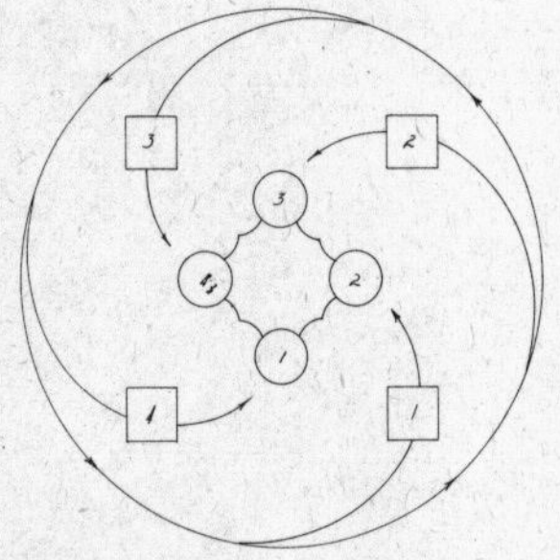

1. *All eight balance, all eight swing.*
   A left allemande and a right hand grand,
   Meet your partners and promenade.

2. a) *Now swing, swing, and everybody swing.*
   b) *Swing them ladies to the center*
   And let 'em stand.
   c) *Gents run away to Alabam'.*
   Pass your partner and swing the next.

   Repeat (b) and (c) three more times, four times in all. On the last repetition calling:

   Pass that gal and swing your own.

3. *Promenade Indian style.*
Lady in the lead and single file.
Stop and swing her once in awhile.

Repeat three more times or until straight.
Repeat 2 and 3 except this time with men to the center, calling:

Gents to the center.
And let 'em stand.
Gals run away to Alabam'.

THE EXPLANATION:

1. See page 151 or substitute any other introduction given there.

2. a) Everyone swings his partner vigorously.
   b) The girls are swung off to the center of the set where they stand back to back.
   c) The men all circle to the right around them (in single file and without holding hands) and continue past

Let 'em stand and the gents run away to Alabam'.

their partners to the next lady with whom they swing.

They repeat this until they come to their original partners and swing them back to the home position.

3. See page 159 or substitute any other ending given there.

The Ocean Wave

(Requiring careful teamwork and careful timing.)

THE CALL:

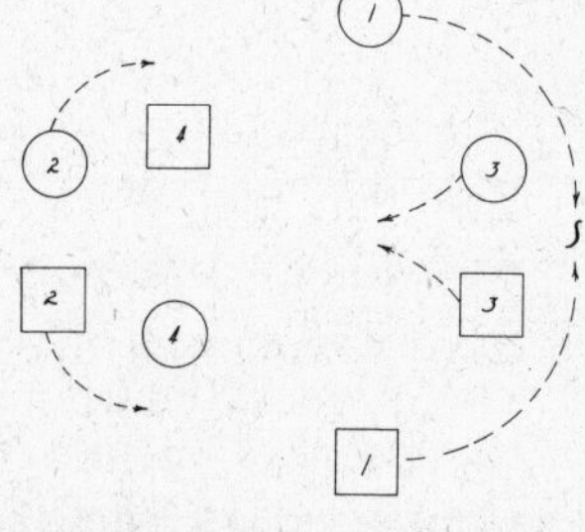

1. *Honors right and honors left,*
   All join hands and circle to the left,
   Break and swing and promenade back.

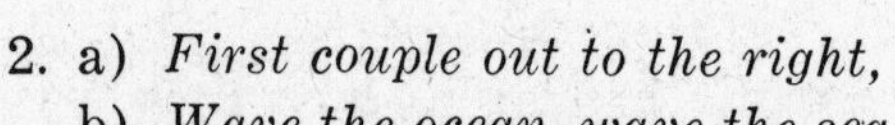

2. a) *First couple out to the right,*
   b) *Wave the ocean, wave the sea,*
      Wave that pretty girl back to me.
   c) *Wave the ocean, wave the shore,*
      Wave this time and a-wave no more.
   d) *On to the next and the second follow up.*
   e) *Wave the ocean, wave the sea,*
      Wave that pretty girl back to me.
      Wave the ocean, wave the shore,
      Wave this time and a-wave no more.
   f) *On to the next and the third follow up.*
   g) *Wave the ocean, wave the sea,*
      Wave that pretty girl back to me.
      Wave the ocean, wave the shore.
      Wave this time and a-wave no more.
   h) *Balance home and everybody swing.*

3. *Now allemande left with your left hand.*
   Right to your partner and right and left grand.
   Meet your partner and promenade.

Repeat for second, third, and fourth couples.

THE EXPLANATION:

1. See page 148 or substitute any other introduction given there.

2. a) First couple advances to second couple.

   b) First couple passes between them, the lady circling around the second man and the gentleman circling around the second lady. The first couple meets in the center and swings once around.

   c) They again pass through and circle the second couple exactly as in (b). They meet and swing a second time.

   d) They advance to the third couple and on the words "second follow up" the second couple swings once in place (in order to give first couple the proper interval of lead), and then the second couple follows the first.

   e) The first couple passes through and around the third couple swinging always when they come back together exactly as in (b) and (c). This time the second

(First couple passing through third couple while second couple is swinging.)

couple follows them through and around the third, swinging in the same way but timing the swings and passage so as not to interfere with the other couple.

f) The first couple after their second swing advances to the fourth couple. While they do so the second couple executes their second swing and on the words "third follow up" the third couple swings in place (in order to give the second couple the proper lead) and then follows the others to the fourth couple.

g) Now a procession of three couples passes between and around the fourth couple exactly as in (b) and (c) and each couple swinging each time they meet in the center. With a little care and careful timing, there will be no confusion or collisions on the part of good dancers. Each must make a good large circle out and around the fourth lady and fourth gentleman, in order to leave adequate time for the other couples to swing. And each couple must be careful not to come together between the swinging couple and the fourth couple, but come in from the side or even a little behind from a good large circle, before they take their swing.

h) Each couple takes the final swing and returns to place. However, if the first couple swings directly to place, they are apt to collide with the second gentleman who at that time is coming in from the side to meet his lady. So, if the first couple swings directly back or towards the second couple's position and then around to its own place, this collision can be avoided. The second couple, of course, goes naturally to its own position and thus avoids collision with the third. While the third swings to place, the fourth couple which has been patiently standing till now also swings in place, and all are ready for the ending.

3. See page 152 for explanation or substitute any other ending given there.

Pokey Nine

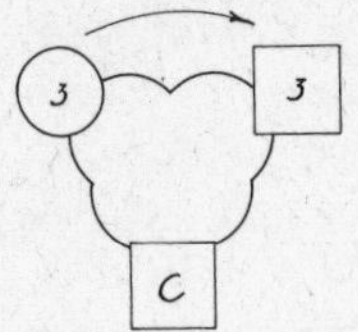

C — EXTRA MAN

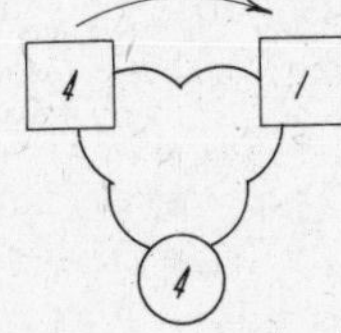

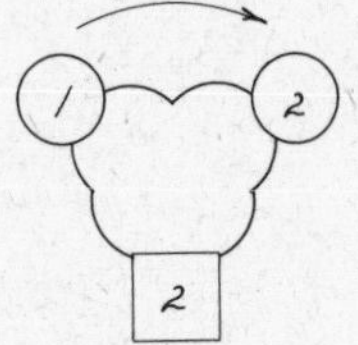

THE CALL:

1. *All eight balance, all eight swing,*
   A left allemande, and a right hand grand,
   Promenade eight when you come straight.

2. a) *First couple balance, first couple swing,*
   Lady go right and the gent go left.

   b) *Three by three in a pokey-nine,*
   Three by three in a pokey-oh,
   Three by three and on you go!

Three by three in a pokey nine.

c) *The lady go on and the gent catch up.*

d) *Three by three in a pokey-nine,*
Three by three in a pokey-oh,
Three by three and on you go.

e) *The lady go on and gent catch up.*
Three by three in a pokey-nine,
Three by three in a pokey-oh,
Three by three and on you go.

f) *The lady stay there and the gent catch up.*
Now circle four, oh, circle four.

g) *And docey-doe with the gent you know,*
The lady go C and the gent go doe.

3. *Balance home and swing 'em all night,*
Allemande left go left and right,
Some'll go right and some'll go le-e-ft.
Promenade, oh, promenade.

Repeat for second, third, and fourth couples.

THE EXPLANATION:

1. See page 151 or substitute any other introduction given there.

2. a) The first lady and gentleman step back from each other four steps, then come together and swing. The lady then goes right to the second couple and the gentleman turns left to the fourth couple.

b) The first lady and second couple join hands and the three circle to the left. At the same time the first gentleman and the fourth couple circle three in the same way. And often the caller joins the third couple making another circle of three and dances while he goes on with the call. Any odd person from the side lines joins the third couple of each other set, so that in each set there will be three circles of three each—for a "pokey-nine." After the word pokey-oh they all reverse and circle right.

c) The lady advances to the third couple, the gentleman advances to the second, and the caller or the odd person in each set advances to the fourth.

d) The three circles turn left again and then reverse as in (b).

e) The first lady advances to the fourth couple, the gentleman to the third, and the caller to the second, and they circle threes again as in (b).

f) The lady remains with the fourth couple while the gentleman advances and joins her there. And the caller or the odd dancer drops out of the set. The first and fourth couples with hands joined circle four to the left, while the other two couples stand still.

g) They then do a *docey-doe* (see page 160 for a description).

3. See page 154 for explanation or substitute any other ending given there.

☼ ☼ ☼

The cowboy pokey is a distant and disinherited relative of the elegant polka. In this dance it has completely forgotten its great grandmother, and is nothing but the gliding walk of the regular square dance.

The Singing Quadrille

To be sung to special music

THE CALL:

1. a) *Dos-a-dos your corners*
   b) *Dos-a-dos your partners.*
   c) *Allemande left your corners,*
   d) *Allemande right your partners*
   And swing them twice around.
   e) *Balance to your corners.*
   f) *Swing your corner lady*
   And promenade the hall.
   Repeat three more times.

2. g) *First couple down center*
   And there they divide.
   The lady goes right
   And the gent he goes left.
   h) *Balance your corner*
   j) *And don't be afraid.*
   k) *Dip to your partner*
   And waltz promenade.
   Repeat for second, third, and fourth couples.

SINGING QUADRILLE—PART ONE
Dos-a-dos your partners.

3\. l) *All join hands and circle*
To the left around the hall,
To the little old log cabin in the lane.

m) *Whoa, you're all going wrong.*
Go back the other way
To the little old log cabin in the lane.

n) *Places now, and balance all,*
And everybody swing
To the little old log cabin in the lane,

o) *Your left hand on your corners*
And your partners by the right
And a grand right and left half around.

p) *The first one by the right hand,*
And the next one by the left
To the little old log cabin in the lane,

q) *And when you meet your partner*
Take your homeward flight
To the little old log cabin in the lane, lane, lane!

THE EXPLANATION:

1\. a) Each gentleman faces the lady to his left and completely encircles her and returns to place without changing the direction in which he is facing. She at

SINGING QUADRILLE—PART TWO
The lady goes right and the gent he goes left.

the same time in the same way advances and encircles him. They pass right shoulders, sidestep to the right passing back to back, and pass left shoulders in returning to place.

b) Each gentleman turns around and does exactly the same as (a) with his own partner.

c) Each gentleman joins left hands with his left-hand or corner lady, and circles around her and back to place.

d) Each gentleman now joins right hands with his partner and circles twice around her (in order to fill out the measure of the music).

e) Each gentleman and his corner lady advance and bow to each other.

f) Each gentleman takes his corner lady in dance position and swings her around and then promenades with her around the square and back to his position. She, however, has left her position and advanced one place. (By the last repetition of the figure she has worked back to her own partner again.)

2. g) The first couple waltzes down the center of the set to the third couple and waltzes between them. Here

SINGING QUADRILLE—PART THREE
Your left hand on your corner.

they separate and the lady then waltzes to the right around the square, while the gentleman turns to the left.

h) Almost back to their own positions each turns and makes a deep bow to their corner. The inactive corners bow to each other at the same time.

j) All four gentlemen now turn to their own partners and make a deep bow.

k) They take their partners in dance position and dip back on their left feet, the women rocking forward on their right feet. (Each rises on the toe of this foot and then sinks; the one-two-three count becoming, step—rise—fall.) The couples then waltz around the square, timing it carefully to be back for the next repetition.

3. l) All eight join hands and circle around to the left.

m) On the word "whoa," they suddenly stop (and if they feel dramatic, look very hurt and surprised). Then each gentleman takes his partner in promenade position, and they march back to their own places.

n) Here each gentleman and his partner step back from each other four steps with a flourish, and then come together and swing twice around.

o) Each gentleman then swings his left-hand lady once around with his left hand (a regular *allemande left)* gives his right hand to his partner and does a regular *right and left grand.* However, since in a Western *right and left grand* each gentleman meets his partner in the opposite position (couple number one meets at number three's position) and there promenades with her, according to the old tradition, this is only a half *right and left.* In the olden times it would have had to continue on until he met her again in their own home position before they promenaded.

p) Therefore he now takes his partner by the right hand. They each pause a moment and make a deep curtsy. They then continue the *right and left* and meet again at their own position.

q) Here they take their partners in promenade position and march around the square.

SINGING QUADRILLE

Figure III

All join hands and cir-cle to the left a-round the hall, To the
Lit-tle Old Log Cabin in the Lane. You are all go-ing
wrong Go back the oth-er way To the Lit-tle Old Log
Cabin in the Lane. Pla-ces now and bal- ance all and
ev-'ry bod-y swing, To the Lit-tle Old Log Cab-in in the
Lane. Your left hand on your corn-er, and your part-ner by your
right, and you grand right and left half a-round.
First by the right hand and next one by the left, To the
Lit-tle Old Log Cab-in in the Lane. And
when you meet your part-ner, you make your home-ward flight, To the
Lit tle Old Log Cab-in in the Lane.

NOTE: Many musicians play eight bars instead of the last sixteen bars as written above, while the dancers waltz around the square. In this case it is best to play the first four bars as written in the top line at the very beginning of the music above, then the 13th to 16th bars instead of the last sixteen bars as written.

Waltz That Girl Behind You

TUNE: The Girl I Left Behind Me, in waltz time can be used as part four of the Singing Quadrille. See previous page.

The whole dance is done with a waltz step and a pronounced dip on the first beat of each measure.

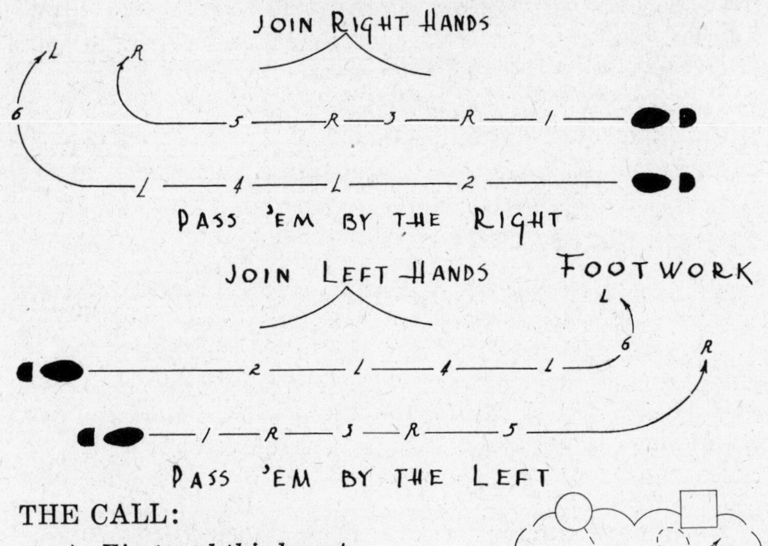

THE CALL:

a) *First and third gents*
To the opposite ladies.
b) *Pass 'em by the right*
Pass 'em by the left,
c) *Swing 'em around*
And back to your own.
d) *All swing that girl beside you.*
e) *Pass 'em by the right*
Pass 'em by the left,
f) *Now bear down eight and mind you.*
g) *Spin 'em behind and single promenade.*
h) *Then waltz that girl behind you.*

Repeat for second and fourth gents.
Then third and first gents.
Then fourth and second gents.

SPIN 'EM BEHIND AND SINGLE PROMENADE

☼ ☼ ☼

The idea and a few of the lines were given us by an old caller who had forgotten the dance. From his suggestions we worked out the dance as given above and in this half-original form it is a great favorite with our dancers. *Bear down eight* is one of his phrases which we have retained, but for beginners, to whom you are teaching the dance *circle eight* would be more easily understood than the original phrase. In singing this to waltz time the caller will find himself adding the syllable, "ah" to many of the words in order to hold the rhythm as:

> *"Pass 'em by the right-ah!*
> *Pass 'em by the left-ah!"*

This adds to the charm of the call.

THE EXPLANATION:

a) The first and third gentlemen waltz across the set to the opposite ladies and take the places of each other.

b) Each faces the opposite lady, and the lady and gentleman, starting with the right foot, advance with a waltz step to each other, taking right hands and passing. They make a half turn back with a sort of waltz-balance step on the second measure. They pass each other touching left hands on the third, and turn back on the fourth.

c) The first and third gentlemen swing the opposite ladies once around with two waltz steps, and with four waltz steps return to places.

Pass 'em by the left.

d) All four gentlemen swing their own partners with a waltz step on the last words of this phrase.

e) All four gentlemen face their partners, and, starting with the right foot, advance with a waltz step touching right hands, pass each other and turn back on a waltz-balance step, pass each other, touching left hands on the third measure, and turn back to each other with a waltz-balance step.

f) They all join hands in a large circle and with a pronounced dip take four waltz steps to the left.

g) Each lady lets go the gentleman in back of her and, still holding her partner's right hand in her own left, she is swung by him toward the center of the circle, once under his arm (rotating leftabout-face) to give her a complete spin and to a position beyond him in the circle. They let go hands and all dance to right around the circle in single file with a waltz step.

h) Each gentleman turns outward from the circle (to the right) and back to the girl behind him (his own partner still) and waltzes with her. (It is better if all four couples do a waltz balance dip at the same time before waltzing. See page 100.)

The music now repeats (e), (f), (g), and (h) (sixteen measures) and in this time each couple have waltzed once around the set, (in promenade direction and all rotating to the right) and should be back in their own positions ready for the next repetition.

☼ ☼ ☼

Pass 'em by the right
And pass 'em by left

offers enough difficulty that it may merit a more detailed analysis of the footwork. The lady and gentleman each use identical footwork.

Advance toward your partner with a right step (at the same time clasping right hands), step on beyond with a left step, and close the right foot to the left. Now step on beyond with a left, but put this left foot down at right angles to your line of motion and pointing directly to your right. Then close your right to the side of your left turning as you do so, and put your left down again in its same position but pointing directly backward to your previous line of motion. As you have taken these last steps you have let go right hands with your partner.

You are now facing your partner again and you clasp left hands with her as you step forward again on your right foot. Step on beyond with your left foot and close your right to your left. Step on beyond with your left, turning left face as you do so and placing the left foot at a ninety-degree angle with your previous line of motion. Now a short-balance step with the right on beyond your left as you complete the turn. And place your left down again in the same position but again reversed and pointing back to your partner with whom you have again broken hand holds.

That is, the partners take right hands, waltz by each other, and do a rightabout-face. Then they take left hands, waltz by, and do a leftabout-face, always starting toward each other with a right step. As they become smoother they become less geometrically accurate and more graceful and natural in their footwork.

Intermingling Dances

With two or more sets involved.

Grand March Change

(All the sets should be in one row down the middle of the floor, for the length of the hall.)

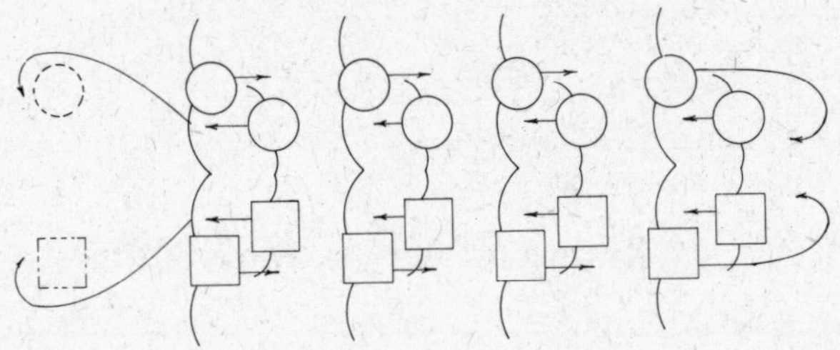

THE CALL:

1. *All eight balance, all eight swing,*
A left allemande and a right hand grand.
And promenade, oh, promenade.

2. a) *First couple balance,*
First couple swing.
First couple promenade
The inside ring
And face the wall.
b) *Second couple balance,*
Second couple swing.
Second couple promenade
The inside ring
And face the wall.
c) *Ends move forward*
And sides fall in.
d) *March! The ladies go right*
And the gents go left.
e) *Ladies circle inside*
Gents circle out;
f) *Now gents circle inside*
Ladies circle out.
g) *Down the center two by two.*

h) *Open your lines*
As you open a book.

j) *Forward all, fall back all.*
Pass right over to the opposite wall.
Forward all, all fall back,
Pass right over to the same old track.
Forward again and take your own.

k) *March! Column right around the hall.*
Now serpentine and see 'em all.

l) *Now down the center with an arbor way,*
'Til you're back in line in the same old way.

m) *Now first couple right*
And the second couple left.

n) *And down the center four by four.*
First four right
And the second four left.
And down the center eight by eight.

o) *Each couple turn with a left pivot swing,*
And march right back.

p) *Now backward march,*
And circle eight.

Down the center four by four.

q) *First and second couple right and left through,*
And the sides the same. Right and left back.
r) *Now the two ladies change,*
And change right back.
s) *Now half promenade,*
And right and left home.

3. *Now swing, swing, and swing 'em all day.*
Now allemande left in the same old way,
And right and left grand around the ring
Hand over hand with the dear little thing.
Promenade, oh, promenade.

¤ ¤ ¤

This can be repeated with the second, third, and fourth couples leading, each time marching in a different direction, or it can be followed directly by any other dance the caller may choose.

THE EXPLANATION:

1. See page 151 or substitute any other introduction given there.

2. a) The first lady and gentleman separate four steps from each other and swing. They then promenade around the set inside the other three couples, and finish in their original position but facing the opposite direction, or "towards the wall" with their backs to the center of the set.
b) The second couple does the same except that they stop directly behind the first couple facing in the same way as the first couple.
c) The third couple steps forward and stands directly behind these two and the fourth couple moves over and gets in line behind the third couple. This puts all the sets on the floor lined up in a column of couples.
d) They all march, forgetting their sets and making one long column. The ladies turn to the right and the gentlemen to the left and each single file circles around the outside of the hall.
e) When they meet at the foot of the hall the ladies pass to the inside and the two files continue past each other.

f) When they meet at the head of the hall, the two lines pass each other again, this time with the men circling on the inside of the ladies.

g) When the two columns meet at the foot of the hall they march up the center two by two, with the ladies back on the same side, to the right of the gentlemen, as when they started.

h) As soon as the double column fills the length of the hall, they stop. The men and women face each other and take four steps backward, separating the two lines.

j) The two lines advance to each other four steps and separate again. They advance and the two lines pass through each other (each person touching his partner by the right hand in passing so as to pass to the left) and continuing on until each line stands in place of the other. Each individual does a rightabout and the two lines advance to each other again and fall back again. Then they advance and pass through to their own places. They all do a rightabout and face each other again, and the two lines advance and form a double column again facing the front of the hall.

k) The column marches to the head of the hall—turns right and marches around the wall to the foot. It marches clear across the foot of the hall and then doubles back on itself, so that every couple passes every other marching in the opposite direction. At the other side it can double back again and thus "serpentine" as long as desired.

l) On the command the column turns down center. The first couple face each other, join hands, and the others pass under their joined hands. As soon as the second couple passes under they too join hands. Then the third. Each couple in turn, as soon as it passes under the last pair of hands, makes the bridge longer for the rest to pass through. When all have passed through the first couple passes under, followed by the second, third, etc., and the column, now reformed, marches ahead in the regular manner.

m) The first couple turns right and the second couple left —every other couple going the opposite direction, so that two columns march around, one along either wall.

n) The couples come together at the foot of the hall, and march four abreast up the middle, when they reach the head the first four turn right and the second left, and so on alternately, forming two columns of four each, marching along the side walls. At the foot the fours pivot and meet and march up the center eight abreast.

o) On the command they stop and each couple pivots in place, the girl circling left around her man who turns in position as a pivot and the new-formed lines of eight now march back toward the foot of the hall.

p) Then on command they all remain facing toward the foot of the hall and at the same time march backward toward the head of the hall. Then the two ends of each group of eight bend around together and they make a ring of eight with hands joined, and all circle to the left.

q) The first and second couple in each set face each other (and at the same time the third and fourth do the same) and pass through each other, each giving the opposite person the right hand in passing, and each couple joining left hands as soon as they have passed through. Each man holding his lady's left hand, puts his right hand behind her back, and turns her leftabout-face around him. The two couples pass back through each other, turn in the same way and are again back where they were, facing each other.

r) The two men stand and send their ladies to the center between them. The ladies take right hands and pass each other, giving their left hands to the opposite men. Each man takes the lady with his left hand, puts his right behind her waist and pivoting, turns her completely around him to the left and back towards her own partner. As the ladies pass they again take right hands and give their lefts to their partners, who pivot again and turn them to place.

s) Each couple now takes promenade position (hands joined in front with partners) and marches to the other couple's place (passing to the right—gentlemen passing left shoulders). They pivot around left face and facing each other do a *right and left* back to place. (Exactly the same as the second half of explanation. (q)).

3. See page 154 for explanation or substitute any other ending given there.

Inside Arch

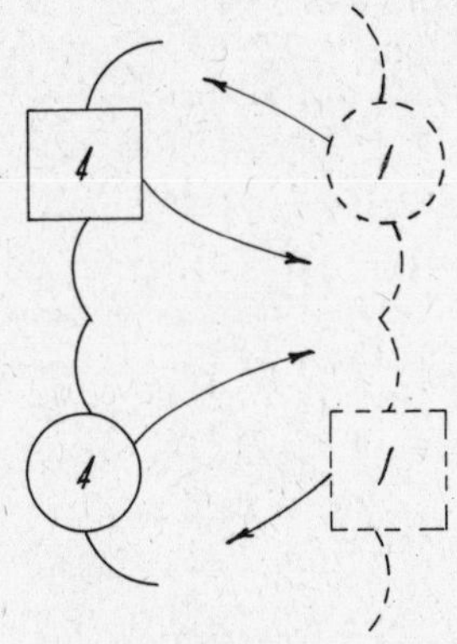

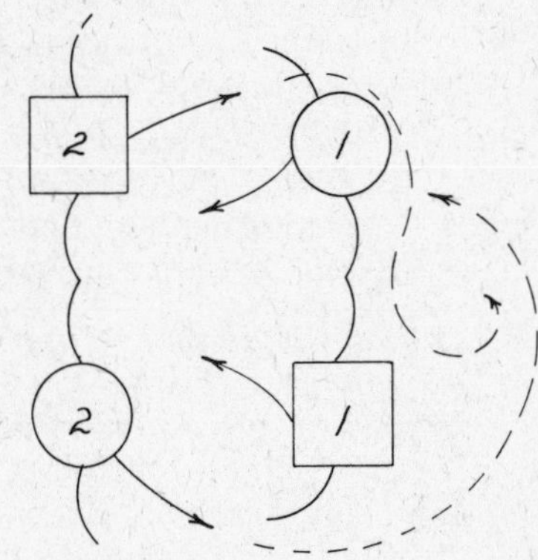

THE CALL:

1. *All eight balance,*
   All eight swing,
   A left allemande
   And a right hand grand.
   And promenade, oh, promenade.

All eight balance.

2. a) *First couple out to the couple on the right*
   With a four and a half.
   b) 1. *Inside arch and the outside under.*
      2. *Inside arch and the outside under.*
      3. *Inside arch and the outside under.*
      4. *Inside arch and the outside under.*
   c) *Now circle four with the odd couple—oh,*
   Around and around and a docey-doe.
   d) *Now on to the next with a four and a half.*
   e) 1. *Inside arch and outside under.*
      2. *Inside arch and outside under.*
      3. *Inside arch and outside under.*
      4. *Inside arch and outside under.*

3. *Balance home and swing 'em all night,*
   Allemande left, go left and right.
   Hand over hand around the ring,
   Hand over hand with the dear little thing.
   Meet your partner and promenade.

   Repeat 2 and 3 for second, third, and fourth couples, or substitute the next dance for second and fourth couples "the length of the hall."

THE EXPLANATION:

1. See page 151 or substitute any other introduction given there.

2. a) The first couple advances to the second couple. They join hands and the four circle halfway round so that the first couple stops with backs to the outside of the set and the second couple with backs to the center of the set.
   b) 1. The second couple raises their arched arms and the first couple, holding hands, passes under the arch.
      2. The first couple continues across the set and raises arched arms, and the fourth couple passes under.
      3. The fourth couple continues and arches, and the second (who have turned around in the meantime) passes under.
      4. The second couple continues, arches, and the first (who have turned around) passes under to the middle of the set.

(This leaves the second couple in the fourth couple's place, and the fourth couple in the second couple's place temporarily.)

c) The first couple now advances to the third (who have stood inactive and unhappy until now) and joining hands circles to the left with them. Then they do a *docey-doe* (see page 160).

d) They now advance to the position of the fourth couple (but the second couple is now standing in this position). They join hands and circle half around with them as in (a). They then do exactly as they did in (b 1, 2, 3, 4), which puts the second and fourth couple back in their own positions, and the first couple in the center of the set. With a balance bow they return to their place.

3. See page 154 for explanation or substitute any other ending given there.

Arch and Under for the Length of the Hall
(Continued)

THE CALL:

2. a) *Second and fourth couples go out to the right*
And four hands full around.
b) *Heads all arch and feet duck under,*
GO, my boys, and go like thunder.
Keep on going till you reach the wall
Then turn right back and through 'em all.

Inside arch and outside under for the length of the hall.

Now touch the wall at the other end
And turn back through till you're home again.
Duck and dive, duck and dive,
Pep up boys and act alive.
Duck and dive, duck and dive,
Regular old time cattle drive.
Duck and dive, duck and dive,
Some'll batch and some'll wive.
Duck and dive, duck and dive,
Cost a one spot, worth a five.
Duck and dive, duck and dive,
Keep on ducking 'til you arrive.

3. *Now you're home and everybody swing.*
A left allemande and a right hand grand.
And promenade.

Repeat 2 and 3 for fourth couple.

☼ ☼ ☼

In calling the two preceding dances, it makes a nice combination to let couple one do inside arch and outside under within the set, then couples two and four do it for the length of the hall, then couple three do it again within the set.

You will note there is no introduction or Part 1 to this call since it starts with couple number two and usually follows some other figure (preferably the preceding dance) done by the first couple.

This dance for the length of the hall is usually done, alas, with only the second couple going out to the right and the fourth couple remaining inactive. It was so given in the first edition of this book, since I had seen it danced in no other way. But this leads to inevitable collisions and disputes as to who shall go over and who shall go under. The more complicated your traffic rules become the more insistent each collider gets that he is right. At last the obvious dawns. Twice as many couples are going one way as are going the other. No traffic rule can keep them out of trouble.

If instead the second and fourth couples both go out to the right there will be as many couples going one way as the other, and everything is solved. The head couple arch over, the foot couple arch under, and since the second couple face the same as the head couple (in fact is head for its group of four) they arch over, and the fourth couple, like the foot couple, arch under. Now by alternating over and under, keeping the spacing even, and by careful timing, it all goes as smoothly as clockwork, and is great fun.

THE EXPLANATION:

2. a) Second couple advances to third couple, joins hands, and the four circle full around, so the second couple is left toward the center of the set. At the same time the fourth couple advance to the first couple, join hands and they circle full around, leaving the fourth couple toward the center of the set. All four couples are in a line with all the other couples down the hall.

   b) The first and second couples raise their arched hands and the third and fourth couples make ready to pass under. On the word GO they pass through and advance right on toward the oncoming couples of the next set. If they have just arched over, they now duck under, then over with the next, then under, and so on and on. In a few moments the whole line has slipped into a continuous flow so that every couple passes alternately over and under each other couple coming from the opposite direction.

   When a couple reaches the end of the hall they turn (the couple pivoting) and accept the rhythm of the oncoming couple. That is, they go either over or under to accommodate the motion of the oncoming couple. This puts them in the correct rhythm to pass back the length of the hall alternately over and under.

   Each couple must continue in the direction they were facing at the time of the first over or under. They must continue in this direction until they reach the end of the hall. Then they turn around and go under in the opposite direction to the other end of the hall. And then they turn and return to their original places on the floor.

   Fix in the mind of each couple that they must go to both ends of the hall and return to place before they have done.

   The duck-and-dive patter, or something like it can be kept going by the caller, or he can settle down for a long rest until all couples are back in place.

3. See page 153 for explanation or substitute any other ending given there.

Three Ladies Change

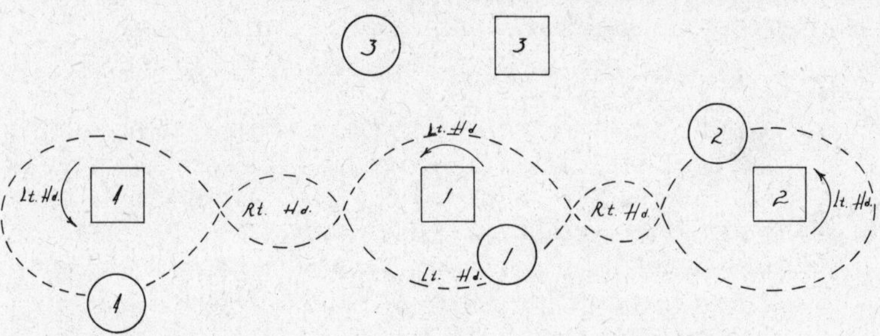

THE CALL:

1. *Honors right and honors left,*
   All join hands and circle to the left,
   Break and swing and promenade back.

2. a) *First couple out to the couple on the right*
   With a four hands full around.

   b) *The two ladies change,*
   Now three ladies change
   On the longer track,
   Three ladies change
   Through the set and back.
   The three gents stand
   Like a rock in the sea

Three ladies change.

And wave them past
Till they've changed all three.
c) *On to the next and circle four.*
Two ladies change and change right back;
d) *On to the next and*
Four hands full around—

Repeat (b) entire for fourth couple.

3. *Now you're home and everybody swing,*
Allemande left with your left hand.
Right hand to partner and right and left grand.
Then promenade, oh, promenade.

Repeat 2 and 3 for second, third, and fourth couples, or substitute the dance on the next page for the second and fourth couples.

THE EXPLANATION:

1. See page 148 for explanation or substitute any introduction given there.

2. a) First couple advances to second couple, joins hands with them and the four circle to the left one full time around, so that the first couple is left again toward the center of the set.

   b) The first and second ladies pass each other, taking right hands. Each gives her left hand to the opposite gentleman. The first lady is turned once around by the second gentleman so she again faces the set. The second lady gives her left hand to the first gentleman

Three ladies change the length of the hall.

who passes her to the other side of himself, where she advances and gives her right hand to the fourth lady who advances to meet her, then her left to the fourth man. She turns around him and faces the set. The first man takes the fourth lady and passes her on so that she joins left hands with the oncoming first lady. Each lady continues in this serpentine fashion from one side of the set to the other and back to where she started from, giving her right hand always to ladies and her left hand to the gentlemen, encircling both the fourth and second men and passing by the first man (who stands in the center) with only a half turn to the left for each lady.

The second and fourth man takes each lady as she comes to him by the left hand, turns her out around him and back into the set again. The first man, standing in the center, keeps turning perpetually to his left, taking a lady with his left hand from one side of the set to the other with each half turn.

c) When all the ladies are back to their own partners again, the first couple advances to the third couple, who have stood inactive thus far. Ladies join right hands and pass each other, then give their left hands to the opposite men, who turn around with them and send them again towards each other. Again they take right hands and pass and each gives her left hand to her partner, who with his right hand behind her back, turns her around to place.

d) The first couple then advances to the fourth couple and does with them exactly as they did with the second couple in section (b). The three ladies take the serpentine route around the men until each comes back to her own partner.

3. See page 152 or substitute any other ending given there.

Four Ladies Change the Length of the Hall

(Continued)

(Can be substituted for the second and fourth couples instead of the simpler form in the preceding dance, provided there are two or more sets in a row down the center of the hall.)

THE CALL:

2. a) *The second and fourth couples*
Go out to the right
With four hands full around.
b) *The two ladies change,*
The three ladies change
To the walls and back,
All ladies change on this longer track.
Keep on changing till you reach a wall.
You're just half through, that isn't all.
Turn right back and keep on trotting,
Keep on changing to the other wall.
Now back to your partner if he ain't forgotten.

3. *Now you're home and everybody swing,*
Allemande ho,
Right hand up and here we go!
Now promenade.
Repeat 2 and 3 for fourth couple.

☼ ☼ ☼

If the sets are arranged the length of the hall it is best to give the simpler dance (see page 346) for couple number one, and keep them changing within the set. Then call the dance given above for couples two and four, sending the several sets the length of the hall. Then repeat the simple dance for the third couple.

THE EXPLANATION:

2. a) Second couple in each set advances to the third couple, joins hands with them and circles to the left once around so that the second couple is again toward the middle of the set. At the same time the fourth couple advances to the first couple and does the same with them, leaving the fourth couple in line toward the middle of the set.

b) The second and third ladies advance to each other, take right hands, pass by each other, and give their left hands to the left hands of the opposite gentlemen. Each gentleman turns half around with the lady so that she continues in the same direction toward the next man, even though he is in the next set. She takes alternately a lady with the right hand, then a man with the left, and continues thus until she reaches the wall at the end of the hall, having passed through all the sets. Here the last man turns her around and sends her back through the line again.

Each man takes a lady coming one direction with his left hand, makes a half turn with her, sending her on in the same direction, and then takes a lady coming from the other direction and gives her a half turn. This makes him turn continuously to the left.

The two men at the extreme ends of the hall each take an oncoming lady, and turn her completely around themselves and back into the line again. The end gentlemen make a full turn each time (but only half as often as the line men) and always turn to their left.

Each lady must go to each end of the hall and be turned back by both of these end men before returning to her partner to stop at the end of the figure.

3. See page 153 for explanation or substitute any other ending given there.

☼ ☼ ☼

If there are enough sets on the floor, this same dance through all the crosswise sets can be done, just as described above for the lengthwise.

Right and Left Through the Length of the Hall

THE CALL:

1. *All eight balance,*
   All eight swing,
   A left allemande,
   And a right hand grand,
   Meet your partner
   And promenade.

2. a) *First and third couple*
   Forward and back.
   b) *Now right and left through the length of the hall,*
   And the sides the same.
   Now right and left back to the other wall.
   And the sides keep shuttling back and forth,
   Going east and west through their south and north.
   c) *Keep on shuttling till you get back home,*

3. *Now swing, swing, and everybody swing.*
   Allemande left with your left hand,
   Right to your partner and right and left grand.
   Promenade eight when you come straight.

☼ ☼ ☼

This call can be repeated with some modification for the second and fourth couples. It would begin:

Right and left the length of the hall.

a) *Second and fourth couples*
Forward and back

b) *Now right and left through the width of the hall*
And the ends the same, etc.

THE EXPLANATION:

1. See page 151 for explanation or substitute any introduction given there.

2. a) First and third couples advance four steps toward each other, then fall back four steps to places.

   b) The first and third couples advance to each other and each person takes the opposite by the right hand and passes beyond him or her. (This means you must pass your opposite to the left.) As soon as the two couples pass through each other in this way, partners take each other by the left hand, and advance toward the oncoming couple from the next set.

   As soon as the first and third couples pass through each other, the second and fourth couples pass through each other in the same way, but crosswise of the hall.

   The first and third couples of each set keep going in the same manner until each couple has been to both end walls and is back in place again. Taking the oncoming couples by the right hands and joining left hands with your partner after passing each couple gives rise to a peculiar action which is soon naturally and effectively exaggerated into a swing of the right hands back and up over the shoulder in a long sweeping curve, timing so they meet the next couple just right.

   When a couple reaches the end or side of the hall, the man stands as a pivot and swings his lady around him in a left turn and then they return down the line.

   The second and fourth couples cross, turn back in this manner, cross and turn, and keep this up until the other couples have completed their travels and are back home.

   c) In case there are several couples crosswise as well as lengthwise of the hall, the side couples go to both side walls, and the whole change becomes very complicated and fascinating. Four sets arranged in a square work out perfectly and symmetrically; but if the arrangement of sets is longer one way than the other, and uneven, when one pair of couples gets back home the other pair in that set may be wandering almost anywhere on the floor. In this case the first pair of couples back home have to shuttle back and forth within the set until their two neighbor couples are back home also.

3. See page 152 for explanation or substitute any other ending.

COMBINATION:

For a complex and delightful combination of intermingling dances (especially fine for exhibitions) the Grand March Change can be called for the first couple, the Arch and Under the Length of the Hall for the second and fourth couples, then the Right and Left Through the Length of the Hall for the first and third couples and finally the Four Ladies Change for the Length of the Hall. By this time they will all know they have been some place, but they will feel quite triumphant and proud.

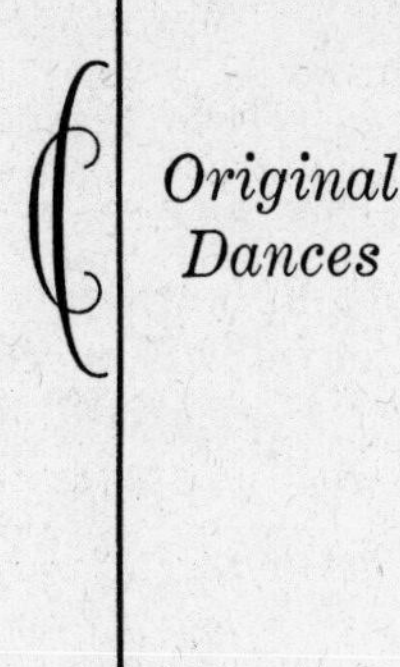

Original Dances

To keep this art vital, each caller must invent a few dances of his own. The following dances of my own invention, are included, not for their excellence but as a challenge for other callers to do better. The first and fourth use familiar figures in a new pattern, the second and third are built upon figures derived from European folk dances.

Forward and Back Eight

THE CALL:

1. *All eight balance, all eight swing,*
   A left allemande and a right and left grand.
   And promenade, oh, promenade!

2. a) *First and third couples forward and back,*
   b) *Forward again and right and left through,*
   The ladies cross left and the gents cross right
   c) *And between side couples remain.*
   d) *Forward eight and fall back eight,*
   Pass right through, don't hesitate.
   Forward eight and fall back eight,
   Pass right back and don't be late.
   e) *Same two couples forward and back,*
   Forward again and circle four.
   f) *Docey-doe with the gent you know*
   The lady goes C and the gent goes doe.

Forward eight and fall back eight.

3. *Balance home and everybody swing,*
Now allemande left with your left hand,
Right to your partner and right and left grand,
Promenade eight when you come straight.

Repeat 2 and 3 for second, third, and fourth couples.

THE EXPLANATION:

1. See page 151 for explanation or substitute any introduction given there.

2. a) The first and third couples advance four steps toward each other and then fall back to place.

   b) They advance again and each person takes the opposite by the right hand as the two couples pass through each other (they thus pass to the left of the opposite). As soon as they have passed, each gentleman takes his lady by the left hand with his left and passes her across in front of him. She continues around the set to the left and behind the side man, while the gentlemen turn right and pass around and behind the side ladies.

   c) The side couples separate so they can come in and stand in line between them. The first gentleman and the third lady are between the second couple; and the first lady and the third gentleman are between the fourth couple, arranged in a line of four, alternately men and ladies.

   d) The two lines of four advance toward each other and fall back to place. Then they advance and pass through to the opposite four's place (passing to the left). They advance and fall back again and then pass back to their own places.

   e) The first and second couples (now temporarily separated) advance toward each other and fall back. Then they advance and join hands in a circle four. This puts each lady on the right side of her own partner.

   f) They do a *docey-doe* in the regular way (see page 160).

3. See page 152 for explanation or substitute any other ending given there.

Double Bow Knot

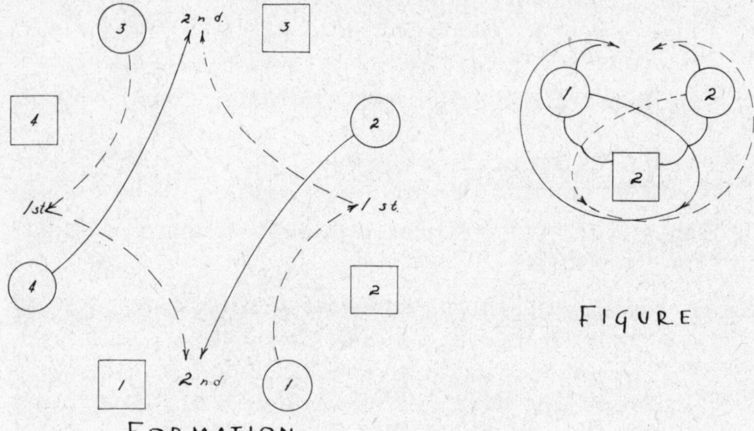

THE CALL:

1. *All jump up and never come down,*
   Grab your honey in your arms and swing her around,
   'Til the hollow of your foot makes a hole in the ground.
   And promenade, oh, promenade.

Tie 'em up in a double bow knot.

2. a) *First and third ladies out to the right,*
   Circle three and get it hot,
   b) *And tie 'em all up in a double bow knot.*
   c) *At the head and feet the side gals meet*
   And circle three and keep 'em hot.
   Tie 'em all up in a double bow knot.
   d) *Now divide to either side*
   And circle three and keep 'em hot.
   Tie 'em all up in a double bow knot.
   e) *Now the head and the feet—*
   With the side gals meet.
   And circle three and keep 'em hot,
   And tie 'em all up in a double bow knot.
   f) *Side gals trot home and everybody swing.*

3. *Now allemande left with your left hand,*
   Right hand to partner and right and left grand.
   Promenade eight when you come straight.

Repeat 2 and 3 for the second and fourth ladies.

☼ ☼ ☼

This dance is adapted from the old Danish dance, "The Crested Hen."

THE EXPLANATION:

1. See page 149 for explanation or substitute any introduction given there.

2. a) The first lady and third lady each leaves her partner and advances to the side couple on her right. She joins hands with them and the three circle to the left with a strenuous skipping step.
   b) The two ladies of each three let go each other's hands and the gentlemen are left in the middle with a lady on either hand. Each gentleman swings the right hand lady under his left arm without letting go the left hand lady. As she passes under, he follows in under his own left arm, and the left hand lady at the same time turns with him in under her right arm (that is, they "turn a dishrag"). As they straighten out he swings the left-hand lady under his right arm and he and the right-hand lady follow under in another dishrag. He again swings the right-hand lady, under

his left arm and turns a dishrag with the left lady and a second time turns the left lady under his right arm and turns a dishrag with the right lady. The grip or hand hold is never changed with either lady during any of the turning. Please be careful always to send the right hand lady through first. Sometimes, with beginners, both ladies try to go under at the same time and a painful collision results. The whole action is so strenuous, with a fast skipping step, that it is easy to "knock the ladies out" if they bump heads.

c) The first and third ladies each continue around the set to the right. At the same time the side ladies go to the left; that is, the first and fourth ladies go to the third gentleman and the third and second ladies to the first gentleman. Each group joins hands and the three's circle to the left. They then do the double bow knot as in (b).

d) Now the ladies divide and go to the side gentlemen, the first and third ladies continuing to the right and the second and fourth ladies to the left. This puts the first and second ladies with the fourth gentleman and the third and fourth ladies with the second gentleman. The three's circle again and do the double bow knot as in (b).

e) The head ladies continue to the right and the side ladies to the left so that the first and fourth ladies meet with the first gentleman and the second and third ladies with the third gentleman. Each three circles and does the double bow knot.

f) The first and third ladies each stay with their own partners while the second and fourth ladies continue left and thus go back to their partners. And everybody swings.

3. See page 152 for explanation or substitute any other ending given there.

☼ ☼ ☼

The head, or active, ladies circle always to the right and the side, or theoretically inactive, ladies to the left, the head ladies beginning the dance and the side ladies ending it. The four gentlemen stay in position waiting for each pair of laides to come to them. In the repetition the side ladies are active and go to the right, while the end ladies go to the left.

lady and the third and second gentlemen with the first lady. They swing arms up and together, separate, and the first and third gentlemen dive again as in (b).

d) The head gentlemen continue to the right and the side gentlemen to the left—so the first and second gentlemen join with the fourth lady and third and fourth gentlemen join with the second lady. They repeat (b) the first and third gentlemen still doing the "diving."

e) The heads continue right and the sides left so the first and fourth gentlemen join the first lady and the third and second gentlemen join the third lady. Then repeat (b) the first and third gentlemen doing the "diving."

f) The second and fourth gentlemen go back to their partners and everybody swings.

3. See page 155 for explanation or substitute any other ending given there.

☼ ☼ ☼

The first and third gentlemen always progress to the right and the second and fourth to the left. And the first and third gentlemen, being active, always do the "diving and rescuing." In the repetition of the dance the second and fourth go right and do the diving, the first and third circle to the left.

Four Gents Cross Right Hands

THE CALL:

1. *All eight balance,*
   All eight swing,
   A left allemande
   And a right hand grand,
   And promenade, oh, promenade.

2. a) *Four gents cross right hands,*
   Circle to your partners.
   b) *Turn 'em with your left hands*
   One time around.
   c) *Double on the right whirl;*
   d) *Back to your partners.*
   e) *All run away*
   With the corner girl.

   Repeat 2 three more times until each man gets his own partner again.

2-3-4 □ THE SAME WITH THEIR PARTNERS

3. *Now you're home and swing 'em all night.*
   Allemande left, go left and right.
   Hand over hand around the ring;
   Hand over hand with a dear little thing.
   Promenade, oh, promenade!

Four gents cross right hands.

THE EXPLANATION:

1. See page 151 for explanation or substitute any introduction given there.

2. a) The four gentlemen advance to the center and join right hands in a star. They circle to the left until they face their partners when they let go each other and return to them.
   b) Each gentleman joins left hands with his partner and circles once around with her.
   c) He returns to the center and again joins right hands with the other gentlemen and circles around to his partner.
   d) He joins left hands with partner and circles once more around with her, and continues on beyond her
   e) To the corner girl, with whom he takes the promenade hold and promenades with her back to his place.

3. See page 154 for explanation or substitute any other ending given there.

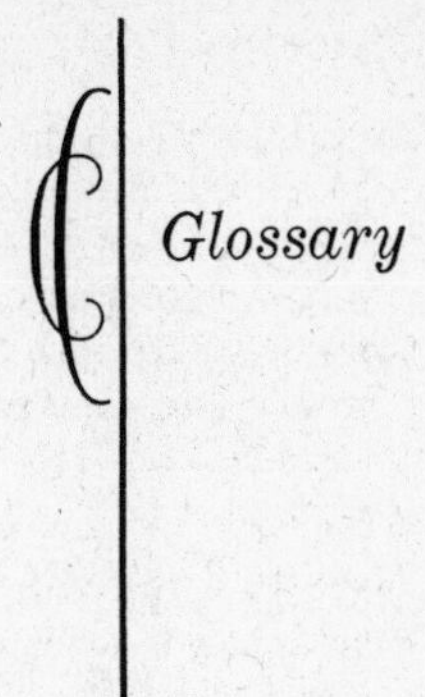

Glossary

Allemande left—the gentleman takes the left hand of the lady on his left with his left hand and walks once around her as she walks around him. Each returns to place. Usually followed by *grand right and left.*

Allemande left just one—the same but not followed by the usual *grand right and left.* Each goes back to his own place, ready for next call.

Allemande right—very uncommon, and usually follows an *allemande left.* Each dancer turns partner around by the right hand, and back to place.

Arch—a couple joins inside or near hands and raises them high for another couple to pass under.

Balance—can be done with anyone according to direction but usually with partner, in which case each steps back from the other four steps, drops into a slight curtsy, and then steps forward four steps together again. Sometimes it is done with only two steps back and forward.

Balance home—as usually danced, it apparently means for a couple to return to their home position, but to be correct they should balance to each other when they get home, and at the same time the three other couples should balance.

Balance-swing—after balancing to each other, the couple takes regular dance position, the lady's right hand in gentleman's extended left hand, her left hand on his right shoulder, and his right arm around her waist. They should stand a little off center, or sideways, right hip touching right hip, and swing rapidly around in place with walking steps so quick and vigorous as to be aware of considerable centrifugal force or swing. The rotation is right-face or clockwise. Most balances are concluded with this swing.

Birdie in a cage—a girl to be alone in a circle or ring of dancers who hold each others' hands. They usually circle clockwise, while she rotates counterclockwise.

Break—to let go hands or holds.

Cast off—to let go holds and move away from each other, usually around the outside of square.

Chain—see ladies' chain.

Change—a) complete call for one square dance.
b) to exchange partners.

Circle four—two couples face each other, join hands and circle to the left, or clockwise.

Circle eight—four couples face center of square, join hands, and circle to the left, or clockwise.

Circle left—a group holding hands circles clockwise.

Circle right—the same except to circle counterclockwise.

Close—to bring one foot to the side of the other.

Come straight—when you come to, or meet your partner, in a *grand right and left.*

Corner—in any square the dancer next to you who is not your partner (see next definition).

Corner lady (or girl)—the lady standing to the gentleman's left in the square.

Corner man—the gentleman standing to the lady's right in a square.

Cut away—usually used with a number such as six, four, or two. To cut away six is to pass through opposite couple, separate from your partner, and each circle around their half of the remaining six, lady to right and gentleman to left. To cut away four—separate from your lady and each pass around the couple on either side—or four in all. To cut away two—separate, and each pass around corner, which is one on each side or two.

Dance position—regular ballroom position—lady and gentleman stand face to face, with the lady's right hand in the gentleman's extended left hand and her left hand on his right shoulder or upper arm. His right arm encircles her, and his right hand should be held about at her left shoulder blade though it is usually and incorrectly lower or farther around.

Dip—the first or introductory step on the first bar of the waltz. The gentleman rocks back on his left foot with his other foot lifted in the air in front while the lady rocks forward on her right foot and holds her other foot free of the floor behind her. The count is step—one, rise on toes, two, fall to heel, three (all done on one foot). On the next bar go directly into regular waltz starting with the foot which has been held in the air during first bar.

Divide the ring—a couple crosses square to opposite couple and passes between them.

Docey-doe—executed while two couples (with each lady on the right of her gentleman) hold hands in a circle of four. Each gentleman passes his lady's left hand from his right hand to his left, and she passes between the opposite couple in making this change. He now passes her behind him around his left side, lets go her hand, and still facing the opposite gentleman reaches with his right hand for the opposite lady who is now coming around from behind the opposite gentleman. He turns her around behind him on his right side and reaches with his left hand for his own partner who has gone around the opposite gentleman and is now coming from behind him. He puts his right hand around her waist and turns her to position. (See page 108 for complete description.)

Docey corners—to *dos-a-dos* or pass back to back with the corner or left hand lady.

Dos-a-dos—to pass back to back with a person. Advance to this person and pass to the left (that is, pass right shoulder to right shoulder), step to the right so you are both back to back, and without changing the direction in which you face, encircle him and back up to your own position. See page 106.

Do-si-do—the same as *docey-doe* and it is the more usual spelling.

Double elbow—a more complicated *right and left grand,* hooking elbows and turning instead of merely taking hands and passing. As the gentleman meets each lady he hooks right elbows with her and turns for four counts, then reverses and hooks left elbows with her and turns for four counts. He then advances to the next lady and does the same with her, and so on around the set. See page 157.

Eight hands round—eight persons join hands in a circle.

Ends—first and third couples in a set.

Feet—the foot couple or third couple. If the second couple is active the fourth couple becomes foot couple.

Figure eight—to pass between two persons (or two couples) encircle one of them, pass through again and encircle the other, in a path which resembles the figure eight.

First couple—the couple standing nearest the head of the hall.

Five hands round—five persons join hands in a circle.

Foot or foot couple—the third couple, or the couple opposite the active couple.

Forward and back—advance four counts and return backwards four counts to place.

Forward two, three, four, six, etc.—as many persons as designated advance four counts.

Four and a half or

Four hands half—two couples join hands in a circle of four and turn to the left until they have exchanged places, that is, a circle of four makes a half turn.

Four hand mill—four persons join right hands shoulder high and pivot clockwise around their joined hands, or join left hands if so directed and circle in the opposite direction.

Four hands full around—two couples join hands in a ring and circle to the left once around so each couple is in same position from which they started circling.

Four hands half—see *four and a half* above.

Four hands round—two couples take hands in a ring and circle to the left—until next direction is given, usually followed by a *docey-doe.*

Four hands up—the same as *four hands round.*

Fourth couple—the couple to the left of the first couple and opposite the second couple.

Gather in (four, six, etc.)—when a couple dancing round with joined hands includes another couple to make a circle of four, or includes yet another couple to make a circle of six, etc.

Gent goes wrong—the gentleman turns to the left when his lady is directed to turn to the right.

Grand right and left—each couple in a square join right hands and pass each other, so that the ladies advance clockwise and the gentlemen advance counterclockwise. Each gentleman touches left hands with the next lady and passes on beyond her while she continues in the opposite direction; he then touches right hands with the next lady and they pass each other. Then he touches left hands with the next and passes her. This brings him to his own lady, with whom he joins right hands, and turns to the promenade position at his side. See page 51.

Grand circle—each gentleman takes his lady to the edge of the hall, and puts her on his right hand and faces center. All couples join hands in one large circle, and all facing center.

Hand over hand—same as *right and left grand.*

Hands round—used with any number such as *six hands round,* means for six people to join hands in a ring and circle clockwise.

Head—the first or head couple.

Head of the hall—the end of the hall which is designated by the caller as the head, usually the end nearest the piano.

Home—the original position of each couple in a square, and to which they return after any maneuver.

Honors all—All gentlemen bow to their partners.

Honors left—each gentleman bows to the lady on his left.

Honors right—each gentleman bows to the lady on his right who is, of course, his partner.

Inside ring—the path a couple follows when they promenade around the set inside the other three couples.

Join hands or join paddies—usually when all four couples of a set join hands in a ring—although smaller rings are sometimes formed.

Ladies' chain—two couples face each other. The two ladies advance, join right hands, and pass each other. Each lady gives her left hand to the opposite gentleman and he pivots with her, turning her completely around. Each lady advances and again joins right hands with the other lady and passes her. She then gives her left hand to her partner's left, and he pivots and turns her around to place. See page 132.

Ladies' doe—often only the preliminary phrase of a *docey-doe* and ignored by the dancers, but more correctly it should precede a *docey-doe,* by the two ladies encircling each other with a *dos-a-dos,* followed by the two gentlemen doing the same, usually to the call *gents you know.* Then the *docey-doe* is done.

Lead out—advance to wherever directed.

Left face—to pivot and face to your own left.

Odd couple—the only inactive couple in a set, as when the first couple is doing a change with the second and fourth couples at the same time, the third couple is left as an odd or inactive couple.

One and a half—a *grand right and left* done with hooked elbows, each gentleman hooking right elbows with his partner and circling one full turn around her and back to his place, continuing a half turn, releasing and going on to the next lady. He hooks left elbows with her, turns once and a half around and on to the next, alternately hooking right or left elbow with each lady he meets. See page 158.

One hand turn—taking a lady by one hand (her right in your right or vice-versa) and turning her around.

Opposite—when two couples face each other—the opposite for each gentleman is the other gentleman's partner, the opposite for each lady the other lady's partner.

Opposite couple—the couple directly across the set from you.

Outside ring—the path taken by a single couple when they promenade around the outside of the other three couples in the set.

Pokey—cowboy pronunciation of polka.

Promenade—to march in couples with the lady on the gentleman's right and their arms crossed and hands clasped in front of them, the lady's right hand in the gentleman's right and her left hand in his left hand. His right arm should be crossed over or in front of her left arm.

Promenade eight—the four couples of a square promenade counter-clockwise around the set and back to their own positions.

Right face—to pivot and face to your right.

Right and left—two couples pass through each other (ladies to the inside) each gentleman taking right hands with the opposite lady as he passes her, and taking his partner's left hand in his left as soon as they have passed through. Usually he makes a left pivot, turning her around with him until the two couples face each other. They now pass back in the same manner, pivot to the left, and face each other in their original positions. Sometimes done without touching hands in passing. And sometimes done without pivoting, but passing directly on to the next oncoming couple. See page 128.

Salute—to make a deep bow to your partner or to the lady directed.

Salute your company—all four gentlemen in a set simultaneously bow to their own partners.

Sashay—to slide to the side with a step—close—step—close—step.

Second couple—the couple to the right of the first couple in a set.

Set—four couples facing each other in a square formation. See page 56.

Seven hands round—seven persons join hands in a ring, all facing to the center, and circle to the left.

Sides—the second and fourth couples.

Side couples—the same as *sides*.

Six hands round—six persons join hands in a ring, facing center, and circle to the left.

Split the ring—a couple advances across a set, passes between the opposite couple, the lady usually turns to her right and the gentleman to his left. They go around the outside of the set, and meet each other at their original position.

Stand-pat—to stand still or in place.

Step—close—to step with one foot and close the other foot to the side of it.

Swing—to take a slightly modified dance position and circle round each other in place, that is, stand face to face with your partner, the gentleman extends his left arm and supports the lady's right hand in his left hand. She places her left hand on his right shoulder or upper arm, and his right arm partly encircles her waist. They usually stand a little off center so their right hips almost touch each other. Then with a light walking step they circle around each other in place, going in a clockwise direction, and usually making two complete circles around each other.

They may also swing around each other holding single hands, both hands, or hooking elbows when so directed.

Three hands round—three persons join hands in a ring facing inward, and circle to the left.

Third couple—the couple opposite the first couple.

Tip—usually when the sets are called out on the floor for a square dance, two complete changes or dances are called, with a slight pause between them. They are called the first tip and the second tip.

Trot 'em home—promenade back to original positions.

Turn right back—in the *grand right and left* when the gentlemen meet their own partners each takes his partner by the right hand and completely encircles her so that he is facing the opposite direction. The *grand right and left* is now repeated in the opposite direction, the gentlemen now circling clockwise while the ladies circle counterclockwise.

Cowboy Dance Tunes *arranged by*

FREDERICK KNORR

6/8 RHYTHM

2/4 AND 4/4 RHYTHM

FIDDLE TUNES

SPECIAL DANCES

Foreword

FREDERICK KNORR is a cellist in the Denver Symphony and a thorough musician. Because of an instinctive love of the virile homely strength of the old dance music, he has taken a genuine interest in our cowboy dancing. Whenever he can get away, he "sets in" with my dance orchestra and strums with it on his guitar or banjo. He is so fascinated with these old dances that for several summers he has played with us for our engagements at Central City, and last fall took the trip with our dance troupe to California as strummer in our little orchestra.

When I asked him to record some of the tunes for me and to make a simple arrangement for those who wanted music to accompany my book *Cowboy Dances,* he was delighted. He sorted over hundreds of tunes and finally made the following selection as most typical and most interesting.

He has scored them as very simple piano arrangements expecting the "fiddler" to play the "top line" or melody. Each pianist uses his own interpretation and is expected to fill out, elaborate, and vary these arrangements however he pleases. And the real "fiddler," of course, takes all the liberties and adds all the flourishes that his ear may dictate. To help the "strummer," Mr. Knorr has indicated the chord to be played by a letter designation. From this simple framework, your orchestra is expected to work out its own best arrangement.

You will notice that most of the pieces are in simple keys using sharps. Most pianists may prefer flats, but "fiddlers" and "strummers" want the sharps, and so you will find most of the old-time music sharpened to their taste, often not a single flat key in a hundred pieces.

Callers, too, prefer certain keys that are easy for their

voices to chord to. A good caller often asks his orchestra to shift a key up or down a little so that his chording chant will fit more easily into his natural voice range. Rather instinctively, a caller pitches his voice on an element of the major chord of the key being played, usually the dominant. Sometimes he chants on the third, occasionally on the tonic itself. He may vary back and forth from one element of the chord to another. But usually he prefers a key that lets him chant his call on the dominant without straining his voice.

Mr. Knorr has arranged his tunes in four groups and suggested that I say a word about each group. In the first group he has tunes in 6/8 rhythm. Many old fiddlers prefer the 6/8 rhythm, but they have to be watched or they will get into such a slow rocking-horse monotony that the dance becomes no fun. In a smooth 6/8 such as "Ocean Wave," the dancers, who step only on the first and fourth beat of each measure, slow the dance down, and if the dancers are young they instinctively have to put in little wiggles or jiggles to keep themselves amused between the slow steps, and that is not so good. However, if the 6/8 melody is faster and sort of spills over itself like running water as in the "Irish Washerwoman" the dancers achieve a quick step and a snappy dance. "Honest John" is a fine tune to dance to. It is speedy enough to establish the quick step, and smooth enough to carry the dancers quite away with it. "Chichester" is a good original tune made up by one of my favorite fiddlers, Ben Chichester.

Six-eight rhythm is sometimes not quite so easy to "call to." A good caller instinctively times his call to counts of four. Regardless of delays caused by backward sets (which never let him call twice alike with any music) he always starts a phrase on a strong beat and builds his phrases on patterns of four. This somehow is often easier to do with the speedier 2/4 or 4/4 time.

The second group of tunes given here are in 2/4 or 4/4 rhythm. Names are always a question. Take the first one, our regular fiddler "Nick" Nichols often plays it, but he doesn't know where he picked it up. So when we ask him the name he says, "I Wonder." The last few tunes in this group are Mr. Knorr's own. We have played them and liked them and asked him to include them here.

The third group are famous old-time fiddle tunes. Made by fiddlers, played by fiddlers, their whirling fast melody isn't difficult for any good fiddler. But when a pianist tries to play that same racing melody in good quick tempo, it is not many repetitions until the muscles in the forearm begin to knot and the pianist can hardly go on. These melodies are very difficult and tiring for a pianist. Some of them are simple enough but do not "lay under the hand" right. So usually the pianist just chords and "plays around" with them, while the fiddler carries the melody at a furious and untiring pace. Amateur pianists had better leave them alone.

And your old-time fiddler will probably say that isn't the way he plays it. Surprising how these standard tunes, transmitted from ear to ear, are each played as individual and personal arrangements. Sometimes, a tune varies so much under the fingers of different fiddlers that you can hardly recognize it as being the same tune. And always, somehow, any good fiddler's tune has a personal magic in it, that can't be put down on paper in eighth and sixteenth notes.

The last selection is a group of special tunes mostly for the round dances described in my book. I have suggested there a single album of old-time dance music, and for each round dance have described just how much of each tune we usually hear in the West, and just how it is played. And so instead of repeating these tunes here, Mr. Knorr has given us some variations. He has given us his own arrangement of the Varsouvianna, built from the many Varsouvianna tunes he has heard, and putting in as many phrases of his own as he liked and writing a new waltz for it. It is a good tune to dance to. The Schottische is his arrangement taken from an old clog—over a hundred years old. The simple little polka is his own and is typical of this style of dance. There are a hundred other polka tunes extant for you to choose from. He has arranged the Rye Waltz as it is played here in the West and as I have described it. And because so many orchestras disagree on chording "Pop Goes the Weasel," he has given an arrangement of this.

The old-time dance tunes are infinite in number. We hope the tunes he has presented here will serve your purpose and add to your joy in cowboy dancing.

LLOYD SHAW

Honest John

D
C
G
Ami
G
D7
G

Chichester

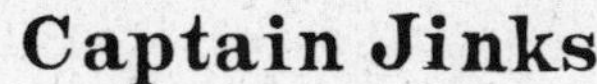

Captain Jinks

Ocean Waves

I Wonder

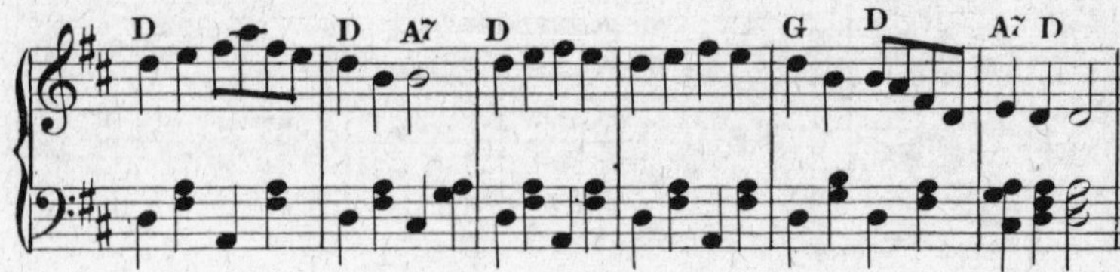

Johnny's Down the River

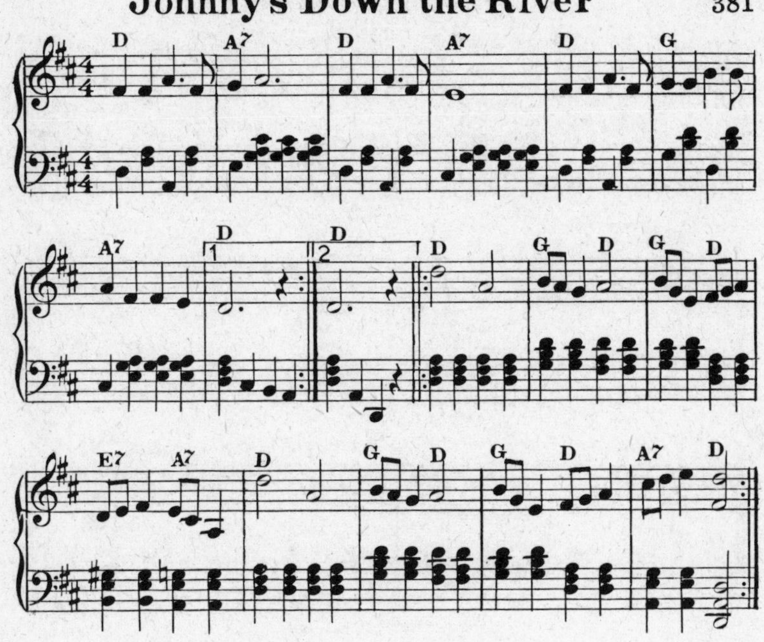

Romping Molly

Buffalo Gals

The Girl I Left Behind Me

Golden Slippers
G
D7
D
D
G
G
Ami
D7
G
G
Ami
D7
G
Soldier's Joy
D
A7
D
D
A7
D
D
A7
D
A7
D
A7
D
D
A7
D

Nellie Bly

Kingdom Come

Whoa Ho Dobbin

Four and Twenty

Cowboy and Indians

Hen and Chickens

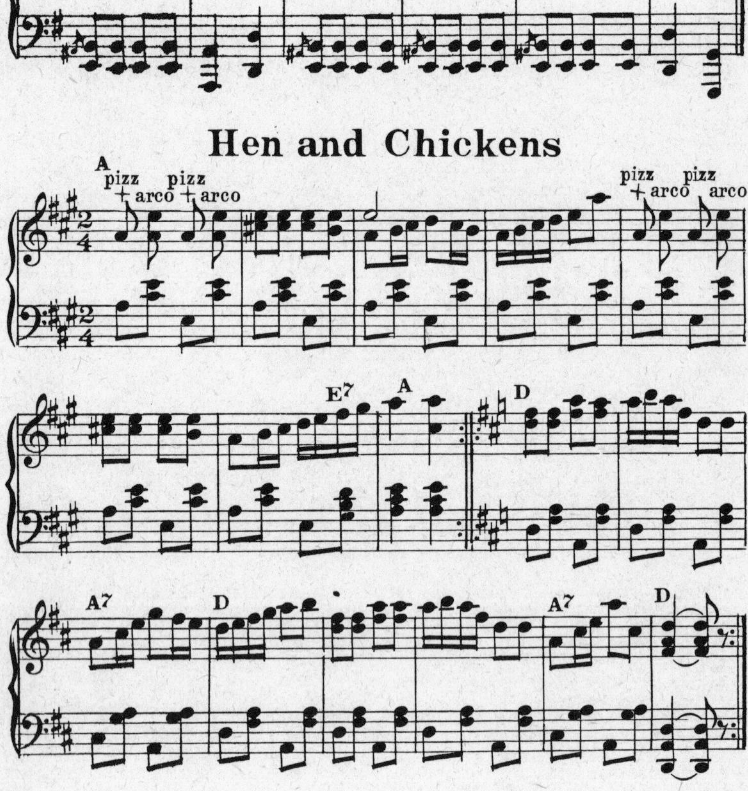

Waggoner
G
gliss
D
G
D7
G
G
D
G
D7
G
Durang
D
A7
D
D
A7
D
D
A7
D
A7
D
A7
D
A7
D
A7
D

Hull's Victory

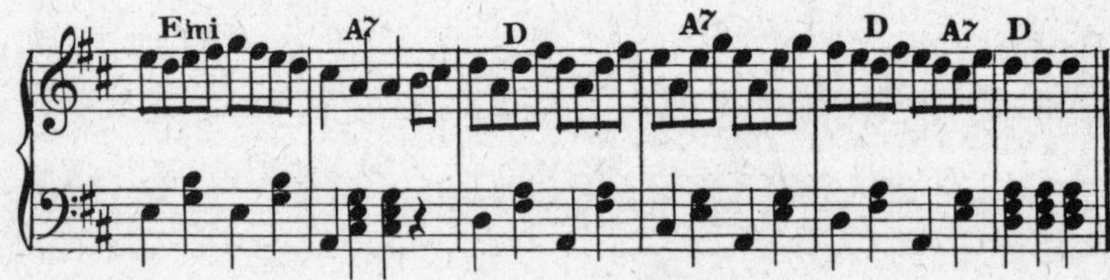

Pigtown Hoe Down

Lamp Lighter

Arkansas Traveler

Devil's Dream

Four White Horses

White Cockade

Cheyenne Varsouvianna

Schottische

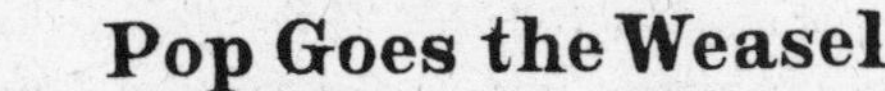

Pop Goes the Weasel

So-So Polka

Rye Waltz

Phonograph Records

AN ORCHESTRA or at least a piano is necessary for good dancing. But in some groups it is impossible to get competent musicians and they have to use phonograph records. The records are never satisfactory for a real dance, but they are good for practice and can be made to work when there is nothing better.

While I have a large collection of records I must confess that I use them so seldom that my experience and my advice are very limited. But since dance teachers and physical education directors from all parts of the country come to my Western Dance Course each summer, and since some of them have to use records with their classes, I decided to ask them which records were best in actual use.

I sent questionnaires to two hundred of them, and was pleased to find that only one fourth of them had to use records. But this meant that only fifty were able to answer my questionnaire. However, these answers were scattered from California to the Columbia River country, from the deep south to New England. They should be typical of the whole country.

I have compiled their answers and give them below. In some cases I am surprised at the records they recommended, and yet they say they have had success with them. In the list below I have given only those records which have been reported as successful by several people. I have omitted all records that had only one mention.

If you order any of these records, be sure to check both name and number, as some numbers may have been changed, or may have been incorrectly reported. And, of course, the record companies have been forced to reduce their stocks, and until the war is over, it may be impossible to secure many of the records listed.

SQUARE DANCES—WITHOUT CALLS

Blackberry Quadrille — Victor 36403
Soldiers Joy — (In Victor Album C-36)

Possum in the 'Simmon Tree — Columbia 36021
Little Brown Jug — (in Columbia Album C-47)

Virginia Reel — Victor 20447
Money Musk

Soldiers Joy — Victor 20592
Lady of the Lake

Old Time Fiddlin' Pieces — (Decca Album No. 66)
Three records played by Clayton McMichen—including: Turkey in the Straw; Old Hen Cackle; Fiddler's Dream; Old Joe Clark; Pretty Little Widder; Shortenin' Bread — Decca 2647

Fire in the Mountain; Ida Red; Sally Gooden; Soldier's Joy; Arkansas Traveler; Mississippi Sawyer — Decca 2648

Sourwood Mountain; Peter Went a Fishin'; Sugar in the Gourd; Devil's Dream; Rickett's Hornpipe; Fisher's Hornpipe — Decca 2649

Flop Eared Mule — Bluebird 5658
Soldier's Joy

Quadrille Figures No. 1 and 2 — Victor 20638

Sicilian Circle — Victor 20639
Quadrille Figure No. 3

Mississippi Sawyer — Bluebird 5433
Georgia Waggoner

Pop Goes the Weasel — Victor 20151
(Norwegian Mt. March)

Medley of Reels — Victor 19964
Money Musk

Plain Quadrille I and II — Ford 101

Lancers Figures I to IV — Ford 104

Lancers Figure V — Ford 106

Oh Dem Golden Slippers — Decca 91803

Many report that they use various polkas for square dancing. Some records with weak calls are used and called **over the call,** such as:

Chicken Reel — Decca 5062
Knickerbocker

SQUARE DANCES—WITH CALLS

Waltz Quadrille — Decca 2561 (in Decca Album 56)

Pop Goes the Weasel — Victor 36400 (Victor Album C-36)

Oh Susanna — Columbia 36019 (Columbia Album C-47)

The Girl Behind Me — Victor 36402 (Victor Album C-36)

Bird in a Cage — Decca 3734 (Decca Album 226)

Boy Round Boy, Etc. — Decca 3735 (Decca Album 226)

Parley Voo — Ford 109

First Two Ladies Cross Over — Columbia 36018
Darling Nellie Gray — (Columbia Album C-47)

(See Discussion of Albums)

POLKAS

Seaside Polka — Victor 19909
Heel and Toe Polka

Little Brown Jug — Bluebird 7294
Crazy

Heel and Toe Polka — Ford 107
Rye Waltz

Beer Barrel Polka	Victor 710
Tinker Polka	Decca 2095
Our Katy	Decca 2097 (Decca Album 19)
Little Brown Jug Varsouvianna	Okeh 05425
Clarinet Polka	Columbia 36142 (Columbia Polka Album C-56)
Little Brown Jug (also listed under Square dance records)	Columbia 36021
Decca Album of Polkas (is the favorite of several experts)	Album 213

SCHOTTISCHES

Military Schottische (Trilby)	Decca 2094 (Decca Album 18)
Schottische Skip	Bluebird 7721
Balen I Karlstad (Mate's Waltz)	Victor 20075
Old Southern Schottische (Hungarian Varsouvianna)	Ford 103
Rustic Schottische	Vocalion 04204
Balen I Karlstad	Columbia 22104
Johanpa Snippin	Okeh 15958
Hailten Jolkeen	Vocalion 4169

(Decca Album of Schottisches—Album 220—not reported on, but very satisfactory)

VARSOUVIANNA

Varsouvianna Schottische Skip	Bluebird 7721
Varsouvianna Veleta Waltz	Decca 2092 (Decca Album 18)
Hungarian Varsouvianna Old Southern Schottische	Ford 103
Put Your Little Foot	Decca 3131

Put Your Little Foot — Vocation 05425

Put Your Little Foot — Bluebird 10579

FAST WALTZES

Skater's Waltz — Victor 35798
Estudiantino

Cuckoo Waltz — Decca 2096
Muziky Polka — (Decca Album 19)

Tales from Vienna Woods — Decca 1774

Album of Strauss Waltzes — Columbia Set C-13
(Al Goodman and his orchestra)

SLOW WALTZES

Rye Waltz — Decca 2090
Duchess — (Decca Album 18)

Veleta — Decca 2092
Varsouvianna — (Decca Album 18)

Isabella — Decca 2095
Tinker Polka — (Decca Album 19)

Old Time Waltz Medley — Decca 2563
Two Faces — (Decca Album 56)

Spanish Waltz — Decca 2093
Moon Winks—Three-step — (Decca Album 18)

Album of Popular American Waltzes — Columbia C-26
(Al Goodman and his orchestra)

Many individual waltz records listed, but above are the only records mentioned by several persons.

TWO STEPS

Old Memories — Decca 2097
Our Katy Polka — (Decca Album 19)

They're Off — Decca 2099
Oh Susannah Schottische — (Decca Album 19)

SPECIAL DANCES REQUIRING SPECIAL MUSIC

Rye Waltz	Decca 2090 (Decca Album 18)
Veleta Waltz	Decca 2092 (Decca Album 18)
Skaters Waltz Bolero (Estudiantino)	Victor 35798
Three Step—Moon Winks	Decca 2093 (Decca Album 18)
Celito Lindo	Decca 1258
Badger Gavotte	Decca 2565 (Decca Album 56)
Rye Waltz	Ford 107
Ten Pretty Girls	Bluebird 10028
Herr Schmidt	Decca 2098 (Decca Album 19)
Oxford Minuet Tuxedo	Decca 2091 (Decca Album 18)

Old Time Albums

THERE are many albums of square dances. Each represents a different type of dancing as done in a different part of the country. Some of them are excellent, some are not so good. None of them are quite typical of the dances described in this book. But try them out. You will find them good fun.

SQUARE DANCES

Square Dances (3—12 inch records) Decca Album 229
Ed Durlacher calling with Al MacLeod's Band

She'll Be Comin' 'Round the Mountain Decca 15033
Billy Boy

The Grapevine Twist Decca 15054
Dip and Dive

Mademoiselle From Armentieres Decca 15055
Cowboy's Dream

An excellent album.

Square dances (4—12 inch records) Victor Album C-36
Floyd C. Woodhull Calling with Woodhull's Old Tyme Masters

Oh Susanna Victor 36400
Pop Goes the Weasel

Captain Jinks Victor 36401
The Wearing of the Green

The Girl Behind Me Victor 36402
Triple Right and Left Four

Blackberry Quadrille (without calls) Victor 36403
Soldier's Joy (without calls)

Another good album and the last record is voted the best square dance record without calls.

Swing Your Partner (4—12 inch records) Victor Album C-34
Paul Conklin calling with Dickensen's
Tuxedo Colonels

Hodge No. 1 Victor 27265
Hodge No. 3
Chase Your Partner Victor 36384
Buffalo Gal

Darling Nellie Gray Victor 36385
Duck the Oyster

Lady 'Round the Lady Victor 36386
Life on the Ocean Wave
(This album is not quite so pleasant to dance to.)

Square dances (4—10 inch records) Columbia Album C-47
Lawrence Loy calling with Carson Robinson and his
Old Timers

The First Two Ladies Cross Over Columbia 36018
Darling Nellie Gray

Oh Susanna Columbia 36019
Buffalo Boy Go 'Round the Outside

Dive for the Oyster, Part 1 Columbia 36020
Part 2

Little Brown Jug (without calls) Columbia 36021
Possum in the 'Simmon Tree (without calls)
(A good album.)

Cowboy Square Dances (3—10 inch records)
Decca Album 226
Roy Rogers calling with Cooley's Buckle Busters

'Round that Couple and Swing When You Meet
Decca 3733
Chase that Rabbit, Chase that Squirrel

Bird in the Cage and Three Rail Pen Decca 3734
Round that Couple Go Through and Swing

Lady 'Round the Lady and the Gent Solo Decca 3735
Boy Around a Boy, Girl Around a Girl
(A good album)

Swing Your Partner — Okeh Record Set No. K2
Arkansas (Arkie) Woodchopper calling with his own dance band. (Impossible to dance to. The calls not properly timed for dancing.)

Arkansas Traveler — Okeh 06296
Mississippi Sawyer

Soldier's Joy — Okeh 06297
Sallie Goodwin

Walkin' Up Town — Okeh 06298
Wagoner

My Love is But a Lassie — Okeh 06299
Light Foot Bill

Running Set (3—10 inch records) — Decca Album 274
Margot Mayo Group

Hog Eyed Sally; Sally Gooden — Decca 18213
Turkey Buzzard; Sugar in the Gourd

Old Granny Hare; Old Joe Clark — Decca 18214
Soldier's Joy; Sugar in My Coffee; Leather Breeches

Sourwood Mountain — Decca 18215
Bigtown Fling
(Excellent for this specialized type of dance.)

Quadrilles with calls (3—12 inch records)
Decca Album No. 277

Marge Mayo, American Square Dance Group

Lancers Quadrille, Figures 1 and 2 — Decca 15060
Same, Figures 3 and 4

Lancers Quadrille, Figure 5 — Decca 15061
Polo Quadrille, Figures 1, 2, and 3

Polo Quadrille, Figures 4 and 5 — Decca 15062
Plain Quadrille, Figures 1, 2, and 3
(The formal New England Type of Quadrille)

Henry Ford
(As individual records or in albums)

Plain Quadrille, Part I (without calls) — Ford 101
Plain Quadrille, Part II

Standard Club Quadrille, Figure I — Ford 102
Standard Club Quadrille, Figure II
(with call)

Standard Club Quadrille, Figure III — Ford 102-C
Jigs and Reels (with calls)

Hungarian Varsovienne — Ford 103
Old Southern Schottische

Lancers "Oriental," Figure I and II (without calls) — Ford 104
Lancers "Oriental," Figure III and IV

Lancers "Oriental," Figures I and II (with calls) — Ford 105
Lancers "Oriental," Figures III and IV

Lancers "Oriental," Figure V (without calls) — Ford 106
Lancers "Oriental," Figure V (with calls)

Heel and Toe Polka — Ford 107
Rye Waltz

Captain Jinks (Singing calls) — Ford 108
The Little Old Log Cabin in the Lane

Hinky-Dinky, Parlee-Voo (Singing Calls) — Ford 109
Life on the Ocean Wave

(Excellent New England type—much slower tempo than in the West.)

Please address all communications to:
HENRY FORD
DEPARTMENT R, BOX 100
DEARBORN, MICHIGAN

SPECIAL ALBUMS WITHOUT CALLS

Old Time Fiddlin' Pieces (3—10 inch records) — Decca Album No. 66
Clayton McMichen (Champion Fiddler)
(Without calls—rather fast tempo)

Turkey in the Straw; Old Hen Cackle; Fiddler's Dream
Old Joe Clark; Pretty Little Widder; Shortenin' Bread — Decca 2647

Fire in the Mountain; Ida Red; Sally Gooden — Decca 2648
Soldier's Joy; Arkansas Traveler; Mississippi Sawyer

Sourwood Mountain; Peter Went a Fishin'; Sugar in the Gourd	Decca 2649
Devil's Dream; Rickett's Hornpipe; Fisher's Hornpipe	

An Album of Polkas (5—10 inch records) Decca Album 213
Freddie "Schnickelfritz" Fisher and his band

Helena Polka Grasshopper Polka	Decca 3678
Jitterbug Polka Earbender Polka	Decca 3679
Beer Barrel Polka (Roll Out the Barrel) The New Okey Dokey Polka	Decca 2384
Emilia Polka Red Raven Polka	Decca 3681
Clarinet Polka Village Tavern	Decca 3682

Let's Polka (4—10 inch records) Columbia Set C-56
Bill Gale and his Music Makers

Clarinet Polka The Bartered Bride Polka	Columbia 36142
Bell Polka Laugh Polka	Columbia 36143
Helena Goofy Gob	Columbia 36144
Beer Barrel Polka Gypsy Polka	Columbia 36145

Album of Schottisches (4—10 inch records)
Decca Album 220
(Several different orchestras)

Oh Susanna Hozauction	Decca 3727
Lena Schottische Le Secret	Decca 3728
Mountain Belle Auf Wiedersehen	Decca 3729
Edna Little Girl Primp Up	Decca 3730

Popular American Waltzes (4—10 inch records)
Columbia set C-26
(Slow American Waltzes)
Al Goodman and his Orchestra

Missouri Waltz — Columbia 35617
Beautiful Ohio

Let Me Call You Sweetheart — Columbia 35618
The Waltz You Saved for Me

Three O'Clock in the Morning — Columbia 35619
That Naughty Waltz

Memories — Columbia 35620
Till We Meet Again

Strauss Waltzes (fast tempo) — Columbia Set C-13
Al Goodman and his Orchestra

Blue Danube Waltz — Columbia 35416
Wiener Blut

Southern Roses Waltz — Columbia 35417
Wine, Women, and Song

Tales from Vienna Woods — Columbia 35418
Voices of Spring

Emperor Waltz — Columbia 35419
Artist's Life

(Note: The old-time American waltz was very slow. The first album listed above averages a metronome reading of about MM 68, and is the most satisfactory of the slow tempo albums. The Strauss Waltzes listed above, are played much faster, at an average Viennese Waltz tempo, of MM 88.

The tendency today is toward the faster or Viennese tempo. You may care to look up the following albums of waltzes (for dancing). They are arranged from slower to fastest. The last of the series, Viennese Waltzes of Waldteufel, you will find very fast.

Victor Herbert Waltzes — Decca Album No. 82
Harry Horlick and his Orchestra
Speed intermediate, MM 78

Waltz Time in Vienna — Columbia Album No. C-17
Al Goodman and his Orchestra
Speed quite fast, MM 86

Favorite Waltzes in Viennese Waltz Time
Decca Album No. 54
Harry Horlick and his Orchestra
Speed faster, MM 88

Favorite Viennese Waltzes Decca Album No. 30
Harry Horlick and his Orchestra
Speed MM 92

Waltzes by Waldteufel Decca Album No. 13
Harry Horlick and his Orchestra
Speed very fast, MM 96

MISCELLANEOUS COLLECTIONS

(These three albums have some excellent records, and others that you probably cannot use.)

Ye Olde Time Dance Night (5—10 inch records)
Decca Album 18
Byran Wolfe's Orchestra

Rye Waltz — Decca 2090
Duchess

Oxford Minuet — Deca 2091
Tuxedo

Veleta — Decca 2092
Varsouvianna

Spanish Waltz — Decca 2093
Three Step—Moon Winks

Military Schottische—Barn Dance — Decca 2094
Trilby

Old Time Dance Music (5—10 inch records) Decca Album 19
Freddie "Schnickelfritz" Fisher and his Orchestra

Isabella and Mariechen Waltz — Decca 2095
Tinker Polka

Cuckoo Waltz — Decca 2096
Muziky, Muziky (Polka)

Old Memories (Two Step) — Decca 2097
Our Katy (Polka)

Herr Schmidt — Decca 2098
Dancing Hour (Schottische)

Oh Susannah (Schottische) They're Off (Two Step)	Decca 2099

More Old Time Dances (5—10 inch records) Byran Wolfe and his Orchestra	Decca Album 56
Waltz Quadrille (Two parts)	Decca 2561
Paul Jones (Two parts—medley of old tunes)	Decca 2562
Old Time Waltz Medley	Decca 2563
Virginia Reel Princess Glide	Decca 2564
Badger Gavotte Montana Dance	Decca 2565

Index